Advanced Unity Game Development

Build Professional Games with Unity, C#, and Visual Studio

Victor G Brusca

Apress®

Advanced Unity Game Development: Build Professional Games with Unity, C#, and Visual Studio

Victor G Brusca
Edison, NJ, USA

ISBN-13 (pbk): 978-1-4842-7850-5   ISBN-13 (electronic): 978-1-4842-7851-2
https://doi.org/10.1007/978-1-4842-7851-2

Managing Director, Apress Media LLC: Welmoed Spahr
Acquisitions Editor: Spandana Chatterjee
Development Editor: Mark Powers
Coordinating Editor: Divya Modi

Cover designed by eStudioCalamar

Cover image designed by Freepik (www.freepik.com)

Distributed to the book trade worldwide by Springer Science+Business Media New York, 1 New York Plaza, New York, NY 10004. Phone 1-800-SPRINGER, fax (201) 348-4505, e-mail orders-ny@springer-sbm.com, or visit www.springeronline.com. Apress Media, LLC is a California LLC and the sole member (owner) is Springer Science + Business Media Finance Inc (SSBM Finance Inc). SSBM Finance Inc is a **Delaware** corporation.

For information on translations, please e-mail booktranslations@springernature.com; for reprint, paperback, or audio rights, please e-mail bookpermissions@springernature.com.

Apress titles may be purchased in bulk for academic, corporate, or promotional use. eBook versions and licenses are also available for most titles. For more information, reference our Print and eBook Bulk Sales web page at http://www.apress.com/bulk-sales.

Any source code or other supplementary material referenced by the author in this book is available to readers on GitHub via the book's product page, located at www.apress.com/9781484278505. For more detailed information, please visit http://www.apress.com/source-code.

Printed on acid-free paper

I'd like to dedicate this book to my Mom. Thank you so much for buying me that Packard Bell 386DX2 66MHZ desktop with 8MB of RAM, 2MB of video RAM, and multimedia CD-ROM. It was one of the most important events of my life. I love you sooo much Mom.

Table of Contents

About the Author

Victor Brusca is an experienced software developer specializing in building cross-platform applications and APIs. He regards himself as a self-starter with a keen eye for detail, an obsessive protection of systems/data, and a desire to write well-documented, well-encapsulated code. With over 14 years of software development experience, he has been involved in game and game engine projects on J2ME, T-Mobile SideKick, WebOS, Windows Phone, Xbox 360, Android, iOS, and web platforms.

About the Technical Reviewer

Pranav Paharia is a game developer who has been working in the gaming industry since 2013. He is proficient with game engines like Unity3D, Unreal Engine 4, and Cocos2dx. He has built games for mobile devices, PCs, and VR in both single-player and multiplayer genres. He has been very passionate about playing games since childhood and, as he grew up, pursued the science of game development. He has also worked on a few game development books in the past to share his knowledge about game development. Building gameplay systems and game mechanics are just two aspects of his vast work experience. His expertise in gametech extends beyond making games; he's also used it provide solutions in various domains like education, medicine, military, emergency training, AEC, VFX/animation and films. The companies he's worked with include Zaha Hadid, DRDO India, Mediamonks, and Line Creative.

Currently, he works in the film and VFX industries in the field of virtual production via game technology.

He loves photography, traveling, and reading.

You can contact him at pranavpaharia@gmail.com.

Acknowledgments

I'd like to take a moment to acknowledge the following people:

Special thanks to Katia Pouleva for fixing up the diagrams and screenshots for this book. You are an amazing graphic artist. I love you dearly, Elkus.

I'd like to acknowledge Carlo M. Bruscani. You are a very special person to me and an important part of my life. I wouldn't be the person I am without knowing you. Thank you so much, Carlo. I love you.

Lastly, I'd like to take a moment to acknowledge Jerry Lawson. Jerry Lawson was an American electronic engineer. He is known for his work in designing the Fairchild Channel F video game console as well as leading the team that pioneered the commercial video game cartridge. Thank you, Mr. Lawson; video games would not be the same without you.

CHAPTER 1

Introduction and Getting Started

Welcome to Chapter 1 of the *Advanced Unity Game Development* text. Unity is a powerful game creation tool. In many ways, it's almost too powerful and complex. This makes it difficult for some game developers to leverage the full potential of the software. Documentation, books, and tutorials are a great way to lower the learning curve. Programming experience, especially in C#, and familiarity with Visual Studio will also greatly improve your time working with Unity.

With all of these different training options available, many of them for free, what does this book offer that the others don't? What makes it stand out from the pack? Well, in most cases, the aforementioned learning material will show you how to accomplish a simple task in Unity. They'll show you a small unfinished game or demo to illustrate the material at hand. This book differs from the rest in that it contains a complete code review, in detail, of a full featured and complete Unity game. This includes the following general topics:

- Code and Classes that run a Complete Game

- Code Structure Essentials

- Project Structure Essentials

- Level/Track Building

- AI Opponents/Players

- Full HUD and Menu System

- Music and Sound Effects

1

© Victor G Brusca 2022
V. G Brusca, *Advanced Unity Game Development*, https://doi.org/10.1007/978-1-4842-7851-2_1

- Player Preferences

- Touch, Mouse, Keyboard, Gamepad Input

- Models, Prefabs, and Scripts

This book will guide you through the game's code, scripts, models, prefabs, and overall structure all the while showing you how the code works with the Unity engine to define a complete, refined, game in Unity. At the conclusion of this text, you'll have gained experience in the following areas of expertise as you are guided through the implementation of a hover car racing game:

- C#: Experience with classes, class management, and project-level aspects of code-like centralization

- Unity Coding: Experience working with classes that extend the Unity Monobehaviour class. Working with components in a component-based game engine

- Visual Studio: Experience navigating projects, viewing, and editing class files

- Unity C# Project Management: Experience working with a complete Unity game and associated C# code

- Unity Environment: Experience navigating the models, prefabs, resources, script files, and scenes of a complex Unity project

- Unity Project Management: Experience working with smaller scenes and associated classes, prefabs, and models

We'll review the details of the game's functionality as well as key concepts in Unity that we encounter throughout the journey. This will give you a solid foundation on which to build your Unity game development future. The general path we'll take is as follows:

1. Review a model of the car, track, track features, and their proposed interactions.

2. Review the code that powers the game. The code is separated into the following groups:

   a. Base Classes

     b. Interaction Classes

     c. Advanced Interaction Classes

     d. Helper Classes

     e. Input Classes

     f. Menu System Classes

     g. Player and Game State Classes

3. Review of the following Unity-related topics:

     a. Input Mappings

     b. Scene Structure and Inactive GameObjects

     c. GameObject Tags

     d. Multiple Camera Setup

     e. Scene Lighting

     f. Music and Sound Effects

     g. AI Opponents

     h. Applying it all to a New Level/Track

At the end of the journey, you'll have all the knowledge and experience you need to make your next great game. Now that we have an idea of what lies before us, let's take the first step on our journey and get our game development environment up and running.

Setting Up Your Environment

Before we can begin, we need to get our environment set up and configured properly. The first thing we'll need to do is open up a browser and navigate to the Unity website. Navigate to `www.unity.com` and create a new account if you haven't already done so. Complete this process and make sure you finish the account verification steps, as you'll need an active account before you can begin with the included racing game project.

At the time of this writing, the correct way to work with Unity is through the Unity Hub application. This application acts as an abstraction layer and centralization point for your Unity projects. The software lets you manage multiple projects, each one using a different version of Unity. Find the downloads page on the Unity site and download the latest version of Unity Hub. Install the software. Once that's done, open Unity Hub and log in with the account you just created.

Currently, Unity Hub will run on Windows, macOS, and certain distributions of Linux. For a quick reference on how to install Unity Hub and what operating systems are supported, navigate your browser to the following URL:

```
https://docs.unity3d.com/Manual/GettingStartedInstallingHub.html
```

Next up we'll install the latest version of Unity. Open up Unity Hub, if you've not done so already, and select the "Installs" tab on the left-hand side of the screen. Select the latest version of Unity available and choose the modules you want to install along with the Unity editor.

For the purposes of this text, we recommend that you select only the modules listed in the following. Of course, if you have your own thoughts on what modules you want installed, please feel free to do so. The only requirement we have is that "Visual Studio" is configured as the default scripting IDE for the Unity editor. You can install Visual Studio separately, but I'll only provide instructions on how to install it as a Unity module.

1. Under "Dev Tools," select "Microsoft Visual Studio Community"; this is required.

2. Select the native build module for your operating system. Choose one of the following depending on your operating system:

a. Linux Build Support (IL2CPP or Mono)

b. Mac Build Support (Mono)

c. Windows Build Support (IL2CPP)

You can install new modules or uninstall existing ones through the Unity Hub software. Select the "Installs" tab and then click the three dots on the tiles of the target Unity editor version. Select "Add Modules" from the context menu and you can customize the modules installed for that version of the Unity editor. Try adding the installation of the Android and WebGL build modules to your setup. With them installed, you'll have some interesting build targets to play around with. Now that we have that taken care of, let's grab a copy of the racing game project associated with this text. Navigate your browser to the following URL:

```
www.middlemind.net/urgbook/[BOOK PUBLICATION https://github.com/Apress/
Advanced-Unity-Game-Development]
```

Find the latest version of the game project. Compare the Unity version listed with the current version of the Unity editor you just installed. If the game project version is older, try to install that version of the Unity editor using the process listed previously. If the older version isn't available in the list of Unity editor versions, then install the oldest available version.

If you find yourself in the second circumstance, an older version isn't available, then I recommend following this process to upgrade the game project. First, open the project with the older version of Unity you've just installed. You should be prompted to upgrade the project. Do so, and when the upgrade process is completed, save the project. With that step done, perform the same steps except this time use the newest version of the Unity editor you have installed. Save the project once it's done upgrading for the second time.

This approach will safely upgrade the project to the latest version of Unity. Let's open up the project and check on a few things. Once the racing game project is done loading, open up the "Preferences" window, "Edit" ➤ "Preferences", and select the "External Tools" tab. Make sure that the "External Script Editor" preference is set to "Visual Studio."

If you don't see "Visual Studio" in the list of available editors, go back and check the installed modules for your version of the Unity editor and make sure that "Visual Studio" is installed. If you're still running into issues, reinstall the Unity editor and make sure to select the "Visual Studio" module.

Playing Hover Racers/Getting Ready

Now that we got that little bit out of the way, let's take the game for a test drive while we have the Unity editor open. Let's check to see which scene has been opened, if any, by default. Look to the Unity editor window's title bar. The name of the currently opened scene should be listed in the window title. If you see the word "Main13" or "Main14" listed in the title, then we're good to go. If not, then we'll have to open the correct scene. Go to the "Project" panel, or if you don't see it, go to the main menu and select "Window" ➤ "Panels" ➤ "Project" and open it.

Find the folder named "Scenes" and open it. Double-click the scene named "Main13". Once the scene loads up, we'll want to locate the "Game" panel. If you can't find it, follow the aforementioned steps to open it. Once the panel opens, select it and you should see a mess of UI and menus on the screen. This is fine. Locate the play button at the top, center, of the editor window. Before you press play, let me review the game's controls.

To control the direction of the car, move the mouse left and right. To accelerate the car, press the up arrow on the keyboard. You can use the left and right arrow keys to "strafe" the car left and right. To slow the car down, use the back arrow key. Ok, now that you've got the basics, press play and then click inside the game to make sure the input is active. Click the "Track 1" button of the main menu and play a few races.

Now that you've had a chance to play the game, let's stop referring to it as "the racing game." Let's now call it "Hover Racers." So from now on, when you see the words "Hover Racers," I'm most likely referring to the project or the game depending on the context. I will use the words car, player, current player, racer, hover racer, or race car to describe the players of the game, both human and AI. Depending on the context, this could mean the current player, the human player, or any opponent player in the game. Be aware of the context.

A little bit about the game. Hover Racers is a complete racing game that supports three race types: easy, classic, and battle. Three difficulties: easy, medium, and hard. And it comes with two built-in tracks. As we've seen, the game has a complete UI implementation including in-game HUD and menu system. Furthermore, the game has background music, sound effects, and win conditions. The main takeaway here is that the game is refined, professional, and complete. It's not a demo or a tutorial project. It's a complete game with a decent set of fully implemented features.

By the conclusion of the book, you'll have a complete understanding of how the Hover Racers game works. At this point, you'll be able to view the project as more a piece of clay to be molded than a final sculpture. You'll be able to see the project for what it is and be able to shape it as you add your own features using the knowledge you've gained here. Furthermore, you can apply that knowledge to any Unity game development project. Including your own, next great game.

We'll review the vast majority of the code together, so you don't necessarily need to be proficient in C#, but some programming experience is recommended. Here are a few tutorials you can read to get a basic understanding of Unity, Visual Studio, and C#:

- `https://docs.microsoft.com/en-us/dotnet/csharp/`
  `tour-of-csharp/tutorials/`
  (introduction to C# tutorial)

- `https://visualstudio.microsoft.com/vs/getting-started/`
  (introduction to Visual Studio tutorial)

- `https://docs.unity3d.com/Manual/LearningtheInterface.htm` (introduction to Unity editor)
- `https://docs.unity3d.com/Manual/CollidersOverview.html` (introduction to Unity collisions)

That brings us to the conclusion of this section. In the next section, we will conclude the chapter with a summary of the material that we've covered.

Chapter Conclusion

This brings us to the conclusion of this chapter. We actually covered a fair amount of ground in this little introduction chapter. Let's take a look at what we've done so far:

1. Listed the Unity game development topics that you'll gain experience with by reading and working through this text

2. Listed the general, overarching skills you'll gain experience with through the use of this text

3. Mapped out a plan to approach the material we need to cover

4. Set up our environment, including installing Unity Hub, the Unity editor, and Visual Studio

5. Played Hover Racers

Now that we have all of that taken care of, we're ready to start reviewing the game's code. But wait! We have to outline the game we're working on. Sure, we have a finished copy of the game, so this seems a bit redundant, doesn't it? Well, we need to really think of this as a guided game review journey. As such, we'll work on the Hover Racers game specifications in the next chapter and we'll review the game's code, in detail, in subsequent chapters.

CHAPTER 2

Game Specifications

In this chapter, we'll outline the Hover Racers' game specifications. This is an important step in game development. You should always take the time to list out some general game specifications. It may seem unnecessary in certain cases, but I would advise you to take the time to do it anyway. More often than not an invaluable thought will pop into your head as you list some of the specifications. That's what we want, new thoughts and concepts formulated around the subject matter at hand. Let's take a look at our specifications list.

1. A racing game where cars race a set number of laps around the track and compete for the fastest speed and first place

2. An in-game HUD indicating information about the current race and the car's status, that is, modifiers

3. Support for six players with video game AI managing the cars that aren't controlled by the human player

4. Track features, including bumper barriers, boost panels (turbo), jump panels, and battle mode modifiers

5. Support for three difficulties: low, medium, and high

6. Support for three game modes: easy, classic, and battle mode

7. Ability to detect off-track, stuck, and wrong direction car states

8. Full menu system including main menu, in-game HUD, end game, and pause game screens

9. Finishing touches like user preferences, input handlers, music, sound effects, and multiple tracks to race on

© Victor G Brusca 2022
V. G Brusca, *Advanced Unity Game Development*, https://doi.org/10.1007/978-1-4842-7851-2_2

The following sections define the basic game mechanics that are needed to power the game when combined with game state management and input classes.

- Model: Car, Track, Sensor

- Model: Car, Boost, Jump, Bounce Modifiers

Now at first glance, this list may seem incomplete, but it's actually pretty spot on at this point. We're not trying to create a list of a hundred bullet points that details every aspect of the game. Even if such a thing were possible, it would almost certainly lead to a rigid, mechanical game of some kind. Our goal here is to loosely define the game so that we can fairly clearly envision most screens in the game without being bogged down by too many details.

For instance, given the preceding description, you might envision the start of the game as a static menu screen the player interacts with before a race. Or it could be that you envision it as an animated scene similar to arcade cabinets, where the game plays itself until the user interacts with the game. The main point here is that we have a general outline of what we want. The details will get filled in at a later time.

Take a moment to review the specification listed previously. Let your imagination run as you read through them. I'll try to make note of it when we address one of the specific entries listed previously, but I would check back to this list every now and then to see how many points we've checked off of the list in case I miss a few. Next, we'll take a look at some of the game's mechanics and detail the model that describes the problem.

Model: Car, Track, Sensor

The first model we'll look at deals with the car, the track, and the car's sensor. This model building exercise will help us detail some of the game's mechanics without having to resort to long descriptions or lists of bullet points. Let's take a look.

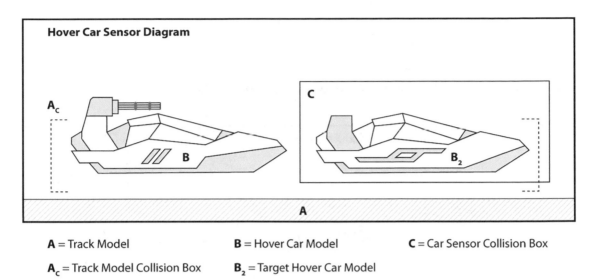

A = Track Model   **B** = Hover Car Model   **C** = Car Sensor Collision Box

A$_c$ = Track Model Collision Box   **B$_2$** = Target Hover Car Model

Figure 2-1. *Car, Track, Sensor Model Diagram*

A diagram depicting the hover racer, track collision box, and car collision box

The model, shown previously, has a side view of the hover racer on a track with its car sensor collision box. The track model, **A**, also has a collision box, **Ac**, that's used to detect if a car is on or off the racetrack. If a car is off the track, the track collision box detects this change and marks the car as being off the track. Another collision box is the car sensor, **C**, shown previously. This collision box is used to detect cars that are in front of the current car.

The model is very simple, but it answers a number of our questions. We now have an idea of how the car and track will interact. This gives us a way to determine if the current player's car has gone off track. This is a common feature of racing games and something we'll have to address at some point anyway, so it's good that we have a plan to work with. Next, we'll take a look at a model that describes how cars should interact with certain track features.

Model: Car, Boost, Jump, Bounce Modifiers

In this model, the second such one, we're attempting to describe, outline, how the player's car interacts with certain track features. In this case, we'll be looking at the jump, bounce, and boost modifiers. These features all change the physics of the hover car. The jump modifier will pop the racer up in the air, while the bounce modifier will bounce the car back in the direction it came from.

The last modifier we'll include in this model is the boost modifier. Similar to the other modifiers we're working with here, the boost modifier also changes the hover car's physics and throws the car forward. Let's take a look at our plan for these game mechanics and how they'll interact with the game's race cars.

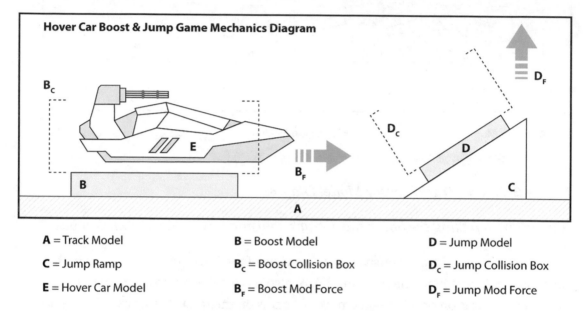

Hover Car Boost & Jump Game Mechanics Diagram

A = Track Model   **B** = Boost Model   **D** = Jump Model

C = Jump Ramp B_c = Boost Collision Box D_c = Jump Collision Box

E = Hover Car Model B_f = Boost Mod Force D_f = Jump Mod Force

Figure 2-2. *Car Boost and Jump Modifier Model Diagram*

A diagram depicting the hover racer, a boot marker, and a jump marker

The first model for this section, shown previously, demonstrates how the boost and jump modifiers interact with the hover racer. The modifiers shown will trigger using standard Unity collision interactions. The **Bc** and **Dc** features indicate collision boxes that detect when the hover racer crosses over the boost or jump modifier. As a result of this collision, a force will be applied to the hover racer. The **Bf** model feature indicates the direction of the boost force applied to the car. Similarly, the **Df** model feature indicates the direction of the jump force applied to the race car. The next model we'll look at is the bounce modifier model.

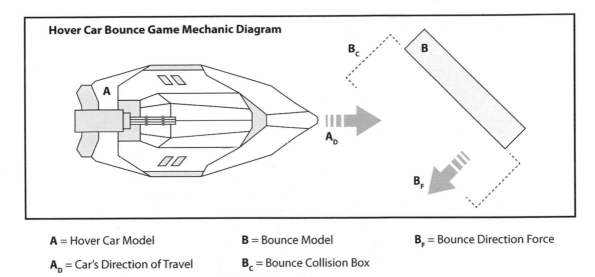

Hover Car Bounce Game Mechanic Diagram

A = Hover Car Model   **B** = Bounce Model B_F = Bounce Direction Force

A_D = Car's Direction of Travel B_C = Bounce Collision Box

Figure 2-3. *Car Bounce Modifier Model Diagram*

A diagram depicting a hover racer interacting with a bounce barrier

The second model of this section is shown previously. In this model, we'll take a look at the bounce modifier and how it will interact with a player's hover racer. The bounce modifier acts like the boost and jump modifiers in that it uses a collision box to detect a hover racer passing over it. When a collision of this kind is detected, a force is applied to the car that is a reflection of its collision angle. This results in the hover racer bouncing off of and away from the bounce object.

The last model we'll take a look at is the hover racer's input handling model. We're going to interpret the input that controls the car from the perspective of the mouse and keyboard. We're doing it this way because we view the mouse and keyboard as the default native support on Windows, macOS, and Linux. The game supports multiple input sources however, but we'll get to that a little later on in the text. Let's have a look!

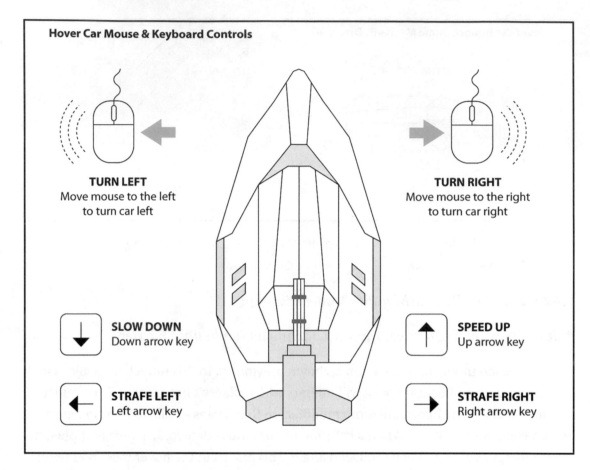

Figure 2-4. *Car Control/Input Diagram*

A diagram depicting the basic hover racer controls

In the previously shown diagram, we've mapped out the basic input from a top-down perspective. The basic keyboard and mouse controls are shown alongside the effective movement of the hover racer. These models and diagrams are like visual extensions to the game's specification list. They are used to help visualize interactions that would be more complicated or confusing to describe in text alone.

The game we'll review in this text uses input mapping to convert multiple inputs into a set of game inputs. An example case, turning the car left or right, can be accomplished by using the keyboard, mouse, or a gamepad. The inputs are mapped to game controls that are handled by a series of game classes to create third-person hover car controls. We'll review each class and the overall controls in detail in upcoming chapters.

Chapter Conclusion

In this chapter, we've mapped out the game's general specifications. The first set of specifications took care of creating a general view of the game as a whole. Our specifications list describes the actual game play, AI opponents, menu systems, sound effects, music, and more. The list loosely describes some game mechanics and interactions.

Following the specifications list, we reviewed a series of diagrams that describe the interactions between the hover racer and different track features. Let's summarize the diagrams that we've reviewed in this chapter in the following list:

1. Car, Track, Sensor Diagram: Depicts the track model and track sensor used to detect on/off track events of the hover racers. Also depicts the car sensor that is used to detect other hover racers in front of the current car.

2. Boost, Jump Diagram: Depicts the boost and jump modifiers and how their collision boxes are used to detect interaction with the current hover racer and subsequently apply a force to the car to alter its path on the track.

3. Bounce Diagram: Depicts the bounce modifier and how collision with a hover racer results in a force applied to the car to make it bounce away from the track's bounce obstacle.

4. Hover Racer Input/Control Diagram: A diagram depicts the basic mouse and keyboard input and how it alters the movement of the hover racer.

The models discussed in this chapter depict a general plan for implementing features such as on/off track functionality via the track sensor, and the ability for cars to detect hover racers in front of them. We also lay out a general plan for how to handle boost, jump, and bounce modifiers that are triggered by track objects and obstacles. Lastly, we mapped out a simple input scheme for controlling the hover racer. In the coming chapters, we'll review the code that powers the Hover Racers game. You'll get to see, in detail, how each game feature is implemented by viewing the code and running special demo scenes that show a given feature in action.

CHAPTER 3

Base Class

The base class is the foundation of most of the classes in the Hover Racers game. For instance, if you open up a class and see the following in the class declaration, ": `BaseScript`", then that class is a `MonoBehaviour` through extension of the `BaseScript` class. Let's quickly review the base script class using the review template discussed in the following section.

Class Review Template

Describing the functionality and use of a code class can be difficult. There can be a lot of context and configuration involved with certain classes. Unity projects are no exception. We'll attempt to overcome this difficulty by reviewing classes in detail using the following template. To clarify the aspects of the classes clouded by context and configuration, we'll demonstrate how classes work whenever possible.

1. Static/Constants/Read-Only Class Members

2. Enumerations

3. Class Fields

4. Pertinent Method Outline/Class Headers

5. Support Method Details

6. Main Method Details

7. Demonstration

Not every class will have topics of discussion for each section of the class review template. In such cases, we'll simply omit those sections without much mention. If you notice a section is missing, it's safe to assume that section doesn't apply to the current class' review.

© Victor G Brusca 2022
V. G Brusca, *Advanced Unity Game Development*, https://doi.org/10.1007/978-1-4842-7851-2_3

Class Review: BaseScript

In this section, we'll do a review of the BaseScript class so that you can get an idea of how class reviews are handled in this text. The BaseScript class is used as a convenient centralization of common functionality. Using this class as a base class simplifies game classes because it takes care of the default preparation, fields and methods, that just about every class needs. There are no enumerations to concern ourselves with, so we'll skip it in the review process and follow the steps listed here:

1. Static/Constants/Read-Only Class Members

2. Class Fields

3. Pertinent Method Outline/Class Headers

4. Support Method Details

5. Main Method Details

6. Demonstration

Class files can be found in one of three directories in the "Project" panel's "Standard Assets" folder:

1. \Character Controllers\Sources\

2. \mmg_scripts\

3. \mmg_scripts\demo_scripts\

Demo scripts are not covered as part of the text, but by the time you finish this text, you'll be an expert with the code base, so reviewing them may be something you plan on doing on your own. The process will lend more value to the associated demonstration scenes.

Static/Constants/Read-Only Class Members: BaseScript

The BaseScript class has a few very important static class members for us to take a look at. First, we'll look at the class' static class field, SCRIPT_ACTIVE_LIST.

Listing 3-1. BaseScript Static/Constants/Read-Only Class Members 1

```
public static Dictionary<string, bool> SCRIPT_ACTIVE_LIST = new
Dictionary<string, bool>();
```

This field is used to store the class initialization results for each class that extends the BaseScript and uses its preparation methods. In this way, the class initialization code is centralized, while the class initialization success data is specific to extended classes only.

Listing 3-2. BaseScript Static/Constants/Read-Only Class Members 2

```
1 public static bool IsActive(string sName) {
2     if (SCRIPT_ACTIVE_LIST.ContainsKey(sName)) {
3         return SCRIPT_ACTIVE_LIST[sName];
4     } else {
5         return false;
6     }
7 }
```

```
1 public static void MarkScriptActive(string sName, bool val) {
2     if (SCRIPT_ACTIVE_LIST.ContainsKey(sName)) {
3         SCRIPT_ACTIVE_LIST.Remove(sName);
4     }
5     SCRIPT_ACTIVE_LIST.Add(sName, val);
6 }
```

Listed previously there are two static class methods for us to review. The first entry is a very important method that is used all over the Hover Racer's code base, the IsActive method. This method is designed to take the current class' name as an argument and check to see if that class has been registered in the list of active scripts. This registration happens as part of the BaseScript class' preparation methods. The second method listed is the MarkScriptActive method. This method is used to set if a script has a true or false associated value, active or inactive. That brings us to the conclusion of this review section. Next, we'll take a look at the class' fields.

Class Fields: BaseScript

The BaseScript class has a number of class fields for us to look at. These fields are common to every class that extends the BaseScript class. I should note that although they are available by extension, not every class uses them.

Listing 3-3. BaseScript Class Fields 1

```
public PlayerState p = null;
public GameState gameState = null;
public bool scriptActive = true;
public string scriptName = "";
public AudioSource audioS = null;
```

The p field is a PlayerState instance and is used to reference the associated player's state information. The next entry is the gameState field, and it's used to hold a reference to the game's central state class instance. This happens to be an instance of the GameState MonoBehaviour and is also a Unity script component attached to a Unity game object labeled "GameState." The following entry, scriptActive, is a Boolean flag with a value that indicates if the current script has been properly initialized.

The scriptName field is a string instance that holds the name of the class extending the BaseScript class. Lastly, there is the audioS field an instance of the AudioSource component. Because sound effects are common, this field has been added to the BaseScript class to simplify other classes in the game's code base. That brings us to the conclusion of this review section. Next, we'll take a look at the class' pertinent methods and class definition.

Pertinent Method Outline/Class Header: BaseScript

The BaseScript class has a few methods for us to cover. Let's take a look.

Listing 3-4. BaseScript Pertinent Method Outline/Class Headers 1

```
//Main Methods
public bool Prep(string sName);
public bool PrepPlayerInfo(string sName);

//Support Methods
public void MarkScriptActive(bool val);
```

This class header, listed subsequently, shows the class declaration and any base classes or interfaces used by the BaseScript class.

Listing 3-5. BaseScript Pertinent Method Outline/Class Headers 2

```
using System.Collections.Generic;
using UnityEngine;

public class BaseScript : MonoBehaviour { }
```

Note that this class uses some C# libraries to power its data structures. Also notice that this class extends the MonoBehaviour class. This means that every class that extends the BaseScript class is also a MonoBehaviour, script component, and can be attached to Unity GameObjects. Let's take a look at the class' support methods next.

Support Method Details: BaseScript

The BaseScript class has only one support method for us to be concerned with. Let's take a look!

Listing 3-6. BaseScript Support Method Details 1

```
1 public void MarkScriptActive(bool val) {
2     scriptActive = val;
3     MarkScriptActive(scriptName, scriptActive);
4 }
```

The MarkScriptActive method is short and sweet. The method updates the scriptActive class field on line 2 and then updates the current script in the active script registry with the call to the static version of the MarkScriptActive method on line 3. Note that the method call uses the class fields scriptName and scriptActive to register the script as active or inactive in the script registry. That brings us to the conclusion of the support methods review section. Up next, let's direct our attention to the class' main methods.

Main Method Details: BaseScript

For the class' main method review section, we have a pair of methods to look at. Both are used to prepare the BaseScript class by finding and loading the necessary Unity GameObjects and their associated components.

Listing 3-7. BaseScript Main Method Details 1

```
1 public bool Prep(string sName) {
2     scriptName = sName;
3     scriptActive = (bool)Utilities.LoadStartingSet(scriptName, out
      gameState)[2];
4     MarkScriptActive(scriptName, scriptActive);
5     return scriptActive;
6 }
```

```
1 public bool PrepPlayerInfo(string sName) {
2     scriptName = sName;
3     scriptActive = (bool)Utilities.LoadStartingSetAndLocalPlayerInfo(
      scriptName, out gameState, out PlayerInfo pi, out int playerIndex,
      out p, gameObject, true)[2];
4     MarkScriptActive(scriptName, scriptActive);
5     return scriptActive;
6 }
```

The first method listed previously is the Prep method. This method is the basic initialization call used by most classes that extend the BaseScript class. One line 2, the class' scriptName field is set followed by a call to the Utilities class' LoadStartingSet method. This method performs the actual work of finding game objects, script components, etc. Note that the second value returned, in the array of results, by this method is a Boolean value indicating if the initialization code was successful or not. This value is stored in the scriptActive class field, line 3. On line 4, the BaseScript class' registry is updated with a call to the MarkScriptActive method that receives both the extended class name and the active flag, line 4. The active flag is returned at the end of the method.

The second method listed is similar to the one we just reviewed, but it supports getting a little more information for us. The PrepPlayerInfo method is used by a few classes that need the starting set and the current player's state loaded at initialization. The only reason we have made a distinction here is due to efficiency. Why do more work than we need to? That's what the Prep method is for. Note the call on line 3 that also returns a Boolean flag indicating the success of the operation stored in array index 2.

Also note that the "out p" method argument is used to update the class' PlayerState field, p, from the method call using the out keyword. The rest of the method is the same as the Prep method, so I'll let you look over it on your own. That brings us to the conclusion of this review section. In the next section, we'll take a look at the class in action.

Demonstration: BaseScript

While there isn't a direct demonstration of this class in action, it's used almost everywhere so we can just load up any demonstration scene and get the same effect. Open the Hover Racer's Unity project and navigate to the "Project" panel. Locate the "Scenes" folder and find the scene named "DemoCollideTrack". Double-click the scene and load it. Once it's done loading, navigate to the Unity editor's "Hierarchy" panel. Notice that the scene elements are organized using parent and child objects to create something like a folder structure that holds game objects.

This isn't a bad thing. Don't think that adding these empty GameObjects and creating the parent/child relationship is going to slow down your game or anything. At most we're adding a few empty objects to the scene which won't cause a slowdown by any means. On the contrary, you should try to organize your scene elements so that you can quickly find what you're looking for. In this case, we're looking for the "Environment" game object. Expand it and locate the child named "Street_30m". Select it and then direct your attention to the "Inspector" panel.

Locate the "Road Script" entry in the "Inspector" panel and expand it. Notice that the fields listed here are not set. The p, gameState, scriptActive, and scriptName fields are all uninitialized. I want to mention that we could have wired this up using the Unity editor and not in the code. For instance, if I dragged and dropped the GameState object, from the hierarchy, into the gameState field in the inspector and filled in the scriptName field, that data would be set and usable by the game. So why not just do that, seems easier right?

The reason for this has a lot to do with the scope and needs of the game you're working on. If your game is simple or a proof of concept, then using this approach is fine. The problem is that wiring things up by hand in the Unity editor isn't really flexible and won't scale with complex games. For instance, if I make changes to the scene and disrupt the GameState object, that will destroy all the wired connections I made. I would have to go back and adjust them once I finished whatever it is that I'm doing with the scene.

By using the programmatic approach, there is nothing to adjust. The code finds the GameObjects and their associated components for us and reports the issue if something goes wrong. That gives us a lot more power and control over the game. That's what we want with a game this size. The game is actually data driven where the data in this case are some preconfigured Unity game objects and script components. The track and players are the data that is loaded up as part of the game's centralized initialization process. This approach ensures that each class has required component references at runtime.

Back to the demonstration. With the inspector panel open, showing the "Road Script" component's details, run the demonstration scene. Notice that once the scene starts up, the gameState and scriptName fields are now properly set.

Think about this for a minute. It's an important distinction, and you may encounter numerous situations where you have to decide if I should wire this up in the editor or use code to connect things. That brings us to the end of the review section.

Chapter Conclusion

In this chapter, we got some important ground work done. We reviewed the BaseScript that is extended by many of the game's classes.

1. Class Review Template: We looked at the framework we'll use to review the game classes and try to interpret and understand how they function and how they are used.

2. BaseScript Class Review: We reviewed, in detail, the BaseScript class which is an important base class that many classes in the game extend.

3. Template in Use: We demonstrated how the class review template is applied to an actual class.

4. Distinction Between Hard Wired and Code Wired: We quickly
    discussed the distinction between hard-wired connections, using
    the Unity editor to set them up, and code-wired connections,
    using script components to make the connection between
    GameObjects and components.

That brings us to the conclusion of this chapter. Even though this is a short chapter, it has a lot of important information in it regarding using and connecting GameObjects in the context of the Hover Racers game but also in the general context of building games in Unity.

CHAPTER 4

Interaction Classes

Welcome to the chapter on interaction classes. In this chapter, we're going to dive into the project and start reviewing the classes that support hover racer modifiers and interactions. I sometimes refer to these interactions as game mechanics, and vice versa, but this is slightly inaccurate. Let me clarify a bit. The interactions we're reviewing here are powered by the Unity engine. They use MonoBehaviour-based classes and collision boxes to determine when the hover racers trigger a collision event.

At this point, the state of the player's hover racer is altered to apply the modifier that was triggered by the collision. The translation from Unity engine interactions to game state adjustments is the actual application of the game mechanic. Because it all happens in sequence and very quickly, it's easy to overlook the distinction. Open the Hover Racers Unity project and locate the "Project" panel. If the panel is not visible, go to the main menu and select "Windows" ➤ "Panels" ➤ "Project." Once the panel is visible, expand the folders until you can see the "Standard Assets" folder in the root directory. Before we look at any code, let's go over the list of classes we'll review. The classes that we'll review in this chapter are as follows:

1. BounceScript

2. RoadScript

3. WaypointCheck

4. TrackHelpScript

Now that we have all of that out of the way, let's jump into some code. Double-click the script named "BounceScript" located in "Assets" ➤ "Standard Assets" ➤ "mmg_scripts" to open it in Visual Studio.

© Victor G Brusca 2022
V. G Brusca, *Advanced Unity Game Development*, https://doi.org/10.1007/978-1-4842-7851-2_4

Class Review: BounceScript

The BounceScript class is responsible for triggering the hover racer's bounce modifier. This game mechanic presents itself on tracks where bounce barriers are used. You can tell when you've collided with an active bounce barrier because your hover racer will fly off in the opposite direction of the barrier. We'll review the class using the aforementioned class review template. The relevant sections are listed as follows:

1. Class Fields

2. Pertinent Method Outline/Class Headers

3. Support Method Details

4. Main Method Details

5. Demonstration

There are no pertinent enumerations to speak of, so we'll skip that review section. As we review the code, I want you to try and imagine how the class and its methods are used. Don't walk away with any concrete observations until you juxtapose your ideas against this class' demo scene.

Class Fields: BounceScript

I'll list the class' fields in groups ranging from roughly 5 to 15 depending on the context. Some fields are private and only used internally by class methods. I won't always list these fields and I won't always go into detail regarding them. Think of them as local variables but registered at the class level. Because this design decision comes up a lot in the code, I want to discuss it a bit. Unity uses C# as a main scripting language. It turns out that C# is a managed memory language.

This means that a C# program runs a garbage collector, watches object reference counts, and cleans up any unused memory from unreferenced objects. Now this is a one-sentence description of a rather complicated process, so let's just overlook any inaccuracies. The main point here is that just because there is a garbage collector running doesn't mean we should give it any work to do.

A garbage collector that's being abused can end up with a lot of work to do. This in turn can negatively impact your game's performance and could affect the frame rate and user experience. In order to prevent the garbage collector from running, as much as possible, local method variables are moved up to private class fields. This prevents the need to allocate and release memory on method calls as the objects in use are still referenced by the class.

I use this approach where it makes sense, in update calls and event handlers. Any code that has potential to be run a few times a second should be adjusted to use private class fields and cause less garbage collection in my opinion. With all that being said, don't abuse this approach either. If a method works fine with local variables, leave it be. You can always come back and refactor the code. Let's take a look at the first set of class fields listed as follows.

Listing 4-1. BounceScript Class Fields 1

```
public float bounceDampener = 0.75f;
public float minBounceVelocityHor = 20.0f;
public float minBounceVelocityVer = 20.0f;
private bool useReflect = false;
```

The bounceDampener field is used to lessen the initial velocity on the X and Z axes. The Y axis, vertical axis, is kept at zero while applying this modifier. The next two class fields, minBounceVelocityHor and minBounceVelocityVer, are used to maintain a minimum strength to the bounce modifier's velocity. This ensures that the bounce effect is prominent at lower collision speeds. When in doubt, go with cartoonish, slightly exaggerated, physics. They tend to be more fun in games, and you can always dial it back if need be.

Next in the list of fields is the useReflect Boolean flag. This field controls the calculation used to determine the car's bounce velocity vector. Often in game development, you are confronted with a situation where you can apply more complex, but more accurate, math to describe the physics of your game. My recommendation is to use a simple, "simulated," approach first and see if you can't get things working adequately.

The only reason I recommend this is because it is often the case that the advanced math will be imperceptible from the simplified approach. In this case, you get the benefit of a more efficient implementation. The second reason I offered this advice is that real-world physics just isn't fun. Again, think cartoon physics. Anyhow let's get back to the class field review. The remaining class fields are private and used internally by class methods. Let's take a look.

Listing 4-2. BounceScript Class Fields 2

```
//***** Internal Variables: BounceObjOff *****
private Vector3 v3;
private float x;
```

```
private float y;
private float z;

//***** Internal Variables: OnTriggerEnter *****
private CharacterMotor cm = null;
```

The fields listed previously are, as mentioned, used internally by the class' BounceOffObj and OnTriggerEnter methods. The v3 field is used to represent the resulting bounce velocity vector. Subsequent fields, x, y, and z, are used to calculate the velocity of the components of the v3, Vector3, field. The end result is a three-dimensional vector with values in the x and z components and a y component value of zero. This constitutes the bounce effect and is applied to the hover racer's movement.

The last class field for us to look at is used by the OnTriggerEnter method. Oftentimes, throughout the game's code, we need to connect from one piece of information, a game object, or a collision event, back to the classes that hold player and game state information. The CharacterMotor field, cm, is a component that allows for the movement of the player's hover racer. This class is the successor to the FPSWalker.js script from Unity 2.x and the predecessor to the FirstPersonController.cs script from Unity 5.x. Yes, at one point in time, you could code in Unity using both JavaScript and C#, side by side. In fact, this game was originally implemented as a JavaScript and C# hybrid project. Next, we'll take a look at the class' pertinent method list and class header.

Pertinent Method Outline/Class Headers: BounceScript

A list of the BounceScript class' pertinent methods are as follows.

Listing 4-3. BounceScript Pertinent Method Outline/Class Headers 1

```
//Support Methods
public void OnTriggerEnter(Collider otherObj);

//Main Methods
public void BounceObjOff(GameObject go, Collider otherObj, PlayerState p,
CharacterMotor cm);

void Start();
```

The class' header shows import statements and the class' declaration including any base classes it extends or interfaces it implements.

Listing 4-4. BounceScript Pertinent Method Outline/Class Headers 2

```
using UnityEngine;

public class BounceScript : BaseScript {}
```

Notice that the BounceScript class is a MonoBehaviour because it extends the base class, BaseScript, which in turn extends the Unity engine's MonoBehaviour class. We'll take a look at the class' support methods first. I'll label the line numbers for each method starting at number one. Feel free to follow along in the Unity editor and Visual Studio as we review different classes.

Support Method Details: BounceScript

The BounceScript class has one support method we'll take a look at next. Sometimes, we'll encounter a class that has a large number of simple support methods like get, set and show, hide methods. Methods with very little in the way of code to review since the methods are simple and direct. In this case, we have a bit of code to review. Let's take a look at the following method.

Listing 4-5. BounceScript Support Method Details 1

```
01 public void OnTriggerEnter(Collider otherObj) {
02     if (BaseScript.IsActive(scriptName) == false) {
03         return;
04     }
05
06     cm = null;
07     if (otherObj != null && otherObj.gameObject != null && otherObj.
       gameObject.CompareTag(Utilities.TAG_PLAYERS)) {
08         Utilities.LoadPlayerInfo(GetType().Name, out PlayerInfo pi, out
           int playerIndex, out p, otherObj.gameObject, gameState, false);
09         if (p != null) {
10             cm = p.cm;
11         }
12
```

```
13        if (p != null && cm != null && p.isBouncing == false) {
14            BounceObjOff(otherObj.gameObject, otherObj, p, cm);
15        }
16    }
17 }
```

This method is a collision detection callback method that's fired as part of the Unity game engine's game object interaction. I'm simplifying things here. There are more components involved with collision detection, but we'll cover them in more detail during the demonstration section of the class review. This method gets a Collider object passed to it as part of the collision event. On lines 2–4, the class is escaped without doing any work if it has encountered a configuration issue and registers a false value in the BaseScript class' initialization results Dictionary, SCRIPT_ACTIVE_LIST.

If the otherObj argument is defined, has a valid gameObject field, and is tagged as a "Player" GameObject, then we process the collision, line 7. On line 8, the call to the utility method LoadPlayerInfo uses the GameObject's PlayerInfo script component to find out the player's index and then uses that information to look up the player's state class, PlayerState, in the game's central state class, GameState. The result is that the class field p is set and can be used to check if that player's character motor, cm, is defined, line 9.

If the necessary fields are defined and the player's hover racer isn't already bouncing, then we apply the bounce modifier by calling the BounceOffObj method, lines 13–14. That wraps up our review of the class' support method. Next up we'll take a look at the class' main methods.

Main Method Details: BounceScript

There are two main methods for us to review. The first is the Start method. This method is part of the Unity engine's component architecture. In short, each component in your game has a Start and an Update callback method. The Start method is called once at the beginning of a component's life cycle. This method, in particular, is considered a point for preparation and configuration. Let's jump into some code!

Listing 4-6. BounceScript Main Method Details 1

```
01 void Start() {
02     base.Prep(this.GetType().Name);
03     if (BaseScript.IsActive(scriptName) == false) {
04         Utilities.wrForce(scriptName + ": Is Deactivating...");
05         return;
06     }
07
08     audioS = GetComponent<AudioSource>();
09     if (audioS == null) {
10         Utilities.wrForce(scriptName + ": audioS is null!");
11     }
12 }
```

The Start method is responsible for initializing the class and as such also has the ability to deactivate the class if the initialization requirements are not met and the class is marked as inactive. The initialization takes place with a call to the Prep method on line 2. Notice that the method's first argument is the name of this class. This string is used to register the result of the initialization and mark the class as active or inactive. One line 3, we test to see if the initialization result was successful.

I chose to add a disable-class feature to prevent classes from throwing tons of exceptions. If the class happens to be used in an Update method, there is potential for a disabling number of exceptions to be logged. This circumstance can clog the "Console" panel and hide the initial cause of the exception. Lastly, on lines 8–11, we load an AudioSource component, if available, to use as a sound effect when applying the bounce modifier. The next main method we'll look at is the BounceOffObj method. Let's jump into some code!

Listing 4-7. BounceScript Main Method Details 2

```
01 public void BounceObjOff(GameObject go, Collider otherObj, PlayerState p,
   CharacterMotor cm) {
02     if (BaseScript.IsActive(scriptName) == false) {
03         return;
04     }
05
```

```
06    v3 = Vector3.zero;
07    x = 0;
08    y = 0;
09    z = 0;
10    p.isBouncing = true;
11
12    x = cm.movement.velocity.x;
13    if (useReflect == true) {
14       x = x * bounceDampener;
15    } else {
16       x = x * -1 * bounceDampener;
17    }
18
19    if (x < 0) {
20       if (x > -minBounceVelocityHor) {
21          x = -minBounceVelocityHor;
22       }
23    } else if (x >= 0) {
24       if (x < minBounceVelocityHor) {
25          x = minBounceVelocityHor;
26       }
27    }
28
29    z = cm.movement.velocity.z;
30    if (useReflect == true) {
31       z = z * bounceDampener;
32    } else {
33       z = z * -1 * bounceDampener;
34    }
35
36    if (z < 0) {
37       if (z > -minBounceVelocityHor) {
38          z = -minBounceVelocityHor;
39       }
40    } else if (z >= 0) {
```

```
41        if (z < minBounceVelocityHor) {
42            z = minBounceVelocityHor;
43        }
44    }
45
46    if (useReflect == true) {
47        v3 = Vector3.Reflect(v3, otherObj.ClosestPointOnBounds(go.
          transform.position).normalized);
48    } else {
49        v3 = new Vector3(x, y, z);
50    }
51
52    cm.movement.velocity = v3;
53    if (audioS != null) {
54        if (audioS.isPlaying == false) {
55            audioS.Play();
56        }
57    }
58    p.isBouncing = false;
59 }
```

Similar to the OnTriggerEnter method, the BounceObjOff method is protected by the IsActive method call and check performed on lines 2–4. The little block of code on lines 6–10 is used to initialize the method's local variables, in this case, private class fields. This method creates a bounce vector with velocity adjusted to make the hover racer bounce away. The x component of the bounce vector is calculated on lines 12–27. The local x component is initialized with the velocity of the hover racer's x component.

If useReflect is enabled, a different calculation is performed. At first, the x component is dampened and reflected if useReflect is false. This is counterintuitive; let me explain. If useReflect is true, we use a Unity reflect calculation. If not, we use a simple simulated reflection. The code block on lines 19–27 is used to force a minimum bounce velocity on the x and z axes. You can also think of them as the x and z components of a Vector3 instance.

A very similar process is used to set the z component of the velocity vector on lines 29–44. Because we're excluding vertical adjustments in our game, this is all we have to do to prepare the bounce velocity vector. If you take a look at lines 46–50, you'll see the creation of the bounce velocity vector. In this snippet of code, if the useReflect flag is true, the class uses the Unity reflect method; otherwise, the very simple simulated reflection is used, line 47.

A subtle but important line of code can be found on line 52. This is where the hover racer game object's character motor has its movement vector adjusted. Finally, on lines 52-56, if the sound effect, AudioSource, is set, the sound is played to indicate a bounce and the player state flag, isBouncing, is set to false, line 58. This field was set to true on line 10 of the method. Using this flag prevents bounce modifiers from doubling up. That completes our review of the BounceScript class. Up next, we'll see how the class works in action.

Demonstration: BounceScript

There is a scene specifically designed to demonstrate the BounceScript in action. Find the "Project" panel and locate the "Scenes" folder. Find and open the scene named "DemoCollideBounce". Before we start the demo, let's talk about what's going on here. You'll be able to start the scene and control the hover racer after a few seconds just like in the normal use of the game. You can use the basic keyboard and mouse controls listed in Chapter 2 to control the hover racer.

In the demo scene, there are three colored pillars surrounded by four bounce barriers. Each group is configured in a different way. The barriers around the green pillar are configured to bounce the car. These barriers have a Box Collider with the "Is Trigger" checkbox checked. This indicates that the collision physics will be handled by a script and not the default physics engine. Running into this barrier will run the operative code from the class we've just reviewed. The car will be bounced away.

The next pillar to discuss is the red pillar. This pillar is also surrounded by barriers, but these barriers are configured a bit differently. These barriers also have BoxCollider, but they have the "Is Trigger" box unchecked. To show that the script no longer matters, the barriers have the script deactivated. Colliding into these barriers will result in default physics behavior. The car will simply run into and stop at the barrier. Try it out!

The last set of barriers to discuss surrounds the purple pillar. These barriers are an example of a misconfiguration. In this case, the barriers have a BoxCollider with the "Is Trigger" box checked just like with the green pillar. The difference here is that these barriers don't have an active script that handles collision events. You'll notice in this case that the car can drive right through the barrier.

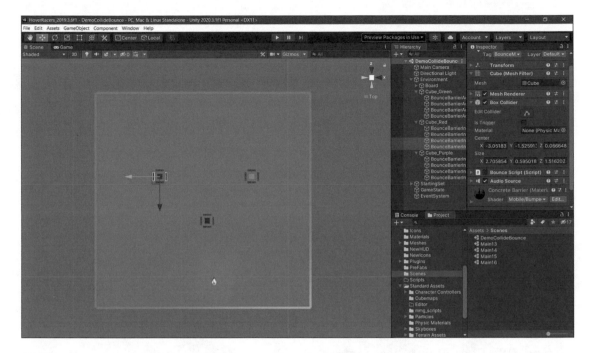

Figure 4-1. *BounceScript Demonstration Scene*

Image showing the bounce demo scene from a top-down view

The image shown previously is a depiction of the demonstration scene used for this class. That brings us to the conclusion of the BounceScript class review. The next class up for review is the RoadScript. This script behaves somewhat similarly to that of the BounceScript.

Class Review: Road Script

The RoadScript class is responsible for detecting if the player's hover car is actively on the track or not. When used in the game, each piece of the racetrack has an attached RoadScript component. This ensures that the player's hover racer is monitored for on-track or off-track status at all times. The relevant sections for this class review are listed as follows:

1. Class Fields

2. Pertinent Method Outline/Class Headers

3. Support Method Details

4.   Main Method Details

5.   Demonstration

There are no pertinent enumerations or static class members to speak of, so we'll skip that review section. Again, try to imagine the class in use as you read through the class review. Try to reserve any final judgements until you take a look at the class' demonstration.

Class Fields: RoadScript

The RoadScript class has a few fields for us to review. Some of these fields are private and used only internally by certain class methods. We won't go into as much detail for private internal fields. The reason for this design decision is that the private class fields are referenced by the class and won't be touched by the garbage collector as long as the class is in use.

Listing 4-8. RoadScript Class Fields 1

```
//***** Class Fields *****
private float delay = 5.0f;
private PlayerState sdp;

//***** Internal Variables: OnTrigger Methods *****
private PlayerState pEntr = null;
private PlayerState pStay = null;
private PlayerState pExit = null;
```

The first class field, delay, is used to add a 5-second delay to the player's hover racer getting its off-track set to true. The following field, sdp, is a PlayerState object that references the current state of the player's car. The next three class fields are used by the class' collision event handlers to hold a reference to the player state associated with the collision object, if any.

Pertinent Method Outline/Class Headers: RoadScript

The RoadScript class' list of pertinent methods is as follows.

Listing 4-9. RoadScript Pertinent Method Outline/Class Headers 1

```
//Main Methods
void Start();

//Support Methods
public void OnTriggerEnter(Collider otherObj);
public void OnTriggerStay(Collider otherObj);
public void OnTriggerExit(Collider otherObj);

public void SpeedUp(PlayerState p);
public void SlowDown(PlayerState p);
public void RunSlowDown();
```

This class header, listed subsequently, shows the class declaration and any base classes or interfaces used by the RoadScript class.

Listing 4-10. RoadScript Pertinent Method Outline/Class Headers 2

```
using UnityEngine;

public class RoadScript : BaseScript {}
```

Let's take a look at the class' support methods.

Support Method Details: RoadScript

The RoadScript class has a few support methods for us to review. We'll start by looking at the collision event handlers. Let's jump into some code.

Listing 4-11. RoadScript Support Method Details 1

```
01 public void OnTriggerEnter(Collider otherObj) {
02     if (BaseScript.IsActive(scriptName) == false) {
03         return;
04     }
05
```

```
06      if (otherObj != null) {
07          Utilities.LoadPlayerInfo(GetType().Name, out PlayerInfo pi, out
            int playerIndex, out pEntr, otherObj.gameObject, gameState,
            false);
08          if (pEntr != null) {
09              SpeedUp(pEntr);
10          }
11      }
12 }
```

```
01 public void OnTriggerStay(Collider otherObj) {
02      if (BaseScript.IsActive(scriptName) == false) {
03          return;
04      }
05
06      if (otherObj != null) {
07          Utilities.LoadPlayerInfo(scriptName, out PlayerInfo pi, out int
            playerIndex, out pStay, otherObj.gameObject, gameState, false);
08          if (pStay != null) {
09              SpeedUp(pStay);
10          }
11      }
12 }
```

```
01 public void OnTriggerExit(Collider otherObj) {
02      if (BaseScript.IsActive(scriptName) == false) {
03          return;
04      }
05
06      if (otherObj != null) {
07          Utilities.LoadPlayerInfo(GetType().Name, out PlayerInfo pi, out
            int playerIndex, out pExit, otherObj.gameObject, gameState,
            false);
08          if (pExit != null && pExit.isJumping == false && pExit.boostOn ==
            false) {
09              sdp = pExit;
```

```
10             Invoke(nameof(RunSlowDown), delay);
11        }
12    }
13 }
```

Because all three of the methods listed previously follow almost an identical pattern, I'll only review the OnTriggerExit method in detail here. Take that knowledge and apply it to the OnTriggerEnter and OnTriggerStay methods. First off, on lines 2–4, we have the active script check. If it returns false, then the method returns without doing any work. This is part of the class' fail-safe lockout. Notice that the lockout affects all instances of the script. Again, we lock out the class' functionality when class configuration has failed. This prevents a cascade of errors from clogging up the console output. Keep in mind this feature can always be commented out for production builds.

On line 6, if the collision object is defined, we use it to load the PlayerState class for the associated player, if there is one, on line 7 with a call to the Utilities class' LoadPlayerInfo method. If the proper criteria match, on line 8, then we set the local field, sdp, to the PlayerState of the game object we just collided with and invoke the RunSlowDown method. Because the OnTriggerExit method fires when a player's hover racer leaves the road sensor, we call the slowdown method to activate the off-track speed penalty.

The stay and enter versions of the collision event handler methods will speed the player's car to normal speeds. The exit collision event handler method will slow the player's car down to off-track speeds as we've just seen. Note that on line 10, the RunSlowDown method is called indirectly by calling the class' Invoke method with the name of the method to run and a time delay. In this case, the player or AI opponent has a few seconds to get back on track before the slowdown penalty triggers.

Listing 4-12. RoadScript Support Method Details 2

```
1 public void SlowDown(PlayerState p) {
2    if (p != null && p.offTrack == false && p.controller.isGrounded ==
     true) {
3        p.offTrack = true;
4        p.SetSlow();
5    }
6 }
```

```
1 public void RunSlowDown() {
2     SlowDown(sdp);
3 }
```

```
1 public void SpeedUp(PlayerState p) {
2     if (p != null && p.offTrack == true) {
3         p.offTrack = false;
4         p.SetNorm();
5     }
6 }
```

The first method listed in the set of support methods detailed previously is the SlowDown method. This method sets the player state to off-track and lowers the hover racer's maximum speed with a call to the PlayerState class' SetSlow method. The next method listed, RunSlowDown, is used to execute the SlowDown method from a call to the Invoke method as we saw a little earlier.

The last method in the set for us to look at is the SpeedUp method. This method essentially reverses the effects of the SlowDown method. On lines 3–4 of the method, the hover racer is marked as being on-track, and its speed is set to the normal speed the hover racer can achieve when on the track. The next section for us to look at is the main method review. Let's have a look, shall we?

Main Method Details: RoadScript

The RoadScript class has only one main method for us to review. The ubiquitous Start method.

Listing 4-13. RoadScript Main Method Details 1

```
1 void Start() {
2     base.Prep(this.GetType().Name);
3     if (BaseScript.IsActive(scriptName) == false) {
4         Utilities.wrForce(scriptName + ": Is Deactivating...");
5         return;
6     }
7 }
```

This method should look familiar. We've seen similar implementations before, and we're certain to see them again. On line 2 of the method, we see a call to the centralized class preparation method, `Prep`, of the base class, `BaseScript`. This method call loads up all the needed default class fields with references to game objects and script components. If the preparation call fails, then the class, by name, is registered with a false value in the `BaseScript` class' registry. Note that on line 4, a log entry is made indicating there was a problem with the class. That wraps up the main method review. Up next, we'll demonstrate the class in action.

Demonstration: RoadScript

There is a scene specifically designed to demonstrate the road script in action. Find the "Project" panel and locate the "Scenes" folder. Find and open the scene named "DemoCollideTrack". Before we start the demo, let me describe how the scene works. In this scene is a 30-meter section of track, with a `RoadScript` script component and a collider with the correct trigger flag settings.

You'll notice some extra text in the bottom left-hand corner of the running demo. This text indicates the off-track status of the hover racer as well as the time in milliseconds that car has been off-track. Note that the off-track flag won't immediately trigger as you go off-track. There is a delay of a few seconds before the flag is flipped, so be patient. Run the demo and check things out. It takes a few seconds for user control to activate. The game is actually running an invisible countdown similar to what it would do in the real game. Next up, we'll take a look at the `WaypointCheck` script.

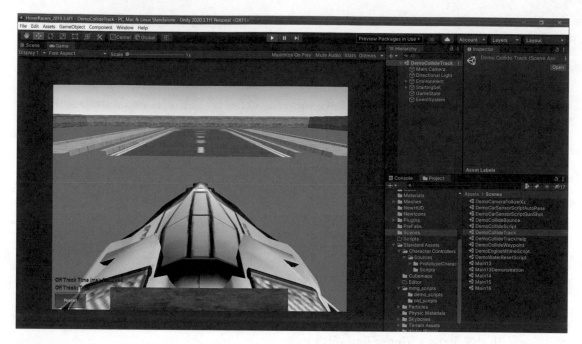

Figure 4-2. *RoadScript Demonstration Scene*

Image showing the on/off-track demo scene from a third person view

Class Review: WaypointCheck

The WaypointCheck script is responsible for detecting the direction and general location of the race cars on the track. I wanted to take a moment to do a deep dive on the game's waypoint system. The AI opponents in the game use the waypoint system to navigate around the track. Let's take a look at a diagram of the model.

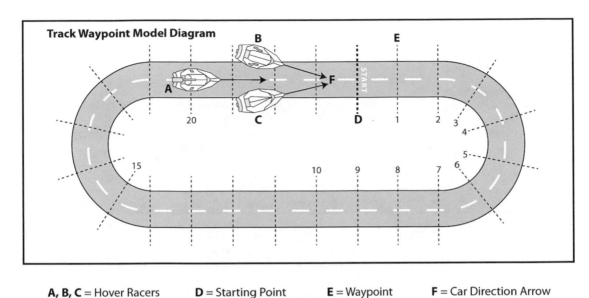

A, B, C = Hover Racers   D = Starting Point   E = Waypoint   F = Car Direction Arrow

Figure 4-3. *Track Waypoint Model Diagram*

A diagram depicting the use of waypoints to define the racetrack

The waypoints provide a scaffolding for the game's AI players. It also provides a quick way to determine a hover racer's general position on the track. And it can be used to indicate the car's direction and subsequently detect cars moving in the wrong direction. Let's take a look at how the AI opponents determine what direction to move in. The following diagram shows the currently implemented logic in a simplified model.

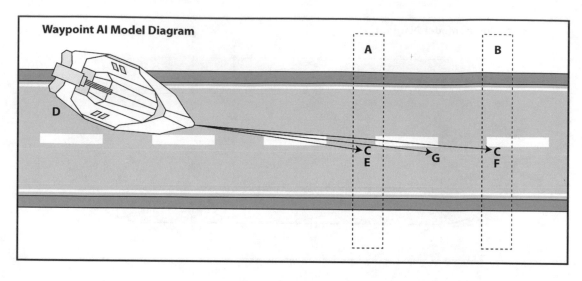

A, B = Waypoints   C = Center   D = Car   E, F = Centerpoint Vectors   G = Calculated Direction

Figure 4-4. *AI Waypoint Logic Model Diagram*

A diagram depicting the use of waypoints to define an AI player's direction

In this diagram, the hover racer uses the known vectors pointing to the center of the next two waypoints. An average of these vectors is taken, **G**, and this is used to direct the car. The waypoints also hold indicators that can slow the AI cars down. This is used to help keep the cars under control as they navigate turns, curves, and jumps. That covers all the prerequisite material. Let's start the class review. The relevant sections we'll cover are listed as follows:

1. Class Fields

2. Pertinent Method Outline/Class Headers

3. Support Method Details

4. Main Method Details

5. Demonstration

And with that, let's begin the class review with the first section.

Class Fields: WaypointCheck

The first set of class fields for us to review, listed as follows, is public and can be viewed through the Unity editor's "Inspector" panel.

Listing 4-14. WaypointCheck Class Field 1

```
public int waypointRoute = 0;
public int waypointIndex = 0;
public float waypointStartY = 4;
public float waypointSlowDown = 1.0f;
public bool isSlowDown = false;
public float slowDownDuration = 100.0f;
```

The first class field listed previously is the `waypointRoute` field. This field is not actually used in the game, everything sort of defaults to route 0, but we'll review it just the same in case you want to further implement waypoint routes. The following class field listed is the `waypointIndex` field. This field should be set during level building in the Unity editor. It is important that the waypoints are numbered properly with incrementing indexes. You can, however, wait to do this at the end of the waypoint placement process.

The `waypointStartY` field is used to assign a Y value to the track waypoint. This is used when placing a player's hover racer back on the track after being off-track, going backward for too long, or falling into the water. It can be used to ensure the hover racer is at the proper height when being replaced. The `waypointsSlowDown` field sets a value that indicates the amount of slowdown applied to AI players. The `isSlowDown` Boolean is a flag field that indicates that the slowdown action is active and should be applied to the AI-controlled hover racers. The last field listed in this set is the `slowDownDuration` field. This field controls how long the slowdown is applied to the car. In the next review section, we'll take a look at the class' pertinent methods.

Pertinent Method Outline/Class Headers: WaypointCheck

The `WaypointCheck` class' pertinent methods are listed as follows.

Listing 4-15. WaypointCheck Pertinent Method Outline/Class Headers 1

```
//Main Methods
void Start();

//Support Methods
public void OnTriggerEnter(Collider otherObj);
public void ProcessWaypoint(Collider otherObj);
```

47

The class header, listed subsequently, shows the class declaration and any base classes or interfaces.

Listing 4-16. WaypointCheck Pertinent Method Outline/Class Headers 2

```
using UnityEngine;

public class WaypointCheck : BaseScript {}
```

Let's take a look at the class' support methods first.

Support Method Details: WaypointCheck

The WaypointCheck class has few support methods for us to review. We'll look at the trigger event handler and its associated support method.

Listing 4-17. WaypointCheck Support Method Details 1

```
01 public void OnTriggerEnter(Collider otherObj) {
02     if (BaseScript.IsActive(scriptName) == false) {
03         return;
04     }
05
06     if (otherObj != null) {
07         ProcessWaypoint(otherObj);
08     }
09 }

01 public void ProcessWaypoint(Collider otherObj) {
02     if (BaseScript.IsActive(scriptName) == false) {
03         return;
04     }
05
06     if (otherObj != null && otherObj.gameObject.CompareTag(Utilities.
       TAG_PLAYERS)) {
07         Utilities.LoadPlayerInfo(GetType().Name, out PlayerInfo pi, out
           int playerIndex, out p, otherObj.gameObject, gameState, false);
```

```
08      if (p != null) {
09          if ((waypointIndex + 1) < p.aiWaypointIndex && ((waypointIndex
            + 1) - p.aiWaypointIndex) <= 3) {
10              p.wrongDirection = true;
11          } else {
12              p.wrongDirection = false;
13          }
14
15          if ((waypointIndex + 1) > p.aiWaypointIndex && ((waypointIndex
            + 1) - p.aiWaypointIndex) <= 5) {
16              if (p.aiWaypointLastIndex != p.aiWaypointIndex) {
17                  p.aiWaypointPassCount++;
18              }
19
20              p.aiWaypointLastIndex = p.aiWaypointIndex;
21              p.StampWaypointTime();
22
23              if (p.IsValidWaypointIndex(waypointIndex + 1) == true) {
24                  p.aiWaypointIndex = (waypointIndex + 1);
25              } else {
26                  if (p == gameState.GetCurrentPlayer() && gameState.
                    gameWon == false) {
27                      gameState.LogLapTime(p);
28                      p.lapComplete = true;
29                  }
30
31                  p.aiWaypointJumpCount = 0;
32                  p.aiWaypointPassCount = 0;
33                  p.aiWaypointIndex = 0;
34                  if (p.currentLap + 1 <= p.totalLaps) {
35                      p.currentLap++;
36                  }
37                  p.ResetTime();
38              }
39
```

```
40                    if (p.aiWaypointIndex == 1 && p.currentLap == gameState.
                      totalLaps && playerIndex == gameState.currentIndex) {
41                        //game over
42                        if (gameState.IsStartMenuShowing() == false) {
43                            gameState.gameWon = true;
44                            gameState.SetPositions();
45                            gameState.ShowEndMenu();
46                        }
47                    }
48                } else {
49                    p.skippedWaypoint = true;
50                }
51
52                if (p.aiOn == true) {
53                    if (isSlowDown == true) {
54                        p.aiSlowDownTime = 0f;
55                        p.aiSlowDownDuration = slowDownDuration;
56                        p.aiSlowDownOn = true;
57                        p.aiSlowDown = waypointSlowDown;
58                    }
59                }
60            }
61        }
62 }
```

The OnTriggerEnter callback method, as we've seen before, is called in response to a collision between the WaypointCheck component's box collider and a hover racer. As we have seen before, the code on lines 2–4 prevents the event handler method from doing any work if the class wasn't configured properly. On lines 6–8, if the given collision object is not null, the ProcessWaypoint method is called, line 7.

The ProcessWaypoint method has the same escape fail safe on lines 2–4. If the collision object is defined and it has the player tag, line 6, we then proceed to load the PlayerState data associated with that player, line 7. If the player's state object is found, line 8, then there are a few things we have to check as part of processing the way point.

The first thing we need to check is if the car is travelling in reverse. This check is handled on lines 9–13. The waypoint index, incremented by one to give the detection a little flexibility, is compared to the car's last waypoint.

If the car's waypoint was ahead of the current waypoint and it was only ahead by three or less, then we mark the hover racer as going in reverse on line 10. If not, we set the value of the field to false, line 12. On line 15, we check to see if the waypoint is ahead of the hover racer's current waypoint by a value of five or less; then we proceed to process it. A quick check is performed to see if the hover racer has passed a waypoint by making sure that the car's previous waypoint is not equal to its current waypoint. If so, the hover racer's `aiWaypointPassCount` is incremented.

Next, on line 20, the player's `aiWaypointLastIndex` is updated to the value of the car's previous waypoint, and on line 21, the `StampWaypointTime` method is called to update the waypoint timestamp. Note that I may refer to the hover racer as the player, at times, because the car is the player's representation in the game. The snippet of code, lines 23–38, is there to detect if we've reached the last waypoint on the track and reset some values for the next lap. On lines 26–29, if the current player is interacting with the last waypoint and the race hasn't ended, then we log the lap time and mark that the lap has completed.

The next responsibility this method has is to check and see if the game has ended. This is handled by the code snippet on lines 40–47. If we've reached the last waypoint for the current lap and this is the last lap of the race, we check to see if the start menu is showing on line 42. If not, meaning we're not running the AI demo of the race, then we mark that the game is over, refresh the car's positions, and then show the ending menu screen.

Last but not least, the method is responsible for guiding AI players by copying the slowdown data into the AI player's state on lines 53 to 58. Note that the data is only set if this waypoint has its `isSlowDown` field set to true. That wraps up the class' support methods. Next, we'll take a look at the class' main methods.

Main Method Details: WaypointCheck

Don't worry, the `WaypointCheck` class has only one main method for us to take a look at. Take a moment to look at the class' start method listed here.

Listing 4-18. WaypointCheck Main Method Details 1

```
1 void Start() {
2    base.Prep(this.GetType().Name);
3    if (BaseScript.IsActive(scriptName) == false) {
4       Utilities.wrForce(scriptName + ": Is Deactivating...");
5       return;
6    }
7 }
```

This start method provides identical class initialization to other class' start methods we've seen previously. As such, I won't go over it in much detail here. Make sure to read over the method and understand how it works before moving on. You'll see very similar if not identical code in just about every game class that extends the BaseScript class. The last class we'll cover in this chapter is the TrackHelpScript. Just like classes we've reviewed thus far, the TrackHelpScript class is a stand-alone collision detector. It provides the interaction that triggers help notifications on a track's first use. Before we get to that class review, let's look at the WaypointCheck class' demonstration scene.

Demonstration: WaypointCheck

The WaypointCheck class has a demonstration scene for us to check out. Before we look at it though, let's talk about what the scene does. First off, like every other demo scene, there is a slight delay before you can actually control the hover racer. Don't worry, this isn't a bug, the game code has been adjusted to support demo scenes, but it still has a few game features, like the countdown at the start of the race. You won't see the countdown numbers, but in just a few seconds, you'll be able to control the car.

If you race the car along the road in the opposite direction as the scene's waypoints, the pillars will turn or stay red. If you race along in the same direction, increasing waypoint indexes, the pillars will turn or stay green. If you click on each waypoint in the "Hierarchy" panel and view its details in the "Inspector" panel, you'll notice one has slowdown information configured. This won't affect your car however, because slowdown information is only used by AI players.

You can find this demo scene in the "Project" panel, in the "Scenes" folder. Look for the scene named "DemoCollideWaypoint". Open it up and play around with it a bit. Take a look at how the scene is set up and pay special attention to the waypoints and their interaction with the player's car. A screenshot of this class' demonstration scene is as follows.

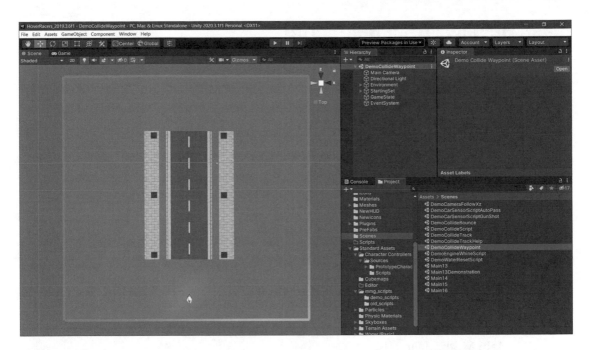

Figure 4-5. *WaypointCheck Demonstration Scene 1*

A top-down view of the waypoint demonstration scene

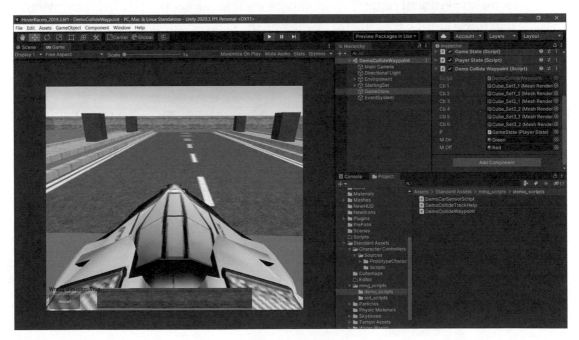

Figure 4-6. *WaypointCheck Demonstration Scene 2*

A screenshot of the waypoint demonstration scene in action

Class Review: TrackHelpScript

The TrackHelpScript class is designed to display help messages when a player races a track for the first time. There is a slight implementation caveat that I'd like to talk about. There are three such help messages supported by the game's HUD. The acceleration, slowdown, and turn help notifications are available for display by the game's HUD screen. The acceleration help notification, however, is not controlled by the TrackHelpScript.

The first of the three supported help messages is actually displayed as part of the race's starting code. As I mentioned before, the TrackHelpScript class is a stand-alone collision event handler very similar to the other classes we've viewed in this chapter. We'll use the following class review sections to cover this class.

1. Pertinent Method Outline/Class Headers

2. Support Method Details

3. Main Method Details

4. Demonstration

There are no pertinent static class members, enumerations, or class fields to review, so we'll skip those sections. Again, try to imagine the class in use as we step through the different review sections of the TrackHelpScript class. The first section we'll look at is the class' pertinent method outline. Let's take a look.

Pertinent Method Outline/Class Headers: TrackHelpScript

The TrackHelpScript class' pertinent methods are as follows.

Listing 4-19. TrackHelpScript Pertinent Method Outline/Class Headers 1

```
//Main Methods
void Start();

//Support Methods
public void OnTriggerEnter(Collider otherObj);
public void ProcessTrackHelp(Collider otherObj);
```

Next, I'll list the class headers, import statements, and class declaration. Pay special attention to any base classes that are used. Take a moment to review those classes if need be.

Listing 4-20. TrackHelpScript Pertinent Method Outline/Class Headers 2

```
using UnityEngine;

public class TrackHelpScript : BaseScript {}
```

In the next section, we'll take a look at the class' support methods.

Support Method Details: TrackHelpScript

The TrackHelpScript class has a similar implementation to that of the other stand-alone collision interaction scripts. The OnTriggerEnter event callback processes a collision event and calls a worker method to handle the necessary collision response.

Listing 4-21. TrackHelpScript Support Method Details 1

```
01 public void OnTriggerEnter(Collider otherObj) {
02     if (BaseScript.IsActive(scriptName) == false) {
03         return;
04     }
05
06     if (otherObj != null) {
07         if (gameState.trackHelpOn == true) {
08             ProcessTrackHelp(otherObj);
09         }
10     }
11 }

01 public void ProcessTrackHelp(Collider otherObj) {
02     if (BaseScript.IsActive(scriptName) == false) {
03         return;
04     }
05
```

```
06      if (otherObj != null && otherObj.gameObject.CompareTag(Utilities.
        TAG_PLAYERS)) {
07          Utilities.LoadPlayerInfo(GetType().Name, out PlayerInfo pi, out
            int playerIndex, out p, otherObj.gameObject, gameState, false);
08          if (p != null) {
09              if (p == gameState.GetCurrentPlayer() && p.aiOn == false) {
10                  if (gameObject.CompareTag("TrackHelpSlow")) {
11                      if (gameState.hudNewScript != null) {
12                          gameState.hudNewScript.HideHelpAccel();
13                          gameState.hudNewScript.HideHelpTurn();
14                          gameState.hudNewScript.ShowHelpSlow();
15                      }
16                      gameState.trackHelpSlowOn = true;
17                      gameState.trackHelpSlowTime = 0f;
18                  } else if (gameObject.CompareTag("TrackHelpTurn")) {
19                      if (gameState.hudNewScript != null) {
20                          gameState.hudNewScript.HideHelpAccel();
21                          gameState.hudNewScript.ShowHelpTurn();
22                          gameState.hudNewScript.HideHelpSlow();
23                      }
24                      gameState.trackHelpTurnOn = true;
25                      gameState.trackHelpTurnTime = 0f;
26                      gameState.trackHelpOn = false;
27                  }
28              }
29          }
30      }
31 }
```

Let's take a look at the OnTriggerEnter method first. The same fail-safe check we've seen before can be found on lines 2–4 of the method. If the collision object is defined, line 6, we check to see if the track help flag is set to true, on line 7, before proceeding. If track help is enabled, then the ProcessTrackHelp method is called on line 8. Moving on to the ProcessTrackHelp method. Lines 2–4 should look familiar so we'll move past it. The method is set to ignore collisions with objects that are not tagged as "Players". This ensures the event will only trigger when a player's car collides with it, line 6.

On line 7, we use a very important method, LoadPlayerInfo, which will find and load the state for the player's hover racer that triggered the collision. You'll see this method used a lot throughout the game's code so make sure you understand how it's used. One of the key features of this method call is the "out p" argument. This special method argument is used to update the p field without using the method's return value. If the call was successful and the p field is defined, the code on lines 9 to 28 executes.

On line 9, we check to see if the colliding player is the current player, and we make sure that the player is not an AI player. Can you figure out why we do this? One reason is that we don't need to display help notifications if the colliding player is not the current active player or AI control is true. This is because the HUD only connects to the current player and there's no need to display help notifications for other cars or if those cars are AI controlled. The TrackHelpScript has the ability to toggle the track help "slow" and "turn" HUD notifications.

Subsequently, on line 10, we check to see if the current Unity GameObject, gameObject field, has the tag "TrackHelpSlow"; then we prepare to display the slowdown help notification. We need to hide any current help notifications, so the code on lines 11–15 checks to see if we can access the game's HUD via the GameState class, gameState. If so, we then hide any other help notifications and show the operative one, line 14. Lines 16–17 reset the fields that control the display of the help notification. These fields are responsible for the timing involved with showing notifications on the game's HUD.

Similar code on lines 18–27 is used to control the track turn help message. Take a look at the code and make sure you understand it before moving on. That brings us to the conclusion of the support methods review section. In the next section, we'll take a look at the class' main methods.

Main Method Details: TrackHelpScript

The TrackHelpScript class has one main method for us to review. We've seen this method before. It's used to initialize the class and set the gameState field among other things. Let's take a look at the code!

Listing 4-22. TrackHelpScript Main Method Details 1

```
1 void Start() {
2    base.Prep(this.GetType().Name);
3    if (BaseScript.IsActive(scriptName) == false) {
4        Utilities.wrForce(scriptName + ": Is Deactivating...");
5        return;
6    }
7 }
```

As we've discussed previously, the start method is responsible for initializing the class. Its main responsibility is to locate the GameState script component located as a component of the GameState Unity GameObject. You'll see this object in the hierarchy for the scene. If everything is successful, then the class is registered, by name, as being active. In other words, the check against the IsActive method uses the results created here, when the class initializes. That brings us to the end of this review section. Coming up next, we'll take a look at the TrackHelpScript in action.

Demonstration: TrackHelpScript

The demonstration scene for the TrackHelpScript component can be found in the "Project" panel, in the "Scenes" folder. Find the scene named "DemoCollideTrackHelp" and open it. Let me take a moment to describe how the demo scene works. A few seconds after the scene starts, the player can take control of the car. The scene should start with the track help acceleration notification flag on, once the player takes control of the car. The notification will only stay on for a few seconds.

While the track help acceleration message is on, the first set of pillars will be colored green. When the message turns off, the pillars will change to red. If you drive forward through the pillars slowly, you'll trigger the next track help notification, the track help slowdown message. To indicate that the second notification is active, the middle set of pillars will turn green for a few seconds. Check the rear-view mirror to see the pillars behind you change back.

Moving the car to the end of the track turns on the last track help notification, track help turn. Note that because the demonstration scene does not have a HUD connected, we're representing when the notifications would be displayed by changing the color of the different pillar sets. The demonstration scene displays the game state with regard to the track help messages in the lower left-hand corner of the game panel. The scene will only cycle through the help notifications once.

If you want to reset the scene, either click the "Restart" button in the lower left-hand corner or start and stop the scene using the Unity editor "Game" panel controls. The following screenshots depict the demonstration scene for this class.

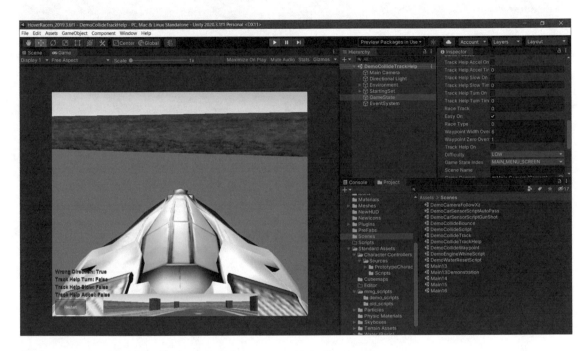

Figure 4-7. *TrackHelpScript Demonstration Scene 1*

Image depicting the track help demonstration scene in use

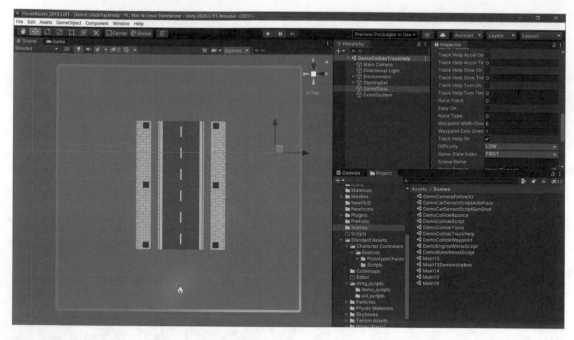

Figure 4-8. *TrackHelpScript Demonstration Scene 2*

Top-down view of the track help script scene

That brings us to the conclusion of the chapter. Let's take a look at the information we've covered in this chapter before moving onto the next topic.

Chapter Conclusion

We've covered a lot of ground in this chapter. Let's review the different classes we've covered here.

1. BounceScript: A stand-alone collision detector that adds a bounce modifier to player cars that collide with specific game objects. The most common game object that supports the bounce modifier is the bounce barrier. The demonstration scene for this class shows different ways the bounce collision script can be activated and deactivated.

2. RoadScript: This class is a stand-alone collision detector that tracks if players' cars are on or off the track. This script is attached to each piece of track in the game. The demonstration scene for this class shows a section of track that toggles the current player's on-track flag.

3. WaypointCheck: This class is used to handle a few different aspects of the game's mechanics. The waypoint system provides scaffolding that an AI-controlled car can use to navigate the racetrack. The waypoint system also provides slowdown queues that can slow AI-controlled cars on curves and other tricky parts of the track. The waypoint system is also used to determine if a car is travelling in the wrong direction and where to restore a car that's fallen off of the track. The demonstration scene for this class shows a small piece of track with three waypoints to test out.

4. TrackHelpScript: This class is responsible for turning on and off different track information messages meant to help the user learn about how to control the hover racer quickly, so they can play the game competently. The demonstration scene for this class shows a series of help messages, represented by colored pillars, being turned on and off as the player drives across a short section of track.

That brings us to the end of the review covering simple, stand-alone, interactions. We've addressed a few points on the game specifications list and model diagrams. In the next chapter, we'll take a look at classes that are centralized, advanced, interaction handlers. That will conclude all interaction-driven game mechanics for us.

CHAPTER 5

Advanced Interaction Classes

In this chapter, we'll take a look at two important centralized interaction handlers: the CollideScript and the CarSensorScript classes. These two scripts round out the game's interaction handlers and their associated game mechanics. The CollideScript handles a number of different interactions that occur when differing game objects collide with a hover racer.

The CarSensorScript is similar but is designed to work with hover racers only. Its main responsibility is to handle car-to-car interactions of varying types. We'll start by reviewing the CollideScript.

Class Review: CollideScript

The CollideScript class is responsible for handling a number of different collision interactions and their associated game mechanics. I'll list the types of interactions supported here:

1. BoostMarker

2. SmallBoostMarker

3. TinyBoostMarker

4. MediumBoostMarker

5. TinyBoostMarker2

6. JumpMarker

7. HealthMarker

8. GunMarker

© Victor G Brusca 2022
V. G Brusca, *Advanced Unity Game Development*, https://doi.org/10.1007/978-1-4842-7851-2_5

9.   InvincibilityMarker

10.   ArmorMarker

11.   Untagged

12.   Hittable

13.   HittableNoY

14.   Players

That's a lot of interactions. Take a moment to look over them. Does anything stand out to you? For the most part, they seem pretty straightforward. The listing named "Players" does seem a bit interesting though. We'll have to keep an eye on that one as we review the CollideScript class.

As I've alluded to earlier, the CollideScript is a centralized interaction that works with the player's hover racer. During the race, as the player's car collides with different objects on the track, the game mechanics activate to adjust the physics of the car. We'll use the following class review template to cover this class:

1.   Static/Constants/Read-Only Class Members

2.   Class Fields

3.   Pertinent Method Outline/Class Headers

4.   Support Method Details

5.   Main Method Details

6.   Demonstration

There are no pertinent enumerations to cover with regard to the CollideScript class, so we'll omit that section. Aside from that, this is a bit more complex of a class than we've previously reviewed. Not to worry, a little diligence goes a long way. Let's jump into some code!

Static/Constants/Read-Only Class Members: CollideScript

The CollideScript class has a few real-only fields for us to review. I'll list them here.

Listing 5-1. CollideScript Static/Constants/Read-Only Class Members 1

```
public readonly float BOUNCE_DURATION = 80.0f;
public readonly float BOOST_DURATION = 200.0f;
public readonly float MIN_JUMP_FORCE = 18.0f;
public readonly float MAX_JUMP_FORCE = 22.0f;
```

The set of previously listed read-only class fields is used to control some aspects of the class' collision interactions. The first entry, BOUNCE_DURATION, is used to control the length of time a bounce modifier is applied to a player's hover racer. Similarly, the BOOST_DURATION field is used to control the length of time a boost modifier is applied to a car. The following two entries are used to set limits on the forces involved with the jump modifier.

Class Fields: CollideScript

The CollideScript has a number of class fields that are used to manage the different game mechanics it's responsible for handling. Some of these fields are private and used internally by certain class methods.

Listing 5-2. CollideScript Class Fields 1

```
private float maxSpeed = 200.0f;
private GameObject player = null;
private CharacterController controller = null;
private CharacterMotor cm = null;
```

The first class field listed, maxSpeed, is used to track the nonboost max speed of the current player's hover racer. The next field listed is the player field. It references the GameObject of the current player's hover racer. This reference is used to adjust the movement of the car based on the applied game mechanic. The next two fields are also used to move the hover racer. The CharacterController instance, controller, is used to move cars along with the CharacterMotor field, cm. That gives us three different ways to control the game's hover racer models in response to different collision-driven game mechanics.

The next set of class fields for us to look at has to do with the forces applied to the hover racers during certain collision interactions. I use the term "force" loosely. We're employing a few different techniques to make the cars bounce, bump, jump, and boost.

In doing so, we'll apply different forces, velocities, and position adjustments to satisfy the game mechanics requirements, and we'll loosely refer to them as "forces" or "velocities."

Listing 5-3. CollideScript Class Fields 2

```
public float forceMultiplier = 2.5f;
public float minForce = 20.0f;
public float maxForce = 80.0f;
public bool lockAxisY = false;
public float bounceDampener = 1.0f;
public float minBounceVelocityHor = 25.0f;
public float minBounceVelocityVer = 25.0f;
public float jump = 9.0f;
```

The first field listed previously, forceMultiplier, is a float value that's used to increase the vertical force of the jump. The next two class fields, minForce and maxForce, are used to set a range for the forces that are applied when a player's race car collides with a hittable object. The subsequent field, lockAxisY, is a Boolean flag that controls whether or not the Y axis, vertical axis, is used when determining the effects of a collision. The bounceDampener field is used to lessen the forces involved with a bounce event.

The following two fields, minBounceVelocityHor and minBounceVelocityVer, are used to ensure that the bounce modifier has sufficient force to really bounce the car. Notice that this modifier works on the horizontal and vertical axes. I should note that this bounce modifier is different from the BounceScript class we reviewed earlier. That class takes care of bounce modifiers activated by a hover racer colliding with an object.

This bounce modifier is activated by two hover racers colliding with each other. The last class field listed in the set is the jump field. This field is used to set a baseline vertical force that is used during the application of the jump modifier. The next set of class fields are private and used internally as local variables in some of the class' methods. Let's quickly take a look at them and describe how they're used.

Listing 5-4. CollideScript Class Fields 3

```
//***** Internal Variables: Mod Markers *****
private GameObject lastHealthMarker = null;
private GameObject lastGunMarker = null;
private GameObject lastInvcMarker = null;
private GameObject lastArmorMarker = null;
```

This next set of class fields are all used to replace battle mode car modifiers that a player can pick up on the track. If you run a battle mode race, this turns on a number of car modifiers throughout the racetrack. In order to replace the modifiers after a few seconds, we keep a copy of the modifier marker that was last activated. As you can see, there is support for the four battle mode modifiers. The next set of class fields for us to review are used by the class' start method.

Listing 5-5. CollideScript Class Fields 4

```
//***** Internal Variables: Start *****
private AudioSource audioJump = null;
private AudioSource audioBounce = null;
private AudioSource audioBoost = null;
private AudioSource audioPowerUp = null;
```

The four entries, listed previously, are AudioSource components that are attached to the parent GameObject of the CollideScript script component. These sound effects are loaded into class fields for use during collision interactions handled by this class. The next block of fields we'll look at are used during hittable object collisions.

Listing 5-6. CollideScript Class Fields 5

```
//***** Internal Variables: PerformHit *****
private float collideStrength;
private float jumpHit = 15.0f;
private Rigidbody body = null;
private Vector3 moveDirection = Vector3.zero;
private Vector3 rotateDirection = Vector3.zero;
private AudioSource phAudioS = null;
```

First, we have the collideStrength field that is used to calculate strength when the car hits an object on the track. In the game, this mechanic manifests itself in hittable oil barrels that are scattered around the track in classic mode. The float instance, jumpHit, is a class field that is used in calculating the Y axis, vertical axis, force when a car collides with a hittable track object. The body field is an instance of the RigidBody class and is used to detect if the hittable object should have forces applied to it.

The next two entries, moveDirection and rotateDirection, are used to determine in what direction and with what rotation a hittable object flies away from the hover racer after a collision. Lastly, the phAudioS field is used to play sound effects during collision events. The next set of class fields to review is a big one. They consist of the fields used to power the bounce mechanic. Now we've seen the bounce mechanic before when applied to bounce barriers.

In that case, the car bounced off of the barrier during a collision event. As I mentioned earlier, in this case, we are implementing a bounce mechanic, but this time it's between two cars instead of a car and a barrier. To support this type of bounce, we need a few fields to hold different information about the car we collided with and activate a bounce modifier on it.

Listing 5-7. CollideScript Class Fields 6

```
//***** Internal Variables: PerformBounce *****
private PlayerInfo lpi = null;
private int lpIdx = 0;
private PlayerState lp = null;
private CollideScript lc = null;
private Vector3 v3;
private float x;
private float y;
private float z;
private bool isBouncing = false;
private bool useReflect = false;
private bool useInverse = false;
private bool bounceHandOff = false;
private Vector3 bounceV3 = Vector3.zero;
private float bounceTime = 0.0f;
```

The first three fields in the previous listing are used to look up player information in the game state using the script components from the car that was collided with. The lc class field is used to hold a reference to the collided-with hover racer's CollideScript. The following four fields, v3, x, y, z, are all used to calculate the force involved with the collision result. The vector component values, x, y, z, are stored in the vector field, v3, at the end of the calculation. The isBouncing field is a Boolean flag that indicates if the hover racer is being bounced.

The subsequently listed fields, useReflect and useInverse, are Boolean flags used to alter the bounce force calculations. The next field, bounceHandOff, is a Boolean used to trigger a bounce from an external source. Can you guess when we'll use this? If you thought about your car triggering a bounce on another car during a collision event, you thought right. The bounceV3 is a Vector3 instance that indicates the direction and force of the resulting bounce. The bounceTime vector keeps track of how long the bounce modifier is being applied to the car. The last set of class fields for us to review corresponds to the boost mechanic.

Listing 5-8. CollideScript Class Fields 7

```
//***** Internal Variables: PerformBoost *****
private float pbAbsX = 0.0f;
private float pbAbsZ = 0.0f;
private bool boostOn = false;
private bool boostHandOff = false;
private Vector3 boostV3 = Vector3.zero;
private float boostTime = 0.0f;
```

The set of class fields in the previous listing are used to power the boost game mechanic. The boost mechanic is as it sounds. It provides a boost to the hover racer, shooting it forward at a new maximum speed. The first two entries are used to determine the absolute value of the hover racer's current X axis velocity. Similarly, the pbAbsZ field tracks the absolute value of the hover racer's current Z velocity. The boostOn field is a Boolean flag that indicates the car has its boost modifier activated. The boostHandOff field is used to trigger a boost modifier from another source. Lastly, the boostV3 vector holds the calculated boost that's applied to the car, while the boostTime float instance tracks the duration of the boost. Next up, we'll look at the fields that control the jump modifier.

Listing 5-9. CollideScript Class Fields 8

```
//***** Internal Variables: PerformJump *****
private bool isJumping = false;
private bool jumpHandOff = false;
private Vector3 jumpV3 = Vector3.zero;
private float jumpStrength;
private float gravity = 10.0f;
```

The first two fields in this set are similar to their boost equivalents. The isJumping field is a Boolean flag that indicates if the current hover racer is jumping. The jumpHandOff field is another Boolean flag that will trigger the jump modifier on the current car. The jumpV3 field is the calculated jump vector that is applied to the hover racer. The float instance jumpStrength is as it seems, a field that tracks the calculated jump strength. Lastly, we have the gravity field that is responsible for estimating gravity and slowly pulling the car back down to the track. Up next, we'll look at the class' pertinent method list.

Pertinent Method Outline/Class Headers: CollideScript

The CollideScript's pertinent method outline is as follows.

Listing 5-10. CollideScript Pertinent Method Outline/Class Headers 1

```
//Main Methods
void Start();
void Update();
public void OnControllerColliderHit(ControllerColliderHit hit);

//Support Methods
public void RecreateHealthMarker();
public void RecreateGunMarker();
public void RecreateInvcMarker();
public void RecreateArmorMarker();

private void CalcCollideStrength();
private float GetMinForce(float v);
private float GetMaxForce(float v);
private float GetBounceVelHor(float v);
private float GetBoostVelHor(int mode, float movVel);

public void PerformHit(GameObject go, ControllerColliderHit hit);

public void PerformBounce(GameObject go, ControllerColliderHit hit)

public void PerformBoost(GameObject go, ControllerColliderHit hit, int mode);

public void PerformJump(GameObject go, ControllerColliderHit hit);
```

Up next, I'll list the CollideScript class' import statements and class declaration. Pay close attention to any base classes used.

Listing 5-11. CollideScript Pertinent Method Outline/Class Headers 2

```
using UnityEngine;

public class CollideScript : BaseScript {}
```

As you can see, the CollideScript class extends the BaseScript class and as such is a MonoBehaviour instance, in other words, a script component. This means that you can attach it to different game objects in a scene. Some of the classes we'll review aren't MonoBehaviours. Keep an eye out for them.

Support Method Details: CollideScript

The CollideScript class is one of the larger classes we'll have to review. Because there are a handful of support methods, we'll list and review them in groups. Let's take a look at the first nine, simpler, support methods.

Listing 5-12. CollideScript Support Method Details 1

```
01 public void RecreateHealthMarker() {
02     lastHealthMarker.SetActive(true);
03 }

01 public void RecreateGunMarker() {
02     lastGunMarker.SetActive(true);
03 }

01 public void RecreateInvcMarker() {
02     lastInvcMarker.SetActive(true);
03 }

01 public void RecreateArmorMarker() {
02     lastArmorMarker.SetActive(true);
03 }
```

```
01 private void CalcCollideStrength() {
02     if (BaseScript.IsActive(scriptName) == false) {
03         return;
04     }
05
06     if (p == null) {
07         collideStrength = 0;
08     } else {
09         collideStrength = (p.speed * forceMultiplier) / maxSpeed;
10     }
11 }
```

```
01 private float GetMinForce(float v) {
02     if (Mathf.Abs(v) < minForce) {
03         if (v < 0) {
04             return -minForce;
05         } else {
06             return minForce;
07         }
08     }
09     return v;
10 }
```

```
01 private float GetMaxForce(float v) {
02     if (Mathf.Abs(v) > maxForce) {
03         if (v < 0) {
04             return -maxForce;
05         } else {
06             return maxForce;
07         }
08     }
09     return v;
10 }
```

```
01 private float GetBounceVelHor(float v) {
02     if (useReflect == true) {
03         v = v * bounceDampener;
```

```
04      } else {
05        if (useInverse == true) {
06            v = v * -1 * bounceDampener;
07        } else {
08            v = v * bounceDampener;
09        }
10      }
11
12      if (v < 0) {
13        if (v > -minBounceVelocityHor) {
14            v = -minBounceVelocityHor;
15        }
16      } else if (v >= 0) {
17        if (v < minBounceVelocityHor) {
18            v = minBounceVelocityHor;
19        }
20      }
21      return v;
22 }
```

```
01 private float GetBoostVelHor(int mode, float movVel) {
02      float v3 = 0.0f;
03      if (mode == 0) {
04        v3 = 200;
05      } else if (mode == 1) {
06        v3 = 50;
07      } else if (mode == 2) {
08        v3 = 25;
09      } else if (mode == 3) {
10        v3 = 100;
11      } else if (mode == 4) {
12        v3 = 15;
13      }
14
```

```
15    if (movVel < 0) {
16        v3 *= -1;
17    }
18    return v3;
19 }
```

The first four methods listed in this group are all pretty much identical. These methods are designed to fire a few seconds after the player collides with a battle mode modifier causing the modifier's game object marker to be deactivated, made invisible. The only difference between the four methods is which marker to reactivate. The next method is the CalcCollideStrength method, this method relies on the p class field which may not have been properly initialized.

Because of this, lines 2–4 have the expected escape check. The method is simple and direct. If p is null, then the collideStrength field gets set to zero; otherwise, a formula is used to determine the correct value, line 9. The next two support methods listed, GetMinForce and GetMaxForce, are very similar. Both methods limit the force passed in and respect the sign of the force. The methods are fairly direct. Read over them and make sure you understand how the methods function.

The next method up for review is the GetBounceVelHor method. This method is used to calculate the bounce velocity on a horizontal axis. The code on lines 2–10 lessens the initial force while taking into account the use of inverse and reflection adjustments. The code on lines 12–20 is there to ensure the calculated velocity has a standard minimum value while taking into account its sign. The final value is returned on line 21.

The last method in this group for us to review is the GetBoostVelHor method. This method is used to calculate the boost modifier's horizontal velocity component. This method supports five different boost types. Based on the mode method argument, a velocity is determined, lines 2–13. If the velocity is negative, the new boost velocity is adjusted and returned, lines 5–18.

The subsequent set of methods for us to review are responsible for actually enacting the modifier. These methods are a bit longer in length, so we'll review them one by one. The first method is the PerformHit method. This method is used as part of the hittable object collision handling.

Listing 5-13. CollideScript Support Method Details 2

```
01 public void PerformHit(GameObject go, ControllerColliderHit hit) {
02     if (BaseScript.IsActive(scriptName) == false || go == null || hit ==
       null) {
03         return;
04     }
05
06     body = hit.collider.attachedRigidbody;
07     if (body == null || body.isKinematic) {
08         return;
09     }
10
11     moveDirection = Vector3.zero;
12     CalcCollideStrength();
13     if (lockAxisY == false) {
14         moveDirection.y = (jumpHit * collideStrength);
15     } else {
16         moveDirection.y = 0;
17     }
18     moveDirection.x = (cm.movement.velocity.x * collideStrength);
19     moveDirection.z = (cm.movement.velocity.z * collideStrength);
20
21     if (minForce > 0) {
22         moveDirection.x = GetMinForce(moveDirection.x);
23         moveDirection.z = GetMinForce(moveDirection.z);
24
25         if (lockAxisY == false) {
26             moveDirection.y = GetMinForce(moveDirection.y);
27         }
28     }
29
30     if (maxForce > 0) {
31         moveDirection.x = GetMaxForce(moveDirection.x);
32         moveDirection.z = GetMaxForce(moveDirection.z);
33
```

```
34        if (lockAxisY == false) {
35            moveDirection.y = GetMaxForce(moveDirection.y);
36        }
37    }
38
39    rotateDirection = (moveDirection * 1);
40    body.rotation = Quaternion.Euler(rotateDirection);
41    body.velocity = moveDirection;
42
43    phAudioS = go.GetComponent<AudioSource>();
44    if (phAudioS != null) {
45        if (phAudioS.isPlaying == false) {
46            phAudioS.Play();
47        }
48    }
49 }
```

As you might expect, lines 2–4 check to see if the class has been properly configured. If not, the method returns without doing any work. On lines 6–9, we check the body of the hit argument to see if the value is null or the body has its isKinematic flag set to true. If it does, then forces and collisions should no longer affect the rigid body. We respect this and check for it in our code.

The value of collideStrength is set on line 12 with a call to the CalcCollideStrength method. The small block of code on lines 13–17 controls whether or not the Y component of the movement vector is part of the collision calculations. The initial horizontal forces are set on lines 18 and 19. The block of code on lines 21–28 filters the component forces to make sure that they have a minimum value.

The same thing is done to make sure the horizontal values are not greater than the maximum allowed value, lines 30–37. The rotateDirection vector is based on the moveDirection vector. The actual rotation of the hit object is set on line 40, while the movement velocity is set on line 41. The code on lines 43–48 is used to play a sound effect when the collision occurs. Next, we'll look at the PerformBounce method.

Listing 5-14. CollideScript Support Method Details 3

```
01 public void PerformBounce(GameObject go, ControllerColliderHit hit) {
02     if (BaseScript.IsActive(scriptName) == false || go == null || hit ==
       null) {
03         return;
04     }
05
06     x = GetBounceVelHor(cm.movement.velocity.x);
07     y = cm.movement.velocity.y;
08     z = GetBounceVelHor(cm.movement.velocity.z);
09
10     if (useReflect == true) {
11         v3 = Vector3.Reflect(v3, hit.collider.ClosestPointOnBounds(player.
           transform.position).normalized);
12     } else {
13         v3 = new Vector3(x, y, z);
14     }
15
16     Utilities.LoadPlayerInfo(GetType().Name, out lpi, out lpIdx, out lp,
       hit.gameObject, gameState, false);
17     if (lp != null) {
18         lc = lp.player.GetComponent<CollideScript>();
19         lc.bounceHandOff = true;
20         lc.bounceV3 = v3;
21     }
22 }
```

The PerformBounce method, as the name suggests, is responsible for applying a bounce modifier to the colliding hover racer. The lines of code at the start of the method, 2–4, prevent the method from doing any work if the configuration step has failed. The x, y, and z components of the bounce vector are set on lines 6–8. Lines 10–14 finalize the bounce vector using one of two techniques shown on lines 11 and 13.

Take a look at the code block on lines 16–21. This is a standard player lookup we've seen time and time again except in this case, we're looking up the player state data for the player we collided with. Notice the code on lines 17–20. We get a reference to the collided-with player's `CollideScript` and trigger a bounce on that player's car by setting the bounceHandOff flag and the bounceV3 field values. The next method we'll look at is the `PerfectBoost` method.

Listing 5-15. CollideScript Support Method Details 4

```
01 public void PerformBoost(GameObject go, ControllerColliderHit hit, int
   mode) {
02    if (BaseScript.IsActive(scriptName) == false || go == null || hit ==
      null) {
03       return;
04    }
05
06    pbAbsX = Mathf.Abs(p.cm.movement.velocity.x);
07    pbAbsZ = Mathf.Abs(p.cm.movement.velocity.z);
08    boostV3 = Vector3.zero;
09
10    if (pbAbsX > pbAbsZ) {
11       boostV3.x = GetBoostVelHor(mode, p.cm.movement.velocity.x);
12    } else {
13       boostV3.z = GetBoostVelHor(mode, p.cm.movement.velocity.z);
14    }
15
16    boostHandOff = true;
17    if (audioBoost != null) {
18       if (audioBoost.isPlaying == false) {
19          audioBoost.Play();
20       }
21    }
22
23    if (p != null) {
24       p.flame.SetActive(true);
25    }
26 }
```

The `PerformBoost`'s method signature is similar to the previous "Perform" methods we've looked at, but it takes an extra argument, a mode value. Lines 2–4 should be familiar to you by now, so we'll move on. Method variables are initialized on lines 6–8. On line 10, determination is made as to which horizontal direction is the dominant direction. The velocity of the vector component is set on lines 11 and 13 using the `GetBoostVelHor` method we reviewed earlier.

On line 16, the `boostHandOff` flag is set to true. This is used to turn on the boost modifier that is applied in the class' update method. A sound effect is played on lines 17–21. Lastly, on lines 23–25, a particle effect is turned on, if available, to indicate the boost modifier. The next method for us to review is the `PerformJump` method. Let's take a look at some code.

Listing 5-16. CollideScript Support Method Details 5

```
01 public void PerformJump(GameObject go, ControllerColliderHit hit) {
02     if (BaseScript.IsActive(scriptName) == false || go == null || hit ==
       null) {
03         return;
04     }
05
06     jumpStrength = ((p.speed) * forceMultiplier) / maxSpeed;
07     jumpV3 = Vector3.zero;
08     jumpV3.y = (jump * jumpStrength);
09
10     if (jumpV3.y < MIN_JUMP_FORCE) {
11         jumpV3.y = MIN_JUMP_FORCE;
12     }
13
14     if (jumpV3.y >= MAX_JUMP_FORCE) {
15         jumpV3.y = MAX_JUMP_FORCE;
16     }
17
```

```
18    jumpHandOff = true;
19    if (audioJump != null) {
20        if (audioJump.isPlaying == false) {
21            audioJump.Play();
22        }
23    }
24 }
```

The PerformJump method follows a similar pattern to the previous methods we've reviewed for this class. The method takes the same parameters we've seen in other "perform" methods. Again, we have the method protection code on lines 2–4. The value of the jumpStrength field is based on the hover racer's speed and is calculated on line 6. The jump velocity variable is initialized on line 7, while the vertical force is set on line 8.

The strength of the jump force is regulated to be within a min and max range by the code on lines 10–16. The jumpHandOff flag is set to true on line 18. This enables the jump modifier in this class' update method. The jump sound effect is handled on lines 19–23. That brings us to the conclusion of the support method details section.

Main Method Details: CollideScript

The CollideScript class has a few main methods for us to review. The first method we'll look at is the Start method. This method is called by the Unity game engine as part of a MonoBehaviour's life cycle.

Listing 5-17. CollideScript Main Method Details 1

```
01 void Start() {
02    base.PrepPlayerInfo(this.GetType().Name);
03    if (BaseScript.IsActive(scriptName) == false) {
04        Utilities.wrForce(scriptName + ": Is Deactivating...");
05        return;
06    } else {
07        player = p.player;
08        maxSpeed = p.maxSpeed;
09        controller = p.controller;
10        cm = p.cm;
11
```

```
12      if (controller == null) {
13          Utilities.wrForce("CollideScript: controller is null!
            Deactivating...");
14          MarkScriptActive(false);
15          return;
16      }
17
18      if (player == null) {
19          Utilities.wrForce("CollideScript: player is null!
            Deactivating...");
20          MarkScriptActive(false);
21          return;
22      }
23
24      if (cm == null) {
25          Utilities.wrForce("CollideScript: cm is null!
            Deactivating...");
26          MarkScriptActive(false);
27          return;
28      }
29
30      AudioSource[] audioSetDst = Utilities.LoadAudioResources(GetCom
        ponentsInParent<AudioSource>(), new string[] { Utilities.SOUND_
        FX_JUMP, Utilities.SOUND_FX_BOUNCE, Utilities.SOUND_FX_BOOST,
        Utilities.SOUND_FX_POWER_UP });
31      if (audioSetDst != null) {
32          audioJump = audioSetDst[0];
33          audioBounce = audioSetDst[1];
34          audioBoost = audioSetDst[2];
35          audioPowerUp = audioSetDst[3];
36      }
37  }
38 }
```

The Start method is a bit longer than most of the methods we've reviewed thus far. Don't worry, it's not as complex as it looks. The code on line 2 is used to load the standard classes and the PlayerState associated with the current player. If the configuration was successful, the active flag check on line 3 will return true, and we then proceed to store references to the player's hover racer model, maximum speed, controller, and character motor in class fields. The snippet of code from lines 12–28 is used to check that the class' required fields are defined, and if not, it marks the class as inactive and returns.

The audio resource loading section of code runs from lines 30 to 36. In this case, we use the utility method, LoadAudioResources, and pass it a reference to an array of connected AudioSources and an array of names to search for. This method searches the audio sources and looks for each of the search targets. The result is a custom array of AudioSource instances. On lines 32 to 35, the individual interaction sound effects are set from the resulting array of audio resources. The next method we'll look at is the Update method.

Listing 5-18. CollideScript Main Method Details 2

```
01 void Update() {
02     if (BaseScript.IsActive(scriptName) == false) {
03         return;
04     }
05
06     if (gameState != null) {
07         if (gameState.gamePaused == true) {
08             return;
09         } else if (gameState.gameRunning == false) {
10             return;
11         }
12     }
13
14     //bounce code
15     if (bounceHandOff == true) {
16         bounceTime = 0f;
17         isBouncing = true;
18         p.isBouncing = true;
19
```

```
20        if (audioBounce != null) {
21            if (audioBounce.isPlaying == false) {
22                audioBounce.Play();
23            }
24        }
25    }
26
27    if (isBouncing == true) {
28        bounceTime += (Time.deltaTime * 100);
29        bounceHandOff = false;
30        controller.Move(bounceV3 * Time.deltaTime);
31    }
32
33    if (isBouncing == true && bounceTime >= BOUNCE_DURATION) {
34        isBouncing = false;
35        p.isBouncing = false;
36    }
37
38    //boost code
39    if (boostHandOff == true) {
40        boostTime = 0f;
41        boostOn = true;
42        p.offTrack = false;
43        p.boostOn = true;
44        p.SetBoost();
45    }
46
47    if (boostOn == true) {
48        boostTime += (Time.deltaTime * 100);
49        boostHandOff = false;
50        controller.Move(boostV3 * Time.deltaTime);
51    }
52
```

```
53      if (boostOn == true && boostTime >= BOOST_DURATION) {
54          boostOn = false;
55          p.boostOn = false;
56          p.SetNorm();
57          p.flame.SetActive(false);
58      }
59
60      //jump code
61      if (controller.isGrounded == true) {
62          cm.jumping.jumping = false;
63          p.isJumping = false;
64          isJumping = false;
65      }
66
67      if (jumpHandOff == true) {
68          p.offTrack = false;
69          cm.jumping.jumping = true;
70          p.isJumping = true;
71          isJumping = true;
72      }
73
74      if (isJumping == true) {
75          jumpHandOff = false;
76          controller.Move(jumpV3 * Time.deltaTime);
77      }
78
79      //gravity code
80      if ((controller.isGrounded == false || cm.movement.velocity.y > 0) &&
        isJumping == true) {
81          jumpV3.y -= gravity * Time.deltaTime;
82      }
83
84      if (player != null && player.transform.position.y >= Utilities.MAX_
        XFORM_POS_Y && cm.movement.velocity.y > Utilities.MIN_XFORM_POS_Y) {
85          cm.movement.velocity.y -= gravity * Time.deltaTime;
```

```
86    } else if (controller.isGrounded == false || cm.movement.velocity.y >
      0 || p.player.transform.position.y > 0) {
87        cm.movement.velocity.y -= gravity * Time.deltaTime;
88    }
89
90    if (controller.isGrounded == false) {
91        cm.movement.velocity.y -= gravity * Time.deltaTime;
92    }
93 }
```

The Update method is called every frame of the game by the Unity game engine. With regard to the CollideScript class, the Update method is responsible for applying the active modifier to the hover racer. The method has the same safety check we've seen before. The code block on lines 6–12 is used to check the state of the game and exit out of the method if certain game states exist.

The first modifier we encounter is the bounce modifier on line 14. The code on lines 15–25 is used to start the bounce modifier and play a sound effect. I should mention that this bounce sound effect is different from the one played in the PerformBounce method. That sound effect is played from the colliding car, not the current player's car as in this case. Notice that on lines 17–18, the modifier status of the CollideScript class is kept in-line with the current player's PlayerState instance. If the bounce modifier is active, the code on lines 27–31 executes. This code applies the bounce modifier, line 30; prevents it from starting again, line 29; and monitors the amount of time it's active, line 28.

The last piece of the bounce modifier logic is the section of code on lines 33–36 that turns off the modifier after the BOUNCE_DURATION expires. The boost modifier code starts on line 38. This section of modifier code is very similar to the bounce code. Let's take a look at the starting code, lines 39–45. If the boostHandOff flag is true, the boostTime is reset, line 40, and the boostOn flags are both set to true, lines 41–42. The boost is turned on for the current player's hover racer on line 43.

Next, on line 47, an active boost modifier is handled. The duration of the boost modifier is incremented on line 48, and the modifier is prevented from turning back on by setting the boostHandOff flag to false. The modifier is applied on line 50. The next block of boost modifier code is on lines 53–58. If the boost duration expires, the boost modifier is deactivated, lines 54–56.

On line 60, the jump modifier section begins. There is a section of code on lines 61–65. This code is designed to turn off the jump modifier when the car touches the ground. Unlike other modifiers handled in this method, the jump modifier is turned off when gravity pulls the car back down to the ground. The jump modifier is started by the jumpHandOff flag in a similar way to the bounce and boost modifiers.

On lines 74–77, the jump modifier is applied. The last block of code on lines 79–92 is used to apply gravity to the car and bring it back down to the ground. The jump force is also lessened over time to help the car float back down from a jump. That wraps up the review of the class' update method. The last main method to look at is the OnControllerColliderHit collision event handler. Let's take a look.

Listing 5-19. CollideScript Main Method Details 3

```
001 public void OnControllerColliderHit(ControllerColliderHit hit) {
002     if (BaseScript.IsActive(scriptName) == false) {
003         return;
004     }
005
006     if (hit.gameObject.CompareTag(Utilities.TAG_UNTAGGED)) {
007         return;
008     } else if (hit.gameObject.CompareTag(Utilities.TAG_HITTABLE)) {
009         lockAxisY = false;
010         PerformHit(hit.gameObject, hit);
011     } else if (hit.gameObject.CompareTag(Utilities.TAG_HITTABLE_NOY)) {
012         lockAxisY = true;
013         PerformHit(hit.gameObject, hit);
014         lockAxisY = false;
015     } else if (hit.gameObject.CompareTag(Utilities.TAG_PLAYERS)) {
016         if (hit != null && hit.gameObject != null) {
017             PerformBounce(hit.gameObject, hit);
018         }
019     } else if (hit.gameObject.CompareTag(Utilities.TAG_BOOST_MARKER)) {
020         if (p.boostOn == true || p.aiIsPassing == false) {
021             PerformBoost(hit.gameObject, hit, 0);
022         }
```

```
023    } else if (hit.gameObject.CompareTag(Utilities.TAG_SMALL_BOOST_
       MARKER)) {
024        if (p.boostOn == true || p.aiIsPassing == false) {
025            PerformBoost(hit.gameObject, hit, 1);
026        }
027    } else if (hit.gameObject.CompareTag(Utilities.TAG_TINY_BOOST_
       MARKER)) {
028        if (p.boostOn == true || p.aiIsPassing == false) {
029            PerformBoost(hit.gameObject, hit, 2);
030        }
031    } else if (hit.gameObject.CompareTag(Utilities.TAG_MEDIUM_BOOST_
       MARKER)) {
032        if (p.boostOn == true || p.aiIsPassing == false) {
033            PerformBoost(hit.gameObject, hit, 3);
034        }
035    } else if (hit.gameObject.CompareTag(Utilities.TAG_TINY_BOOST_2_
       MARKER)) {
036        if (p.boostOn == true || p.aiIsPassing == false) {
037            PerformBoost(hit.gameObject, hit, 4);
038        }
039    } else if (hit.gameObject.CompareTag(Utilities.TAG_JUMP_MARKER)) {
040        if (p.isJumping == false) {
041            PerformJump(hit.gameObject, hit);
042        }
043    } else if (hit.gameObject.CompareTag(Utilities.TAG_HEALTH_MARKER)) {
044        if (audioPowerUp != null) {
045            if (audioPowerUp.isPlaying == false) {
046                audioPowerUp.Play();
047            }
048        }
049
050        if (p.damage - 1 >= 0) {
051            p.damage -= 1;
052        }
053
```

```
054        p.aiHasGainedLife = true;
055        p.aiHasGainedLifeTime = 0;
056        hit.gameObject.SetActive(false);
057        lastHealthMarker = hit.gameObject;
058        Invoke(nameof(RecreateHealthMarker), Random.Range(Utilities.
           MARKER_REFRESH_MIN, Utilities.MARKER_REFRESH_MAX));
059    } else if (hit.gameObject.CompareTag(Utilities.TAG_GUN_MARKER)) {
060        if (audioPowerUp != null) {
061            if (audioPowerUp.isPlaying == false) {
062                audioPowerUp.Play();
063            }
064        }
065
066        if (p.ammo <= Utilities.MAX_AMMO) {
067            p.ammo += Utilities.AMMO_INC;
068        }
069
070        p.gunOn = true;
071        p.ShowGun();
072        hit.gameObject.SetActive(false);
073        lastGunMarker = hit.gameObject;
074        Invoke(nameof(RecreateGunMarker), Random.Range(Utilities.MARKER_
           REFRESH_MIN, Utilities.MARKER_REFRESH_MAX));
075    } else if (hit.gameObject.CompareTag(Utilities.TAG_INVINC_MARKER)) {
076        if (audioPowerUp != null) {
077            if (audioPowerUp.isPlaying == false) {
078                audioPowerUp.Play();
079            }
080        }
081
082        p.invincOn = true;
083        p.invincTime = 0;
084        p.ShowInvinc();
085        hit.gameObject.SetActive(false);
086        lastInvcMarker = hit.gameObject;
```

```
087        Invoke(nameof(RecreateInvcMarker), Random.Range(Utilities.MARKER_
           REFRESH_MIN, Utilities.MARKER_REFRESH_MAX));
088      } else if (hit.gameObject.CompareTag(Utilities.TAG_ARMOR_MARKER)) {
089        if (audioPowerUp != null) {
090          if (audioPowerUp.isPlaying == false) {
091            audioPowerUp.Play();
092          }
093        }
094
095        p.armorOn = true;
096        hit.gameObject.SetActive(false);
097        lastArmorMarker = hit.gameObject;
098        Invoke(nameof(RecreateArmorMarker), Random.Range(Utilities.
           MARKER_REFRESH_MIN, Utilities.MARKER_REFRESH_MAX));
099      }
100 }
```

The OnControllerColliderHit method is the central point for processing collisions and deciding what action to take. The first type of collision that's handled is a collision with an untagged object. In this code, nothing is done, and the method returns. Next is the hittable collision type. This modifier is applied on line 10 after the lockAxisY field is set to true.

Following the hittable collision type is a similar collision type, HittableNoY, except that it doesn't use Y axis forces in the applied modifier vector. Line 12 has the lockAxisY field set to true before a call to the PerformHit method. Subsequently, the lockAxisY is set back to false on line 14. On lines 15–18, the bounce modifier is processed. This modifier is slightly different from the others in that it applies to the collided-with player's car and not the current player's car.

The block of code from line 19 to line 38 is for handling boost marker collisions. There are five different types of boost markers that can be processed. I'll list them here along with their associated speed. All of the entries are the same except for the mode value that gets passed into the PerformBoost method. Note that the boost modifier won't fire if the modifier is already on, or the car is in passing mode.

- BoostMarker: 200

- SmallBoostMarker: 50

- TinyBoostMarker: 25

- MediumBoostMarker: 100

- TinyBoostMarker2: 15

The last of the physical modifiers starts on line 39. If the current player's hover racer isn't already jumping, then a jump modifier is performed on line 41. The remaining collision types are all specific to the game's battle mode. In battle mode, hover racers can shoot at one another using an automated firing system. During battle mode races, there are markers on the track that activate health, gun, armor, and invincibility modifiers.

The health marker is the first battle mode marker handled by the OnControllerColliderHit method on line 43. Every battle mode marker will play a sound when it's triggered. That can be seen on lines 44–48 with regard to the health marker. If the player has damage to heal, this is handled on lines 50–52. More player state adjustments are made on lines 54 and 55. The next three lines of code are important because they appear for every other battle mode marker.

What this code does is deactivate the marker, store a reference to the marker, and then schedule a method invocation to reactivate the marker. The remaining battle mode markers (gun, invincibility, and armor) have similarly structured code. Read over the remaining method code and make sure you understand it before moving on. That wraps up the review of the OnControllerColliderHit method and the CollideScript's main method review section. In the next section, we'll take a look at a demonstration scene for this class.

Demonstration: CollideScript

The CollideScript class has an interesting demonstration scene named "DemoCollideScript". You can find the scene in the "Project" panel in the "Scenes" folder. Before you open it, let me talk a little bit about how the scene works. After a few seconds, you'll be able to control the hover racer. There are a number of different objects in the demo scene you can interact with. From the starting position of the car, on the left, there are a number of boost markers you can try out. They are surrounded by a set of red pillars.

Next to this, on the right, are a set of jump ramps in between two purple pillars. These ramps will trigger the jump modifier for you to check out how it works. Following these features are a set of green pillars. These pillars actually mark a series of waypoints and an AI-controlled, opponent, hover racer. It takes a little doing but you can line up the cars and collide them together. This is an example of the car bounce modifier at work.

Beyond the center line of interactive features, there are two stacks of oil drums. You can crash into these and send them flying. This is an example of the hittable modifier in action. Last but not least, there are a series of battle mode markers lining the far wall. If you collide into these, they'll disappear for a while. One will even enable the car's gun. Try them out. They constitute the battle mode marker modifiers we covered in this class.

That brings us to the end of this class review. The next class we'll take a look at is the second centralized interaction class; we'll review and conclude all of the game's collision-driven interactions and game mechanics. Take a moment to look back at the game specifications list as we complete more and more game features.

Class Review: CarSensorScript

The last interaction class for us to look at is the `CarSensorScript`. This script powers the car sensor that is designed to track opponent cars that are in front of, and close to, the current player's hover racer. Using this sensor setup, the following car can trigger a "passing" modifier if it tracks a car closely enough for a long enough time.

The other responsibility of the `CarSensorScript` is to run the automated gun that simulates shooting at another hover racer. This happens if the following car has ammo and can keep the car in front of it close and in the sensor until the target tracking completes and the gun goes off. A random dice roll takes care of determining a hit, and if the hit car has no more health points, it gets respawned a few waypoints back as a penalty. We'll use the following class review template to cover this class:

1. Static/Constant/Read-Only Class Members

2. Class Fields

3. Pertinent Method Outline/Class Headers

4. Support Method Details

5. Main Method Details

6. Demonstration

Let's take a look at some code!

Static/Constants/Read-Only Class Members: CarSensorScript

The CarSensorScript class has a number of static and read-only class fields we'll need to review.

Listing 5-20. CarSensorScript Static/Constants/Read-Only Class Members 1

```
public static float BASE_BOOST = 200.0f;
public static float BASE_NON_BOOST = 25.0f;
public static string AUDIO_SOURCE_NAME_GUN_SHOT = "explosion_dirty_rnd_01";

public static string AUDIO_SOURCE_NAME_TARGETTING = "alien_crickets_lp_01";

public static readonly float TRIGGER_TIME_DRAFTING = 2.5f;

public static readonly float TRIGGER_TIME_PASSING = 2.5f;
```

The first two fields listed, BASE_BOOST and BASE_NON_BOOST, are used to track the boost and nonboost default forces. Subsequent fields, AUDIO_SOURCE_NAME_GUN_SHOT and AUDIO_SOURCE_NAME_TARGETTING class fields, are used to load AudioSource components and should reflect the name of the audio resource used. The last two fields in the set, TRIGGER_TIME_DRAFTING and TRIGGER_TIME_PASSING, are used to control the timing and duration of the passing game mechanic.

Listing 5-21. CarSensorScript Static/Constants/Read-Only Class Members 2

```
public static float TRIGGER_SPEED_PASSING = 0.90f;
public static readonly float SAFE_FOLLOW_DIST = 80.0f;

public static readonly float GUN_SHOT_DIST = 160.0f;
public static readonly float GUN_RELOAD_TIME = 500.0f;

public static readonly float MIN_TARGET_TO_FIRE_TIME = 100.0f;

public static readonly float MAX_EXPLOSION_TIME = 120.0f;
```

The first field listed, TRIGGER_SPEED_PASSING, is used to trigger the car passing game mechanic. You need to have at least 90% of your max speed as part of the trigger requirements. The SAFE_FOLLOW_DIST field is the maximum distance you can follow an opponent's car to trigger the passing mechanic. The GUN_SHOT_DIST is the maximum distance to be able to still fire the gun at the car in front of you.

The GUN_RELOAD_TIME field is the amount of time, in milliseconds, that it takes to reload the gun for the next shot. The next field represents the minimum amount of time necessary to keep a car locked into the sensor to fire a shot at it. The MAX_EXPLOSION_ TIME represents the maximum amount of time to run the gunshot explosion effect. That brings us to the conclusion of this review section. Up next, we'll take a look at the remainder of the class' fields.

Class Fields: CarSensorScript

The CarSensorScript class has a few class fields for us to look at.

Listing 5-22. CarSensorScript Class Fields 1

```
//***** Class Fields *****
private AudioSource audioGunShot = null;
private AudioSource audioTargetting = null;
private ArrayList cars = null;
private GameObject player = null;
```

The first two fields are references to audio components attached to the player's car for use as sound effects, audioGunShot and audioTargetting. The next field listed in this set is the cars ArrayList instance. This data structure is used to track the opponents that are currently in the car's sensor. The player class field is used to hold a reference to a player's GameObject instance. The next set of class fields we'll review is those used by the SetBoostVectors method. Let's have a look.

Listing 5-23. CarSensorScript Class Fields 2

```
//***** Internal Variables: SetBoostVectors *****
private float absX = 0;
private float absZ = 0;
private Vector3 passLeftV3 = Vector3.zero;
private Vector3 passGoV3 = Vector3.zero;
private Vector3 passV3 = Vector3.zero;
```

The first two fields listed in the set are the absX and absZ fields that are used in force calculations by the SetBoostVectors method. The next three fields are all Vector3 instances: passLeftV3, passGoV3, and passV3. These fields are used to set the forces of the vectors used to move the car around another car when passing. We'll look at class fields used by the PerformShot method next.

Listing 5-24. CarSensorScript Class Fields 3

```
//***** Internal Variables: PerformShot *****
private PlayerState p2 = null;
private int r2 = 0;
```

The fields listed previously are used to look up the "shot" player's state info to potentially apply the gunshot hit modifier. The p2 field stores a reference to the associated player's state object, while the integer, r2, is used to support the random dice roll used in determining a hit. The next, and last, set of fields up for review are used by the class' Update method.

Listing 5-25. CarSensorScript Class Fields 4

```
//***** Internal Variables: Update *****
private Collider obj = null;
private int i2 = 0;
private int l2 = 0;
private bool tb = false;
private Vector3 t1 = Vector3.zero;
private Vector3 t2 = Vector3.zero;
private float dist = 0.0f;
private float moveTime = 0.0f;
private bool explosionOn = false;
private float explosionTime = 0.0f;
private Collider target = null;
```

The Collider field, obj, is used to reference the Collider object that gets recorded when the car sensor collides with another player's hover racer. The i2 and l2 fields are used to control the loop that runs through the list of cars picked up by the sensor. The tb field is a Boolean flag that's used to indicate that the auto passing mechanic should turn on for the current player's car. The t1 and t2 fields are used to determine the distance of the tracked cars. The dist field is used to hold the calculated distance between the current player's hover racer and the tracked cars.

Next up, the moveTime field is used to control how the passing mechanic is applied over time. The next three fields are involved with the gunshot mechanic. These fields track if there are any effects that need to run during the gunshot. The explosionOn field indicates that the gunshot explosion effect should be shown. The explosionTime field tracks how long the explosion effect has been running. Lastly, the target field represents the car being fired upon. In the next review section, we'll look at the class' pertinent method outline.

Pertinent Method Outline/Class Headers: CarSensorScript

The CarSensorScript is a MonoBehaviour, via BaseScript class extension, that has a number of main and support methods for us to review. The method outline is listed as follows.

Listing 5-26. CarSensorScript Pertinent Method Outline/Class Headers 1

```
//Main Methods
void Start();
void OnTriggerEnter(Collider otherObj);
void OnTriggerExit(Collider otherObj);
void Update();

//Support Methods
public void SetBoostVectors();
public void PerformGunShotAttempt(Collider otherObj);
public void CancelTarget();
```

The CarSensorScript class' import statements and headers are listed next.

Listing 5-27. CarSensorScript Pertinent Method Outline/Class Headers 2

```
using System.Collections;
using UnityEngine;

public class CarSensorScript : BaseScript {}
```

Next, we'll take a look at the class' support methods.

Support Method Details: CarSensorScript

The CarSensorScript class has a few support methods that are used to power the car passing and gunshot game mechanics. We'll take a look at the SetBoostVectors method first.

Listing 5-28. CarSensorScript Support Method Details 1

```
01 public void SetBoostVectors() {
02    if (p == null) {
03       return;
04    } else if (BaseScript.IsActive(scriptName) == false) {
05       return;
06    }
07
08    absX = Mathf.Abs(p.cm.movement.velocity.x);
09    absZ = Mathf.Abs(p.cm.movement.velocity.z);
10    passLeftV3 = Vector3.zero;
11    passGoV3 = Vector3.zero;
12    passV3 = Vector3.zero;
13
14    if (absX > absZ) {
15       passGoV3.x = BASE_BOOST;
16       if (p.cm.movement.velocity.x < 0) {
17          passGoV3.x *= -1;
18       }
19
20       passLeftV3.z = BASE_NON_BOOST;
21       if (p.cm.movement.velocity.z < 0) {
22          passLeftV3.z *= -1;
23       }
24
25       passV3.z = passLeftV3.z;
26       passV3.x = passGoV3.x;
27    } else {
28       passGoV3.z = BASE_BOOST;
```

```
29        if (p.cm.movement.velocity.z < 0) {
30            passGoV3.z *= -1;
31        }
32
33        passLeftV3.x = BASE_NON_BOOST;
34        if (p.cm.movement.velocity.x < 0) {
35            passLeftV3.x *= -1;
36        }
37
38        passV3.x = passLeftV3.x;
39        passV3.z = passGoV3.z;
40    }
41 }
```

The SetBoostVectors method is used to set certain force components of a Vector3 instance used to make the current player's hover racer pass the target car in front of it. The code on lines 2–6 prevents the method from doing any work if certain prerequisites are not met. The next little block of code for us to look at prepares the methods' local variables. The absX and absZ class fields are set to the current player's speed. We are only really concerned with the horizontal axes of X and Z.

Subsequently, the three Vector3 objects used in the passing game mechanic are reset on lines 10–12 in preparation for the results of the current calculations. The speeds involved are absolute values. We do this in an attempt to simplify the detection of which direction the car is moving in. If the X axis is the dominant component, line 14, we execute the code on lines 15–26. Because the X axis is the dominant axis, we'll infer it's the main direction the hover racer is moving in.

As such, we set the velocity of the X component of the passGoV3 field to the BASE_ BOOST speed. On lines 16–18, we take into consideration the original sign of the given velocity. The forward velocity vector is set, but we need a little side movement to help the passing car get around the car that it's passing. On line 20, the passLeftV3 field has its Z axis velocity set to the value of BASE_NON_BOOST. Again, the sign of the original velocity is taken into consideration on lines 21–23.

On lines 25–26, we take the calculated velocities for the X and Z axes and store them in the passV3 field. The code on lines 28–39 follows the same patterns as the code we've just reviewed except we're working with the Z axis here. We'll see these vectors in use in just a bit during the Update method review. The next method up for review is the PerformGunShotAttempt method.

Listing 5-29. CarSensorScript Support Method Details 2

```
01 public void PerformGunShotAttempt(Collider otherObj) {
02    if (BaseScript.IsActive(scriptName) == false) {
03      return;
04    }
05
06    if (otherObj.gameObject.CompareTag(Utilities.TAG_PLAYERS)) {
07      Utilities.LoadPlayerInfo(GetType().Name, out PlayerInfo pi2, out
         int playerIndex2, out p2, otherObj.gameObject, gameState, false);
08      if (p2 != null) {
09        r2 = Random.Range(1, 6);
10
11        explosionOn = true;
12        explosionTime = 0f;
13        if (p2 != null && p2.gunExplosion != null) {
14          p2.gunExplosion.SetActive(true);
15        }
16
17        if (audioGunShot != null) {
18          if (audioGunShot.isPlaying == false) {
19            audioGunShot.Play();
20          }
21        }
22
23        if (r2 == 1 || r2 == 2 || r2 == 4 || r2 == 5) {
24          p2.isHit = true;
25          p2.isMiss = false;
26          p2.isMissTime = 0f;
27          p2.PerformGunShotHit();
28        } else {
29          p2.isHit = false;
30          p2.isMiss = true;
```

```
31                p2.isHitTime = 0f;
32            }
33
34        CancelTarget();
35        }
36    }
37 }
```

The `PerformGunShotAttempt` method starts off in much the same way you'd expect, the safety check on lines 2–4 prevents the method from doing any work if the class isn't properly configured. We check to see that the `otherObj` argument is a player object on line 6. On line 7, the standard utility method call loads up `GameState` and `PlayerState` references except in this case, we apply it to the `otherObj` method argument. On line 9, a random number is generated and stored in the `r2` field.

Because the gun is fired to perform the shot, we set the `explosionOn` field to true, and the `explosionTime` field is set to zero. An explosion effect is activated on line 14 if the player and explosion effect are defined. Next up, on lines 17–21, a sound effect is played to indicate a gunshot has occurred. Subsequently, we have to apply the results of the gun shot, lines 23–32. If the hit roll results in a value of 1, 2, 4, or 5, the shot is a hit. Pretty good odds. If not, the shot is a miss, and nothing happens to the target car.

On lines 24–27, the hit is registered on the target car and the `PerformGunShotHit` method of the associated player's `PlayerState` object is called. On lines 29–31, a miss is handled. Last but not least, the `CancelTarget` method is called to clear the targeting system.

Listing 5-30. CarSensorScript Support Method Details 3

```
01 public void CancelTarget() {
02    if (BaseScript.IsActive(scriptName) == false) {
03        return;
04    }
05
06    if (audioTargetting != null) {
07        audioTargetting.Stop();
08    }
09
10    target = null;
```

```
11    if (p != null) {
12        p.aiHasTarget = false;
13        p.aiHasTargetTime = 0f;
14        p.aiCanFire = false;
15    }
16 }
```

The CancelTarget method starts off much like we'd expect with a quick safety check. Any audio is stopped on line 7. The target class field is set to null, and the current player's targeting fields are reset on lines 11–15. That wraps up the review of the class' support methods.

Main Method Details: CarSensorScript

The CarSensorScript's main methods are generally more geared to callback methods used by the Unity game engine or collision detection events. Let's take a look at the class' main methods.

Listing 5-31. CarSensorScript Main Method Details 1

```
01 void Start() {
02    cars = new ArrayList();
03    base.PrepPlayerInfo(this.GetType().Name);
04    if (BaseScript.IsActive(scriptName) == false) {
05        Utilities.wrForce(scriptName + ": Is Deactivating...");
06        return;
07    } else {
08        player = p.player;
09        AudioSource[] audioSetDst = Utilities.LoadAudioResources(
           GetComponentsInParent<AudioSource>(), new string[] {
           AUDIO_SOURCE_NAME_GUN_SHOT, AUDIO_SOURCE_NAME_TARGETTING });
10        if (audioSetDst != null) {
11            audioGunShot = audioSetDst[0];
12            audioTargetting = audioSetDst[1];
13        }
14    }
15 }
```

The Start method begins by initializing the cars ArrayList used to hold reference to the hover racers being tracked by the car sensor, line 2. On line 3, the base class' more complex configuration method, PrepPlayerInfo, is called to initialize the GameState and PlayerState references. If the class configuration has failed in some way, the method returns after printing some debugging text on lines 4–7. If the class configuration is successful, the player class field is set to the current players' game object, line 8.

An array of found audio resources is set on line 9 with a call to the utility method LoadAudioResources. This method takes an array of AudioSource components and an array of target strings as arguments. If there are results to process, we extract the sound effects for gunshot and targeting game mechanics, lines 11–12. The next method we'll look at handles collision events for the class.

Listing 5-32. CarSensorScript Main Method Details 2

```
01 void OnTriggerEnter(Collider otherObj) {
02     if (BaseScript.IsActive(scriptName) == false) {
03         return;
04     }
05
06     if (p != null && otherObj.CompareTag(Utilities.TAG_PLAYERS)) {
07         if (cars.Contains(otherObj) == false) {
08             cars.Add(otherObj);
09         }
10
11         if (cars.Count > 0) {
12             p.SetDraftingBonusOn();
13         }
14     }
15 }
```

The CarSensorScript receives collision events from different objects as a player's car races around the track. The method is escaped without doing any work if the class configuration had errors. If the game object that was collided with has a tag set to "Players," then the code on lines 7–13 is executed. If the player encountered is not already registered by the targeting system, it is added to the cars ArrayList, line 8. The last little bit of code on lines 11–13 activates a small drafting bonus if there are any cars in the current player's tracking system. Next, we'll take a look at the OnTriggerExit method.

Listing 5-33. CarSensorScript Main Method Details 3

```
01 void OnTriggerExit(Collider otherObj) {
02     if (BaseScript.IsActive(scriptName) == false) {
03         return;
04     }
05
06     if (p != null && otherObj.CompareTag(Utilities.TAG_PLAYERS)) {
07         if (cars.Contains(otherObj) == true) {
08             cars.Remove(otherObj);
09         }
10
11         if (cars.Count == 0) {
12             p.SetDraftingBonusOff();
13         }
14
15         if (target == otherObj) {
16             CancelTarget();
17         }
18     }
19 }
```

The OnTriggerExit method fires when an opponent's car exits the current player's car sensor. The standard safety check code can be found on lines 2–4. If the object leaving the hover racer's sensor is tagged as a player's game object, the code on lines 7–17 will execute. If the cars list contains the given game object, line 7, it's removed from the player's tracking system. On lines 11–13, if there are no cars being tracked, the drafting bonus is turned off.

Take a look at the code on lines 15–17. If the player's car that exited the tracking sensor was being targeted, the CancelTarget method is called on line 16. The last main method for us to review is the CarSensorScript class' Update method. This method is called once per game frame by the Unity game engine. The method is somewhat long, so I'll break it into snippets of code for us to look at.

Listing 5-34. CarSensorScript Main Method Details 4

```
01 void Update() {
02     if (p == null) {
03        return;
04     } else if (BaseScript.IsActive(scriptName) == false) {
05        return;
06     } else {
07        if (gameState != null) {
08           if (gameState.gamePaused == true) {
09              return;
10           } else if (gameState.gameRunning == false) {
11              return;
12           }
13        }
14     }
15
```

The first snippet of code is from the beginning of the Update method, listed previously, which handles escaping the method call if certain prerequisites are not met. This code is a little bit different than previous code blocks we've looked at. In this case, care is taken to prevent the method from doing any work if the game is paused or not running.

Listing 5-35. CarSensorScript Main Method Details 5

```
16     //Process Car Sensor Targets
17     if (p.aiPassingMode == 0 && p.aiIsPassing == false) {
18        l2 = cars.Count;
19        tb = false;
20        for (i2 = 0; i2 < l2; i2++) {
21           obj = (Collider)cars[i2];
22           t1 = obj.gameObject.transform.position;
23           t2 = player.transform.position;
24           dist = Vector3.Distance(t1, t2);
25
```

```
26          //Auto Passing Check
27          if (dist <= SAFE_FOLLOW_DIST && p.speed >= (TRIGGER_SPEED_
            PASSING * p.maxSpeed)) {
28             tb = true;
29             break;
30          }
31
32          if (gameState.gameSettingsSet == 2) {
33             //No Gun Play
34             continue;
35          }
36
37          //Targeting Check
38          if (dist <= GUN_SHOT_DIST && p.gunOn == true && p.ammo > 0 &&
            p.aiHasTarget == false && p.aiIsReloading == false) {
39             target = obj;
40             p.aiHasTarget = true;
41             p.aiHasTargetTime = 0f;
42
43             if (audioTargetting != null) {
44                if (audioTargetting.isPlaying == false) {
45                   audioTargetting.Play();
46                }
47             }
48          } else if (dist <= GUN_SHOT_DIST && p.gunOn == true && p.ammo
            > 0 && p.aiHasTarget == true && p.aiCanFire == true &&
            p.aiIsReloading == false) {
49             p.aiHasTarget = false;
50             p.aiHasTargetTime = 0f;
51             p.aiCanFire = false;
52             p.ammo--;
53
```

```
54              if (p.ammo <= 0) {
55                  p.ammo = 0;
56                  p.HideGun();
57              }
58
59              if (audioTargetting != null) {
60                  audioTargetting.Stop();
61              }
62
63              PerformGunShotAttempt(obj);
64              p.aiIsReloading = true;
65              p.aiIsReloadingTime = 0f;
66          } else if (dist > GUN_SHOT_DIST) {
67              if (audioTargetting != null) {
68                  audioTargetting.Stop();
69              }
70              target = null;
71              p.aiHasTarget = false;
72              p.aiHasTargetTime = 0f;
73              p.aiCanFire = false;
74          }
75      } //end for loop
76
```

In the next snippet of code, listed previously, the Update method handles processing the hover racers currently being tracked by the car's targeting system. If the current player's car is not in passing mode, line 17, the local variable l2 is updated with the number of cars currently being tracked by the targeting system, while the Boolean flag, tb, is set to false, lines 18–19. Lines 20–21 are used to loop over the cars being tracked. Next, lines 21–24 set the object being targeted, the position of the target, the position of the current player, and lastly on line 24 the distance between the target and the player. An auto passing game mechanic is checked for on line 27.

If the target is within the safe following distance and the current player is moving fast enough, then the auto passing flag is toggled and the for loop is broken out of, lines 28 and 29. On lines 32–35, there is a check to make sure that the current race supports the battle mode game mechanics; if not, we skip past the target player's entry, line 34.

The targeting system is checked to see if there is currently a target, line 38. The target and player state information are updated on lines 39–41. This block of code starts off the targeting process by setting the target.

Next, on line 48, if the target hover racer is still in range and the current player's car can fire its gun then a shot is taken. The small block of code on lines 49–52 resets the player's car sensor script's targeting and firing fields. The player's ammo is decreased on line 52. On lines 54–57, we check to see if the current player is out of ammo. If so, we make sure that the ammo is set to zero and hide the gun. The targeting sound effect is stopped on lines 59–61. The shot is performed on line 63, and the reloading state is set on lines 64–65.

The last block of code in this large snippet runs from line 66 to line 74. This block of code is used to turn targeting off. The targeting sound effect is stopped, line 68, and the target field is set to null on line 70. The player state targeting fields are reset on lines 71–73. The next snippet of code we'll look at handles the start of the hover racer's auto passing code.

Listing 5-36. CarSensorScript Main Method Details 6

```
77        //Auto Passing Start
78        if (tb == true) {
79            p.aiPassingTime += Time.deltaTime;
80            if (p.aiPassingTime > TRIGGER_TIME_PASSING && p.aiPassingMode
                 == 0) {
81                p.aiPassingMode = 1;
82                p.aiIsPassing = true;
83                p.aiPassingTime = 0f;
84                moveTime = 0f;
85                p.SetBoost();
86                p.SetCurrentSpeed();
87                SetBoostVectors();
88            }
89        } else {
90            p.aiPassingMode = 0;
91            p.aiIsPassing = false;
92            p.aiPassingTime = 0f;
93            moveTime = 0f;
```

```
94          p.SetNorm();
95          p.SetCurrentSpeed();
96      }
97  } //main if statement
98
```

If the tb field, set earlier in the Update method, if set to true, line 78, then auto passing is initiated, and the aiPassingTime field is incremented on line 79. After the required amount of time, the passing mode moves from zero to one, and the code on lines 81–87 is executed. Take a look at the code and make sure that it makes sense to you. If the tb flag is false, then the code on lines 90–95 executes, turning off any passing mode flags and resetting any timers. Up next, we'll take a look at the application of the auto passing game mechanic.

Listing 5-37. CarSensorScript Main Method Details 7

```
099  //Auto Passing Applied
100  if (p.aiIsPassing == true) {
101      moveTime += Time.deltaTime * 100;
102      if (p.aiPassingMode == 1) {
103          p.controller.Move(passLeftV3 * Time.deltaTime);
104          if (moveTime >= 50) {
105              p.aiPassingMode = 2;
106              moveTime = 0;
107          }
108      } else if (p.aiPassingMode == 2) {
109          p.controller.Move(passGoV3 * Time.deltaTime);
110          if (moveTime >= 100) {
111              p.aiPassingMode = 0;
112              p.aiIsPassing = false;
113              p.aiPassingTime = 0f;
114              p.SetNorm();
115              moveTime = 0f;
116          }
117      }
118  }
119
```

```
120    //Auto Passing End
121    if (p.isJumping == true) {
122        p.aiPassingMode = 0;
123        p.aiIsPassing = false;
124        p.aiPassingTime = 0f;
125        p.SetNorm();
126        moveTime = 0f;
127    }
128
```

The next snippet of code in the CarSensorScript's Update method is responsible for applying the auto passing game mechanic. On line 100, if the aiIsPassing Boolean flag is set to true, we start updating the moveTime field, line 101. If the aiPassingMode field is equal to one, line 102, the current player's car moves left for 50 milliseconds, and then the aiPassingMode is set to 2 and the moveTime field is reset to track the duration of the next movement in the auto passing game mechanic.

If the passing mode has a value of 2, line 108, then the current player's car is thrust forward for the next 100 milliseconds, lines 109 and 110. After the 100-millisecond time interval expires, the passing mode, speed, and move time are all reset, lines 111–115. The last bit of auto passing code on lines 121–127 is responsible for turning off the auto passing mode if the current player's hover racer is jumping. That brings us to the end of the auto passing code. Next, we'll wrap up the method review with some targeting related code.

Listing 5-38. CarSensorScript Main Method Details 8

```
129    //Targetting to Fire
130    if (p.aiHasTarget == true && p.aiIsReloading == false) {
131        p.aiHasTargetTime += Time.deltaTime * 100;
132        if (p.aiHasTargetTime >= MIN_TARGET_TO_FIRE_TIME) {
133            p.aiHasTargetTime = 0f;
134            p.aiCanFire = true;
135        }
136    } else if (p.aiIsReloading == true) {
137        p.aiIsReloadingTime += Time.deltaTime * 100;
138        if (p.aiIsReloadingTime >= GUN_RELOAD_TIME) {
139            p.aiIsReloading = false;
```

```
140            p.aiIsReloadingTime = 0f;
141        }
142    }
143
144    //Targetting Gun Explosion Effect
145    if (explosionOn == true) {
146        explosionTime += Time.deltaTime * 100;
147    }
148
149    if (explosionOn == true && explosionTime >= MAX_EXPLOSION_TIME) {
150        explosionOn = false;
151        explosionTime = 0f;
152        p.isHit = false;
153        p.isMiss = false;
154        if (p != null && p.gunExplosion != null) { // &&
               p.gunExplosionParticleSystem != null)
155            p.gunExplosion.SetActive(false);
156            //p.gunExplosionParticleSystem.emit = false;
157        }
158    }
159 } //method end
```

The last snippet of code we have to review handles targeting responsibilities like reloading, checking if the current car can fire, and showing the gunshot explosion effect, if the particle effect has been implemented. I've left some particle effect customizations up to you. The code on lines 130–136 executes if the tracking system has a target and the gun is not reloading. This code sets the player's aiCanFire field to true on line 134. The code on lines 136 to 142 handles the timing of the gun's reloading mechanism. The code on lines 145–147 handles tracking the duration of the explosion effect. The last block of code on lines 144–158 handles turning off the explosion effect once the duration expires.

Make sure to look over and understand this code before moving on. That brings us to the end of the main method review section. Up next, we'll look at a demonstration of the CarSensorScript in action.

Demonstration: CarSensorScript

The CarSensorScript class is a bit complex, so there are actually two demonstration scenes for us to review. As always, control of the car takes a few seconds to kick in. The first demonstration scene is named "DemoCarSensorScriptAutoPass". You can find it in the "Project" panel in the "Scenes" folder. In this scene, if you slowly get behind and close to the hover racer in front of you, the auto pass feature will activate. Try it out and make sure to think about the code as you try it out.

In the second demonstration scene, "DemoCarSensorScriptGunShot", you'll have to arm your hover racer using one of the two battle mode modifiers on the board. Next, get close to the opponent car and wait a few moments until you hear the targeting chirp sound effect. Next, listen for the boom of the gunshot. If you fire a number of times, the opponent's car will jump as it's repositioned to a previous waypoint for respawning.

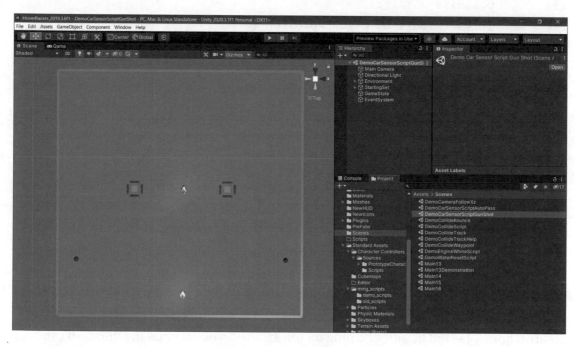

Figure 5-1. *CarSensorScript Demonstration Scene 1*

Screenshot depicting the CarSensorScript's gunshot demo scene

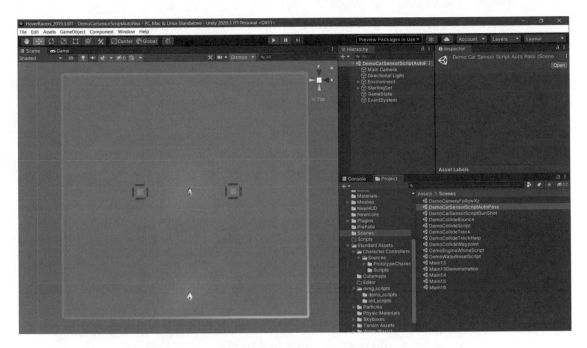

Figure 5-2. *CarSensorScript Demonstration Scene 2*

Screenshot depicting the CarSensorScript's auto passing demo scene

The screenshots, shown previously, depict the two different scenes used to demonstrate this class. That brings us to the conclusion of the class review.

Chapter Conclusion

This brings us to the conclusion of this chapter. Let's take a look at the material we've covered here. This should wrap up all of the game's interaction-driven game mechanics listed in the game specification in Chapter 2.

1. CollideScript: This class is a centralized point of interaction that supports a few different game mechanics:

   a. Untagged: Ignored game objects.

   b. Hittable: Objects that fly off when collided with; think of "oil drums."

   c. Boost: Several different boost markers that accelerate the car when collided with.

      d. Jump: An interaction marker that causes the player's car to jump when collided with.

      e. Battle Mode Markers: Interaction markers that are only available during battle mode. These markers control battle mode modifiers such as:

         i. Ammo

        ii. Gun

      iii. Health

      iv. Armor

       v. Invincibility

2. CarSensorScript: This class is a second centralized point of interaction that supports a few different game mechanics:

      a. Auto Passing: Following a car close enough at a certain speed and distance will trigger an auto passing game mechanic.

      b. Gun Shot Attempt: Follow a car closely and for a long enough time, while you have the gun enabled, and your car will target and attempt to shoot the car in front of you.

With these new game mechanics, we almost have a complete racing game. All we need is a central game state, input handlers, and a few helper classes. Notice how different script components can control the current player's car and AI-controlled cars through the centralized GameState and PlayerState class instances we've seen in use. This approach to looking up player state data helps hover racers interact with their environment and one other. In the next chapter, we'll slow things down a little bit and take a look at some helper classes.

CHAPTER 6

Helper Classes

In this chapter, we're going to be reviewing the various helper classes that support different features of the Hover Racers game. Helper classes are, generally speaking, smaller classes that are used to assist in certain game-related processes. In general, the chapter should be less intense than the previous chapter with most classes being simple and direct. In some cases, and I'll try to make note of it ahead of time, we'll abandon our class review template in exchange for a shorter, more direct process. The first two classes we'll review are used to handle cars or objects that have flown off the track.

Class Review: DestroyScript

The DestroyScript class is responsible for handling game objects that have fallen off of the board. Instead of allowing them to fall indefinitely, you should design your levels to handle occurrences of objects ending up in strange places. The default tracks for hover racers are designed to handle objects and hover racers falling off of the track or even the board. Let's take a look at some code! In this case, we'll list the full class in one review step.

Listing 6-1. DestroyScript Class Review 1

```
1 public class DestroyScript : WaterResetScript {
2    public override void OnTriggerEnter(Collider otherObj) {
3        if (otherObj.gameObject.CompareTag(Utilities.TAG_PLAYERS)) {
4            base.OnTriggerEnter(otherObj);
5        } else {
6            Destroy(otherObj.gameObject);
7        }
8    }
9 }
```

© Victor G Brusca 2022
V. G Brusca, *Advanced Unity Game Development*, https://doi.org/10.1007/978-1-4842-7851-2_6

Notice that the class extends the WaterResetScript class. The only method defined here, and overridden, is the OnTriggerEnter method. This method triggers during a collision with another Unity GameObject. If the object collided with is tagged as a player object, then the base class method is called. For any other type of game object, that object is destroyed, line 6. As you can tell, the class is designed to clean things up. Let's take a look at the WaterResetScript class next.

Class Review: WaterResetScript

The WaterResetScript class is responsible for putting hover racers back on the track when they fly off into the water hazard. This class is a bit longer than the DestroyScript we just reviewed, so we'll employ the stand class review process:

1. Pertinent Method Outline/Class Headers

2. Support Method Details

3. Main Method Details

4. Demonstration

The WaterResetScript class extends the BaseScript class and as such is a MonoBehaviour. There are no static class members, enumerations, or class fields to speak of, so we'll begin the class review process with the pertinent method outline section.

Pertinent Method Outline/Class Headers: WaterResetScript

The WaterResetScript class' pertinent method outline is listed as follows.

Listing 6-2. WaterResetScript Pertinent Method Outline/Class Headers 1

```
//Main Methods
void Start();
public virtual void OnTriggerEnter(Collider otherObj);

//Support Methods
public void ProcessWaterReset(Collider otherObj);
```

Next, I'll list the class' import statements and declaration.

Listing 6-3. WaterResetScript Pertinent Method Outline/Class Headers 2

```
using UnityEngine;

public class WaterResetScript : BaseScript {}
```

This brings us to the conclusion of the method and class declaration outline. The next section up for review is the class' support methods.

Support Method Details: WaterResetScript

The WaterResetScript class has one support method for us to review, listed as follows.

Listing 6-4. WaterResetScript Support Method Details 1

```
01 public void ProcessWaterReset(Collider otherObj) {
02    if (BaseScript.IsActive(scriptName) == false) {
03       return;
04    }
05
06    if (otherObj.gameObject.CompareTag(Utilities.TAG_PLAYERS)) {
07       Utilities.LoadPlayerInfo(GetType().Name, out PlayerInfo pi, out
         int playerIndex, out p, otherObj.gameObject, gameState, false);
08       if (p != null) {
09          if (p.waypoints != null && p.waypoints.Count > 0) {
10             //move car to waypoint center
11             if (p.aiWaypointIndex - 5 >= 0) {
12                p.aiWaypointIndex -= 5;
13             } else if (p.aiWaypointIndex - 4 >= 0) {
14                p.aiWaypointIndex -= 4;
15             } else if (p.aiWaypointIndex - 3 >= 0) {
16                p.aiWaypointIndex -= 3;
17             } else if (p.aiWaypointIndex - 2 >= 0) {
18                p.aiWaypointIndex -= 2;
19             } else if (p.aiWaypointIndex - 1 >= 0) {
20                p.aiWaypointIndex -= 1;
```

```
21              } else {
22                  p.aiWaypointIndex = 0;
23              }
24
25              if (p.aiWaypointIndex >= 0 && p.aiWaypointIndex <
                p.waypoints.Count) {
26                  p.MoveToCurrentWaypoint();
27              }
28
29              p.offTrack = false;
30              p.offTrackTime = 0;
31          }
32      }
33    }
34 }
```

On lines 2–4, the method is escaped if there is a configuration issue detected. Line 6 checks to see if the collision object is tagged as a "Player" or not. If so, the player state for the collision object's associated player is loaded on line 7. The key results are stored in the p class field inherited from the BaseScript class. If p is defined, line 8, and if the track's waypoint data is defined, line 9, we look for a previous waypoint index. On lines 11–23, we look for a previous waypoint starting at five indexes behind the current waypoint index.

If a valid index is found, the value of the aiWaypointIndex field of the PlayerState class is updated. Now that a waypoint index has been chosen, we double-check that it is indeed valid, line 25; then we move the colliding player's hover racer to that waypoint index on line 26. Lastly, the player's off-track status is reset on lines 29–30.

Main Method Details: WaterResetScript

The WaterResetScript class has two main methods for us to review: the Start and OnTriggerEnter methods. I'll list them as follows, and then we'll quickly review them.

Listing 6-5. WaterResetScript Main Method Details 1

```
01 void Start() {
02     base.Prep(this.GetType().Name);
03     if (BaseScript.IsActive(scriptName) == false) {
04         Utilities.wrForce(scriptName + ": Is Deactivating...");
05         return;
06     }
07 }

01 public virtual void OnTriggerEnter(Collider otherObj) {
02     if (BaseScript.IsActive(scriptName) == false) {
03         return;
04     }
05     ProcessWaterReset(otherObj);
06 }
```

The Start method is called as part of the MonoBehaviour's life cycle in the Unity game engine. In this case, the method is called as part of the MonoBehaviour's initialization. The Prep method is called to load up GameState and PlayerState information for the current player. If any issues are encountered, the class is marked as inactive by name. A quick test for this result is performed on line 3 followed by some logging on line 4. This is a standard, simple, implementation of an extension of the BaseScript class' Start method we've seen before.

The second main method listed previously is the OnTriggerEnter callback method. This method is called in response to a collision event. If the script is inactive, the method returns without doing any work, lines 2–4. If not, then the ProcessWaterReset method is called on line 5. That brings us to the conclusion of the main method review. We'll look at the class' demonstration section next.

Demonstration: WaterResetScript

Because the DestroyScript extends the WaterResetScript, I decided to demonstrate both scripts in this review section. The DestroyScript is very similar to the WaterResetScript in functionality, so we won't explicitly demo it here. We will, however, explicitly demonstrate the WaterResetScript in action.

117

Go to the "Project" panel and find the "Scenes" folder. Locate the "DemoWaterResetScript" scene but don't open it just yet. I want to describe how the demo scene works first. After a few seconds, you'll be able to control the hover racer. Click inside the game window and make sure it's activated for input. In front of the car will be two green pillars, drive through them, and aim for the jump in between the purple pillars. You'll fly through the air for a bit until you hit the invisible WaterResetScript-enabled plane.

This game object is labeled as "WaterReset" in the "Hierarchy" panel. The script will trigger upon collision and send the player back a few waypoints. The DestroyScript class would function the same way except that it would destroy any objects that collide with it and don't have the "Player" tag. Play around with the demonstration scene for a bit and make sure you understand how it works before moving on. The next class up for review controls the hover racer's engine sound effect.

Class Review: EngineWhineScript

The EngineWhineScript class is responsible for controlling the audio, volume, and pitch of the engine sound effect. The script component adjusts the play-back attributes of the AudioSource component, creating louder, higher-pitch engine sounds at faster speeds. Take a moment to think about this class in the context of all the other classes we've reviewed. Does anything stand out?

One thing you might have noticed is that script components are somewhat compartmentalized. They configure themselves and make adjustments to game objects during the Update method call or other collision event callback methods. Let's start the class review with the following review steps:

1. Static/Constants/Read-Only Class Members

2. Class Fields

3. Pertinent Method Outline/Class Headers

4. Support Method Details

5. Main Method Details

6. Demonstration

Without further ado, let's take a look at some code!

Static/Constants/Read-Only Class Members: EngineWhineScript

The EngineWhineScript class has one static field for us to review, listed subsequently.

Listing 6-6. EngineWhineScript Static/Constants/Read-Only Class Members 1

```
public static string AUDIO_SOURCE_NAME_WHINE = "car_idle_lp_01";
```

The field listed has the name of the AudioSource component that will be used for the engine sound effect. We'll take a look at the remaining class fields next.

Class Fields: EngineWhineScript

The EngineWhineScript class has one field that is used internally by the class' Update method.

Listing 6-7. EngineWhineScript Class Fields 1

```
//***** Internal Variables: Update *****
private float pTmp = 0.0f;
```

The pTmp field is used by the class to hold a copy of the player's speed percentage. This value is used to set the pitch and volume of the AudioSource component referenced by the audioS base class field.

Pertinent Method Outline/Class Headers: EngineWhineScript

The EngineWhineScript class' pertinent method outline is as follows.

Listing 6-8. EngineWhineScript Pertinent Method Outline/Class Headers 1

```
//Main Methods
void Start();
void Update();
```

The class' import statements and declaration are listed here.

Listing 6-9. EngineWhineScript Pertinent Method Outline/Class Headers 2

```
using UnityEngine;

public class EngineWhineScript : BaseScript { }
```

In the upcoming review section, we'll take a look at the class' main methods.

Main Method Details: EngineWhineScript

The EngineWhineScript class has two main methods for us to review. Both of these methods should look familiar. Let's take a look.

Listing 6-10. EngineWhineScript Main Method Details 1

```
01 void Start() {
02     base.PrepPlayerInfo(this.GetType().Name);
03     if (BaseScript.IsActive(scriptName) == false) {
04         Utilities.wrForce(scriptName + ": Is Deactivating...");
05         return;
06     }
07
08     audioS = Utilities.LoadAudioResources(GetComponents<AudioSource>(),
       new string[] { AUDIO_SOURCE_NAME_WHINE })[0];
09     if (audioS != null) {
10         audioS.volume = 0.2f;
11         audioS.pitch = 0.2f;
12     }
13 }
```

This Start method is a bit more complex than the default, standard, method that only loads up the game state info with a call to the base class' Prep method. This method calls the more complex PrepPlayerInfo base class method. This method will also load player state info along with the game state. It also uses the LoadAudioResources utility method to find and load a reference to the AudioSource component with a name that matches the AUDIO_SOURCE_NAME_WHINE static class field. If the audio resource is found, line 9, then the sound effect's volume and pitch are adjusted to a default value of 0.2.

Notice that each class that extends the BaseScript class and uses one of the two class preparation methods, Prep or PrepPlayerInfo, calls the GameState class' PrepGame method. The reason for this redundancy is that we can't guarantee which GameObject's Start method will be called first. To be safe, just about every script component in the game checks to make sure the game has been prepared as part of the class' configuration. Let's take a look at the Update method next.

Listing 6-11. EngineWhineScript Main Method Details 2

```
01 void Update() {
02     if (BaseScript.IsActive(scriptName) == false) {
03         return;
04     }
05
06     if (p != null) {
07         pTmp = p.speedPrct;
08         if (audioS != null) {
09             audioS.pitch = Mathf.Clamp(pTmp * 4.1f, 0.5f, 4.1f); //p is
                clamped to sane values
10             audioS.volume = Mathf.Clamp(pTmp * 0.6f, 0.2f, 0.6f);
11         }
12     }
13 }
```

The Update method is escaped on lines 2–4 in the same way we've seen time and time again. On line 6, we check to see if the PlayerState instance, p, is defined. If so, then we update the pTmp class field with the hover racer's current speed percentage on line 7. Because we're explicitly adjusting the hover racer's engine sound, we can only proceed if the audio resource, audioS, has been properly defined, line 8. If the field is not null, then we adjust the pitch and volume of the engine whine sound effect on lines 9 and 10. Notice that the values are based on the pTmp field. In other words, the pitch and volume are based on the hover racer's current speed. This brings us to the end of the main method review section. In the next section, we'll take a look at the demonstration scene for this class.

Demonstration: EngineWhineScript

The demo scene for this class can be found in the "Project" panel's "Scenes" folder. Locate the scene named "DemoEngineWhineScript". This demonstration is simple and direct. Just drive around the board and go as fast as you can. Notice the value of the pitch and volume shown at the bottom left-hand corner of the screen. Keep in mind that the values are based on the hover racer's current speed. That brings us to the conclusion of the EngineWhineScript class' review. The next class we'll look at is the LapTime class.

Class Review: LapTime

The LapTime class is not a MonoBehaviour-based class; it's just a plane old C# class. This class is responsible for wrapping the track time information and provides methods for serializing and deserializing the class' lap time to and from a string representation. This class is somewhat long, but I still think we can review it in one shot. We'll do a direct review of the class next.

Listing 6-12. LapTime Class Review 1

```
01 public class LapTime {
02     public string time = "";
03     public int timeNum = 0;
04     public int track = 0;
05     public int type = 0; //0=easy, 1=battle, 2=classic
06     public int diff = 0; //0=low, 1=med, 2=high
07     public int lap = 0;
08
09     public string Serialize() {
10         string t = time;
11         string tN = timeNum + "";
12         string tr = track + "";
13         string ty = type + "";
14         string df = diff + "";
15         string l = lap + "";
```

```
16      string col = "~";
17      return (t + col + tN + col + tr + col + ty + col + df + col + l);
18   }
19
20   public override string ToString() {
21      string ret = "";
22      ret += "Time: " + time + "\n";
23      ret += "Time Number: " + timeNum + "\n";
24      ret += "Track: " + track + "\n";
25      ret += "Type: " + type + "\n";
26      ret += "Difficulty: " + diff + "\n";
27      ret += "Lap: " + lap + "\n";
28      return ret;
29   }
30
31   public bool Deserialize(string s) {
32      if (s != null && s != "") {
33         char[] c = "~".ToCharArray();
34         string[] cs = s.Split(c);
35         if (cs.Length == 6) {
36            time = cs[0] + "";
37            timeNum = int.Parse(cs[1]);
38            track = int.Parse(cs[2]);
39            type = int.Parse(cs[3]);
40            diff = int.Parse(cs[4]);
41            lap = int.Parse(cs[5]);
42            return true;
43         } else {
44            return false;
45         }
46      } else {
47         return false;
48      }
49   }
50 }
```

The LapTime class declaration is shown on line 1. The class fields are listed on lines 2–7. The first field, time, holds a string representation of the current lap time. The timeNum field represents the lap time as a large integer. The track field is an integer value that represents which track is being raced on. The type field is an integer value that represents the type of race being run: easy, battle, or classic. Next, the diff field is used to track the race' difficulty: low, medium, and high. Lastly, we have the lap class field. This represents the lap number associated with the current lap time.

The LapTime class has three methods for us to review. The first two methods, Serialize and ToString, are used to represent the class as a string. The Serialize method converts all the string representations of class fields into a long string with entries separated by the col variable, line 17. The ToString method is similar to the Serialize method.

In the ToString method, the class fields are given labels and separated by line breaks, lines 21–27. The resulting string is returned on line 28. The last method for us to review is the Deserialize method. This method reverses the serialization process and updates the values of the class fields based on the decoded data. The passed in string argument is split on line 34. If the expected length is found, the data is converted and assigned, lines 36–41. The method returns a Boolean indicating the success of the deserialization process. We'll skip the demonstration section for this class because we'll see it in use when we review the LapTimeManager class next.

Class Review: LapTimeManager

The LapTimeManager class is responsible for managing a set of recorded lap times. Similar to that of the LapTime class, the LapTimeManager class is not a MonoBehaviour; it's just a plane old C# class. The LapTimeManager class is sufficiently complex that we would be well served to use the more structured class review process we've used previously.

1. Static/Constants/Read-Only Class Members

2. Class Fields

3. Pertinent Method Outline/Class Headers

4. Support Method Details

5. Main Method Details

6. Demonstration

There's nothing out of the ordinary to discuss with regard to this class, so without further ado, let's take a look at some code!

Static/Constants/Read-Only Class Members: LapTimeManager

The LapTimeManager class has two static members for us to look at.

Listing 6-13. LapTimeManager Static/Constants/Read-Only Class Members 1

```
public static int CLEANING_START_INDEX = 33;
public static int LAST_NOT_CLEANED_INDEX = 32;
```

The first field listed is used to mark the index that will be used when attempting to clean entries from the lap time manager. The second field listed is the last index that won't be cleaned by the class' cleaning process. What this means is that as the saved lap times build up and the cleaning code executes, only the first 32 entries will be preserved. Entries 33 and up are all subject to being cleaned. Notice that the LapTimeManager and LapTime classes do not extend the BaseScript class. Can you think of a reason why?

The main reason is that these classes are not Unity MonoBehaviours, script components. They are standard C# classes. As such, the classes are initialized by calling class constructors and other class config methods. MonoBehaviours, however, are components of the Unity game engine and are initialized by component life cycle callback methods like Awake and Start. These initialization methods act upon the live game environment and have to be able to handle missing configuration resources at runtime. That's why we have support to disable classes that extend the MonoBehaviour class' functionality by registering the class as inactive. Let's move on to the class' remaining fields.

Class Fields: LapTimeManager

The LapTimeManager class has a few public fields and some private fields that are used as local method variables.

Listing 6-14. LapTimeManager Class Fields 1

```
//***** Class Fields *****
public List<LapTime> lapTimes = new List<LapTime>();
public LapTime lastEntry = null;
public LapTime bestEntry = null;

//***** Internal Variables: FindBestLapTime *****
private LapTime retFbt = null;
private int lFbt = 0;
private int iFbt = 0;

//***** Internal Variables: CleanTimes *****
private LapTime ltFbt = null;
private int lCt = 0;
private int iCt = 0;
```

The first class field in the set is the lapTimers list. The list is responsible for storing individual lap time records. The following two fields are used to reference important lap times. The lastEntry field holds the last recorded lap time, while the bestEntry field holds the best recorded lap time. The next group of class fields is used by the FindBestLapTime and CleanTimes methods. The retFbt field is a LapTime instance that is used to hold a return value.

The lFbt and iFbt fields are loop control variables and are used to loop over the list of recorded lap times. The ltFbt field is another LapTime instance used to hold the current lap time when looping over a list of them. Lastly, the lCt and iCt fields are used to control looping over the list of recorded lap times when cleaning out old entries. The next two sets of fields are used by the Serialize and Deserialize methods.

Listing 6-15. LapTimeManager Class Fields 2

```
//***** Internal Variables: Serialize/ToString *****
private string retSer = "";
private int lSer = 0;
private int iSer = 0;
private string retTs = "";
private int lTs = 0;
private int iTs = 0;
```

```
//***** Internal Variables: Deserialize *****
private char[] cDes = null;
private string[] csDes = null;
private int lDes = 0;
private int iDes = 0;
private string tmpDes = "";
private LapTime ltDes = null;
```

The first field listed previously, retSer, is a string that is used to build the serialized list of recorded lap times. The lSer and iSet fields are used as loop control variables during the serialization process. Similarly, the retTs field is used to build a to-string representation of the class, and the lTs and iTs fields are used as loop control variables during the to-string operation. The next set of fields are used by the Deserialize method.

The cDes field is used to represent the dividing character used to split a list of lap times in string form. Subsequently, the csDes field is used to hold the results of said split. The lDes and iDes fields are loop control variables used during the deserialization process. The tmpDes field is used to hold the deserialized string as the set is looped over. Lastly, the ltDes field, a LapTime instance, is used to deserialize the string to a LapTime object that is stored in the lapTimes list. In the next section, we'll take a look at the class' pertinent method outline.

Pertinent Method Outline/Class Headers: LapTimeManager

The LapTimeManager class' pertinent method outline is as follows.

Listing 6-16. LapTimeManager Pertinent Method Outline/Class Headers 1

```
//Main Methods
public string Serialize();
public bool Deserialize(string s);
public override string ToString();
public void CleanTimes();
```

```
//Support Methods
public void AddEntry(LapTime lt);
public LapTime FindBestLapTimeByLastEntry();
public LapTime FindBestLapTime(int track, int type, int diff, int timeNum);
public string ToStringShort();
```

Next, I'll list the class' import statements and declaration. Note that this class does not extend Unity's MonoBehaviour class.

Listing 6-17. LapTimeManager Pertinent Method Outline/Class Headers 2

```
using System.Collections.Generic;


public class LapTimeManager {}
```

In the next review section, we'll take a look at the class' support methods.

Support Method Details: LapTimeManager

The LapTimeManager class has a few support methods for us to review. Let's take a look.

Listing 6-18. LapTimeManager Support Method Details 1

```
01 public void AddEntry(LapTime lt) {
02     lapTimes.Add(lt);
03     lastEntry = lt;
04 }
```

```
01 public LapTime FindBestLapTimeByLastEntry() {
02     return FindBestLapTime(lastEntry.track, lastEntry.type, lastEntry.
       diff, lastEntry.timeNum);
03 }
```

```
01 public LapTime FindBestLapTime(int track, int type, int diff, int
   timeNum) {
02     retFbt = null;
03     ltFbt = null;
```

```
04     if (lapTimes != null) {
05         lFbt = lapTimes.Count;
06         for (iFbt = 0; iFbt < lFbt; iFbt++) {
07             ltFbt = (LapTime)lapTimes[iFbt];
08             if (ltFbt != null) {
09                 if (ltFbt.track == track && ltFbt.type == type && ltFbt.diff
                    == diff) {
10                     if (ltFbt.timeNum < timeNum) {
11                         retFbt = ltFbt;
12                     }
13                 }
14             }
15         }
16     }
17     bestEntry = retFbt;
18     return retFbt;
19 }
```

```
01 public string ToStringShort() {
02     return "Lap Times: " + lapTimes.Count;
03 }
```

The first method listed, AddEntry, is used to append a new lap time record to the current list of lap times, line 2. Notice that the lastEntry field is updated when this method is called, line 3. The next method for us to review is a convenience method, FindBestLapTimeByLastEntry, that calls the class' FindBestLapTime method with information about the last entry lap time, line 2. That brings us to the FindBestLapTime method.

The FindBestLapTime method is used to search through the list of known lap times to find the entry that matches the race settings - track, type, and difficulty arguments - and has the lowest time duration. On lines 2–3, method variables retFbt and ltFbt are reset to null. On line 4, if the lapTimes field is not null, then we loop over the entries searching for a match with the lowest duration, lines 5–6. Each entry in the lapTimes list is assigned to the ltFbt local variable on line 7. If the lap time entry is defined, matches the search criteria, and has a lower time duration, the lap time is set as the data being returned by the method, lines 8–11.

The last method in the set is the ToStringShort method. This method is very simple and returns a string indicating the number of lap times managed by the class. As you can see, this class is very helpful when working with lap time data. Next up, we'll take a look at the LapTimeManager class' main methods.

Main Method Details: LapTimeManager

The LapTimeManager class has a few main methods used to manage the lap time records stored in the class. I'll list the main methods in one group here.

Listing 6-19. LapTimeManager Main Method Details 1

```
01 public string Serialize() {
02     retSer = "";
03     if (lapTimes != null) {
04         lSer = lapTimes.Count;
05         for (iSer = 0; iSer < lSer; iSer++) {
06             if (lapTimes[iSer] != null) {
07                 retSer += ((LapTime)lapTimes[iSer]).Serialize();
08                 if (iSer < lSer - 1) {
09                     retSer += "^";
10                 }
11             }
12         }
13     }
14     return retSer;
15 }
```

```
01 public bool Deserialize(string s) {
02     lapTimes = new List<LapTime>();
03     if (s != null && s != "") {
04         cDes = "^".ToCharArray();
05         csDes = s.Split(cDes);
06         if (csDes != null && csDes.Length > 0) {
07             lDes = csDes.Length;
```

```
08          for (iDes = 0; iDes < lDes; iDes++) {
09              tmpDes = csDes[iDes];
10              if (tmpDes != null) {
11                  ltDes = new LapTime();
12                  ltDes.Deserialize(tmpDes);
13                  lapTimes.Add(ltDes);
14              }
15          }
16          return true;
17      } else {
18          return false;
19      }
20  } else {
21      return false;
22  }
23 }
```

```
01 public override string ToString() {
02     retTs = "";
03     if (lapTimes != null) {
04         lTs = lapTimes.Count;
05         for (iTs = 0; iTs < lTs; iTs++) {
06             if (lapTimes[iTs] != null) {
07                 retTs += "Lap Time Entry: " + (iTs + 1) + "\n";
08                 retTs += ((LapTime)lapTimes[iTs]).ToString() + "\n";
09             }
10         }
11     }
12     return retTs;
13 }
```

```
01 public void CleanTimes() {
02     if (lapTimes != null && lapTimes.Count > 1) {
03         if (lapTimes.Count > LAST_NOT_CLEANED_INDEX) {
04             lCt = lapTimes.Count;
```

```
05              for (iCt = CLEANING_START_INDEX; iCt < lCt; iCt++) {
06                  lapTimes.Remove(lapTimes[iCt]);
07                  lCt--;
08              }
09          }
10      }
11  }
```

The first method in the group is the Serialize method. This method is used to convert the LapTimeManager class to a string representation so it can be stored in the game's player preferences. This will allow it to persist across multiple uses of the game. Why go through all of this serialization trouble? Why not just store the data directly? As it turns out, it's much easier and more powerful to rely on serialization because it simplifies interaction between the game, recorded lap times, and Unity's PlayerPrefs simple data persistence class.

If you think back to our review of the LapTime class recall that it also supports conversion to and from string form. What this means is that you can turn a string into a C# object instance and vice versa. The power here comes from the fact that you can interact with the classes programmatically and, with one method call, convert the class to string form. Knowing that, let's see how the lap time manager utilizes this capability.

The variable that's used for the return value is reset on line 2. If the lapTimes field is defined, we prepare loop control variables and loop over the stored lap times, lines 3–5. If the lapTimes entry is defined, line 6, we serialize the class and append it to the retSer variable on lines 7–10. If we have more entries to process, we append a special character, '^', in between them. The result is a serialization of the lap times stored in the LapTimeManager class.

In the Deserialize method, we reverse the process and convert a string, a serialized list of lap time strings, into a list of LapTime object instances. The lapTimes class field is reset on line 2 of the method. If the method argument, s, is defined and has data, we prepare the method variables, lines 4–5. If the string split on the special character returns results, we prepare the loop control variables and proceed to loop over the split string. The tmpDes variable is used to hold each string fragment on line 9.

On lines 10–12, if the entry is defined, we use it as the argument to the Deserialize method of a new lapTime instance. The newly configured LapTime instance is added to the lapTimes class field on line 13. The remainder of the method returns a Boolean value indicating the success of the operation. When this method is completed, we'll have restored this class to its state at the time its Serialize method was called.

The ToString method is used to create a string representation of the class for logging purposes. The method return variable, retTs, is reset on line 2, and if the lapTimes field is defined, we loop over the list on lines 3–5. Each entry is processed and appended to the return variable on lines 6–9. The generated string is returned on line 12. Next, we'll take a look at how we prune the recorded lap times.

The CleanTimes method is used to trim the number of lap times stored by the manager class. If there are lap times to process and if there are more than the specified number of entries, we prepare to loop over the excess entries, lines 3–5. For each excess entry found, we remove the value and decrement the loop control variable on lines 6–7. That wraps up our review of the LapTimeManager class. Up next, we'll check out how the class is actually used.

Demonstration: LapTimeManager

To demonstrate the LapTimeManager class, and subsequently the LapTime class, we'll take a look at how some class functionality is used in the actual game. First, we'll see how the manager is used to persist lap time data. If you load up the GameState class and search for the LogLapTime method, take a look at the method's last few lines of code.

Listing 6-20. LapTimeManager Demonstration 1

```
1 lapTimeManager.AddEntry(lt);
2 lapTimeManager.CleanTimes();
3 lapTimeManager.FindBestLapTimeByLastEntry();
4 PlayerPrefs.SetString("LapTimes", lapTimeManager.Serialize());
```

It's a bit underwhelming, but that's because our class is well encapsulated and focused in its design. In the example listed previously, a new lap time entry is appended to the list. The manager then cleans the list to make sure its length is capped. Lastly, the serialized list of lap times is stored in the Unity APIs PlayerPrefs class, line 4. Up next, we'll take a look at how deserialization is used.

Listing 6-21. LapTimeManager Demonstration 2

```
1 string tmpStr = PlayerPrefs.GetString("LapTimes", "");
2 lapTimeManager = new LapTimeManager();
3 if (tmpStr != null && tmpStr != "") {
4    Utilities.wr("Found lap times: " + tmpStr);
5    lapTimeManager.Deserialize(tmpStr);
6 }
```

The reverse of the serialization process is just as simple. We load up the last stored lap times string; if one doesn't exist, an empty string is returned, line 1. Then we initialize the lapTimeManager class field and check to see if there is any data to process, lines 2–3. The data we found is logged, and the lapTimeManager class is restored with a call to the Deserialize method. That wraps up our LapTimeManager class review. The next class up for review is the PopupMsgTracker class.

Class Review: PopupMsgTracker

The PopupMsgTracker class is used to keep track of the pop-up notifications that are displayed on the HUD screen in response to certain track events. Because multiple notifications may fire in rapid succession, we can end up with multiple notification images to display. To help us manage this information, we've introduced the PopupMsgTracker class. Let's take a look. Because this class is so concise, we'll forgo the usual class review process and just list the class next.

Listing 6-22. PopupMsgTracker Class Review 1

```
1 public class PopupMsgTracker {
2    public int index = 0;
3    public Image image = null;
4    public int posIdx = 0;
5    public bool movingUp = false;
6    public int type = 0;
7 }
```

This class is very simple; it's just a set of class fields. Let's review them quickly. The first field is an integer value, index, and it's used to track an image notification's position in a vertical list of notifications. The next class field is an instance of the Unity Image class. This field references the image that is displayed on the screen, the actual notification. The next field, posIdx, is an integer value that represents the notification's position index, or the index of the display slot in a preset list of available display slots.

The next class field is a Boolean flag indicating that this notification is moving up in the list of available display slots, movingUp. Lastly, the type field is an integer value that represents the type of notification this class is tracking: a warning, a modifier, a help message, etc. That's pretty much all there is to this class. Notice that it's not based on the MonoBehaviour class; it's just a plain old C# class. The next class we'll look at is a centralized utility class. But before we get to it, let's look at a demonstration of the PopupMsgTracker class in action.

Demonstration: PopupMsgTracker

To demonstrate the PopupMsgTracker class, we'll take a look at how it's used by the GameHUDNewScript class. This script is responsible for displaying the notifications, among other things, on the in-game HUD. Let's take a look at how the message tracker class is used.

Listing 6-23. PopupMsgTracker Demonstration 1

```
1 public void UndimYourHit() {
2     if (imgYourHit.gameObject.activeSelf == false) {
3         imgYourHit.gameObject.SetActive(true);
4         imgYourHit.gameObject.transform.position =
          posPopupMsg[posPopupMsgIdx];
5         AddPopupMsgTracker(imgYourHit, posPopupMsgIdx, 0);
6         CheckPopupMsgIdx();
7     }
8 }

1 public void AddPopupMsgTracker(Image i, int idx, int tp) {
2     pt = new PopupMsgTracker();
3     pt.index = posPopupMsgVis.Count;
4     pt.posIdx = idx;
```

```
5    pt.image = i;
6    pt.type = tp;
7    posPopupMsgVis.Add(pt);
8    posPopupMsgIdx++;
9 }
```

The first method we'll look at is the `UndimYourHit` method. This method is used by the HUD to show a "you're hit" notification during battle mode races. If the notification image is not visible, line 2, activate it on line 3. The position of the notification image is set based on the available display slots tracked by the `posPopupMsgIdx` field, line 4. Notice the index is used to look up a set display position in an array of display positions.

Next, on line 5, the pop-up notification is tracked with a call to the `AddPopupMsgTracker` method. The last line of code checks to see if the next `posPopupMsgIdx` value is a valid one and, if not, cycles the index value back to zero. This will reset the position of the next notification to be displayed. The next demonstration method listed is the `AddPopupMsgTracker` method. Notice that the index is the notification's position in the list of visible notifications, line 3.

The `posIdx` field is set to the argument, `idx`, which is the value of `posPopupMsgIdx`. This indicates the actual render position of the notification, line 4. The pop-up message is added to the list of visible notifications on line 7 and the `popupMsgIdx` is subsequently incremented line 8. That brings us to the conclusion of the `PopupMsgTracker` class review. Next, we'll focus our attention on the `Utilities` class.

Class Review: Utilities

The `Utilities` class is also not a `MonoBehaviour`. It's just a plain C# class that happens to handle some important responsibilities. The Utilities class is used as a central initialization, logging, and settings class. The class is designed as a static, quick access class. As such, it has only static class members. We'll adapt our review process a bit to take into account the static nature of the class. We'll use the following review steps:

1. Static Class Fields

2. Static Class Methods

3. Demonstration

We'll start by looking at the class' static fields. Let's see what we've got.

Static Class Members: Utilities

There are a fair number of static class fields to review, so we'll look at them in groups.

Listing 6-24. Utilities Static Class Fields 1

```
public static bool LOGGING_ON = true;
public static string SOUND_FX_JUMP = "buzzy_jump_01";
public static string SOUND_FX_BOUNCE = "cute_bounce_01";

public static string SOUND_FX_BOOST = "rocket_lift_off_rnd_06";

public static string SOUND_FX_POWER_UP = "powerup_01";

public static string TAG_TRACK_HELP_SLOW = "TrackHelpSlow";

public static string TAG_TRACK_HELP_TURN = "TrackHelpTurn";

public static string TAG_PLAYERS = "Players";
```

The first set of static fields for us to review is listed previously. The first entry, LOGGING_ON, controls the class' logging functionality. The next field, SOUND_FX_JUMP, is the name of the target jump sound effect to use in the game. The SOUND_FX_BOUNCE is the name of the target bounce AudioSource to use as a bounce sound effect. The next two entries are the names of the target AudioSource to use as a sound effect for the boost and power-up game mechanics, respectively.

The next group of three fields, those that start with TAG_, are used to check the tag assigned to a game object. Tags are used to categorize game objects. They are a low-level way to differentiate between game objects and are often used in collision handling. If you think back to some of the code we've reviewed thus far, we've checked tags quite a bit. The first two tag entries are used to detect help system marked objects. The last entry, TAG_PLAYERS, is a very important field. It's used to determine if a game object is a hover racer or not.

Listing 6-25. Utilities Static Class Fields 2

```
public static string TAG_UNTAGGED = "Untagged";
public static string TAG_HITTABLE = "Hittable";
public static string TAG_HITTABLE_NOY = "HittableNoY";
```

```
public static string TAG_BOOST_MARKER = "BoostMarker";

public static string TAG_SMALL_BOOST_MARKER = "SmallBoostMarker";

public static string TAG_TINY_BOOST_MARKER = "TinyBoostMarker";

public static string TAG_MEDIUM_BOOST_MARKER = "MediumBoostMarker";

public static string TAG_TINY_BOOST_2_MARKER = "TinyBoostMarker2";
```

The first field listed in this set, TAG_UNTAGGED, is used to identify game objects marked as untagged. There are default system tags, untagged is one of them, and then there are user-defined tags. Unity game objects are marked as "untagged" by default. I'll mention the game mechanic these tags are associated with as we review them. The next two entries are tags used for hittable objects. The most obvious example of this tag and game mechanic are the oil drums that fly off when collided with.

The next few entries are all used to define different boost markers. If you recall from our review of the game's interaction classes. Boost markers accelerate the player's vehicle forward at different rates of speed. Using this system, all you need to do to change a boost marker is to change its tag to a different boost marker tag type.

Listing 6-26. Utilities Static Class Fields 3

```
public static string TAG_JUMP_MARKER = "JumpMarker";
public static string TAG_HEALTH_MARKER = "HealthMarker";

public static string TAG_GUN_MARKER = "GunMarker";
public static string TAG_INVINC_MARKER = "InvincibilityMarker";

public static string TAG_ARMOR_MARKER = "ArmorMarker";

public static int MAX_AMMO = 6;
public static int AMMO_INC = 3;
```

The next five fields listed in the preceding set are all battle mode–related tags. Each tag is used to identify a different battle mode marker that, when collided with, modifies the player's state. The next two static fields define the maximum amount of ammo a player can hold followed by the AMMO_INC field that indicates how much ammo is added from a gun/ammo marker. There's one more set of fields to review, listed as follows.

Listing 6-27. Utilities Static Class Fields 3

```
public static string NAME_GAME_STATE_OBJ = "GameState";

public static string NAME_PLAYER_ROOT = "HoverCar";
public static string NAME_START_ROOT = "StartPosition";

public static float MAX_XFORM_POS_Y = 50.0f;
public static float MIN_XFORM_POS_Y = 12.0f;
public static int MARKER_REFRESH_MIN = 60;
public static int MARKER_REFRESH_MAX = 90;
```

The next static class field is an important one. We've seen this field in use before, in a lot of classes, in the BaseScript class' preparation methods. The NAME_GAME_STATE_OBJ field is used to find the game object with the same name. In the Hover Racers game as is, the game state is tracked by, you guessed it, the GameState class. This class has been added to an empty Unity GameObject with the same name.

This is why each and every MonoBehaviour in the game searches for the GameState game object to see if it has a GameState script component associated with it. Examples of this can be seen in the preparation methods of the Utilities class, which is used by the BaseScript class. The next two fields, MAX_XFORM_POS_Y and MIN_XFORM_POS_Y, are used in determining if a player's hover racer is in the air and should be pulled down by gravity. Last but not least are two fields that are used to determine the refresh time for a given battle mode marker.

When a player's hover racer collides with a marker, that marker disappears for a few seconds before becoming visible again. The MARKER_REFRESH_MIN and MARKER_REFRESH_ MAX fields are used to generate a random amount of time to wait before the marker becomes visible again. That concludes the class' static fields. Up next, we'll take a look at the class' static class methods.

Listing 6-28. Utilities Static Class Methods 1

```
1 public static void wr(string s) {
2    if (LOGGING_ON) {
3        Debug.Log(s);
4    }
5 }
```

```
1 public static void wrForce(string s) {
2     Debug.Log(s);
3 }
```

```
1 public static void wr(string s, string sClass, string sMethod, string
  sNote) {
2     if (LOGGING_ON) {
3         Debug.Log(sClass + "." + sMethod + ": " + sNote + ": " + s);
4     }
5 }
```

```
1 public static void wrErr(string s) {
2     if (LOGGING_ON) {
3         Debug.LogError(s);
4     }
5 }
```

```
1 public static void wrErr(string s, string sClass, string sMethod, string
  sNote) {
2     if (LOGGING_ON) {
3         Debug.LogError(sClass + "." + sMethod + ": " + sNote + ": " + s);
4     }
5 }
```

The Utilities class has a number of useful logging methods for us to peruse. The first method listed, wr, is for logging calls that respect the logging control variable. The wrForce method is for logging calls that must display. This method ignores the class' logging control field, LOGGING_ON. The second version listed takes more arguments; it handles writing formatted text to the logs but otherwise functions similarly to its counterpart. The subsequent two methods, wrErr and the more complex version of the wrErr method, are used in the exact same way as their non-error cousins. The main difference here is that the wr methods call Unity's Debug.Log method while wrErr calls the Debug.LogError method. Next up, let's take a look at the class' audio support methods.

Listing 6-29. Utilities Static Class Methods 2

```
01 public static void SafePlaySoundFx(AudioSource audioS, string sClass,
   string sMethod, string sNote, string name) {
02    Utilities.wr("Playing sound " + name, sClass, sMethod, sNote);
03    SafePlaySoundFx(audioS);
04 }

01 public static void SafePlaySoundFx(AudioSource audioS) {
02    if (audioS != null) {
03       if (audioS.isPlaying == false) {
04          audioS.Play();
05       }
06    }
07 }

01 public static AudioSource[] LoadAudioResources(AudioSource[]
   audioSetSrc, string[] audioSetNames) {
02    AudioSource[] audioSetDst = null;
03    int count = 0;
04    if (audioSetSrc != null && audioSetNames != null) {
05       audioSetDst = new AudioSource[audioSetNames.Length];
06       for (int i = 0; i < audioSetSrc.Length; i++) {
07          AudioSource aS = (AudioSource)audioSetSrc[i];
08          for (int j = 0; j < audioSetNames.Length; j++) {
09             if (aS != null && aS.clip.name == audioSetNames[j]) {
10                Utilities.wr("Found audio clip: " + audioSetNames[j]);
11                audioSetDst[j] = aS;
12                count++;
13                break;
14             }
15          }
16
```

```
17          if (count == audioSetNames.Length) {
18             break;
19          }
20       }
21    }
22    return audioSetDst;
23 }
```

The first two entries in the methods listed previously support centralized audio playback. The first method takes a few extra parameters that it uses for logging purposes, line 2, followed by a call to the simple version of the SafePlaySoundFx method on line 3. Directing our attention to the SafePlaySoundFx method that takes a single argument, an AudioSource instance audioS. This method checks that the audio resource is defined and, if so, plays the sound. The last method in this group is the LoadAudioResources method. We've encountered this method a few times in certain class Start methods where audio resources are loaded.

This method takes two arrays as arguments. The first is an array of audio resources to search through. The second is an array of strings that constitute the target audio resources to extract from the first array. The method is fairly straightforward. If the method arguments are defined, then we prepare our loop control variables and return array on lines 2–5. For each audio resource in the audioSetSrc array, we loop over the audioSetNames array to find a match. If one is found, we add it to the results array and increment a counter, lines 11–12. We then break out of the inner loop and move onto the next audio resource. If we've found everything that we're looking for, we exit the outer loop, lines 17–19. The method's findings are returned on line 22, presumably after locating all the required audio resources. The next set of methods for us to review are used to load game and player state data. Let's have a look.

Listing 6-30. Utilities Static Class Methods 3

```
01 public static object[] LoadStartingSet(string className, out GameState
   gameState) {
02    GameObject gameStateObj = GameObject.Find(Utilities.NAME_GAME_STATE_OBJ);
03    if (gameStateObj != null) {
04       gameState = gameStateObj.GetComponent<GameState>();
05       if (gameState != null) {
```

```
06          gameState.PrepGame();
07          return new object[] { gameStateObj, gameState, true };
08      } else {
09          Utilities.wrForce(className + ": gameState is null!
            Deactivating...");
10          return new object[] { gameStateObj, gameState, false };
11      }
12  } else {
13      Utilities.wrForce(className + ": gameStateObj is null!
        Deactivating...");
14      gameState = null;
15      return new object[] { gameStateObj, gameState, false };
16  }
17 }
```

```
01 public static object[] LoadStartingSetAndLocalPlayerInfo(stri
   ng className, out GameState gameState, out PlayerInfo pi, out int
   playerIndex, out PlayerState p, GameObject g, bool inParent) {
02    GameObject gameStateObj = GameObject.Find(Utilities.NAME_GAME_STATE_OBJ);
03    if (gameStateObj != null) {
04        gameState = gameStateObj.GetComponent<GameState>();
05        if (gameState != null) {
06            gameState.PrepGame();
07        } else {
08            Utilities.wrForce(className + ": gameState is null!
              Deactivating...");
09            pi = null;
10            playerIndex = -1;
11            p = null;
12            return new object[] { gameStateObj, gameState, false, pi,
              playerIndex, p };
13        }
14    } else {
```

```
15        Utilities.wrForce(className + ": gameStateObj is null!
          Deactivating...");
16        gameState = null;
17        pi = null;
18        playerIndex = -1;
19        p = null;
20        return new object[] { gameStateObj, gameState, false, pi,
          playerIndex, p };
21    }
22
23    if (g != null) {
24        if (inParent) {
25            pi = g.GetComponentInParent<PlayerInfo>();
26        } else {
27            pi = g.GetComponent<PlayerInfo>();
28        }
29        if (pi != null) {
30            playerIndex = pi.playerIndex;
31            p = gameState.GetPlayer(playerIndex);
32            if (p != null) {
33                return new object[] { gameStateObj, gameState, true, pi,
                  playerIndex, p };
34            } else {
35              Utilities.wrForce(className + ": p is null!
                  Deactivating...");
36              p = null;
37              return new object[] { gameStateObj, gameState, false, pi,
                  playerIndex, p };
38            }
39        } else {
40            Utilities.wrForce(className + ": pi is null! Deactivating...");
41            pi = null;
42            playerIndex = -1;
43            p = null;
```

```
44        return new object[] { gameStateObj, gameState, false, pi,
          playerIndex, p };
45      }
46    } else {
47      Utilities.wrForce(className + ": g is null! Deactivating...");
48      pi = null;
49      playerIndex = -1;
50      p = null;
51      return new object[] { gameStateObj, gameState, false, pi,
          playerIndex, p };
52    }
53 }
```

```
01 public static object[] LoadPlayerInfo(string className, out PlayerInfo
   pi, out int playerIndex, out PlayerState p, GameObject g, GameState
   gameState, bool inParent, bool verbose = false) {
02    if (g != null && gameState != null) {
03      if (inParent) {
04        pi = g.GetComponentInParent<PlayerInfo>();
05      } else {
06        pi = g.GetComponent<PlayerInfo>();
07      }
08      if (pi != null) {
09        playerIndex = pi.playerIndex;
10
11        p = gameState.GetPlayer(playerIndex);
12        if (p != null) {
13          return new object[] { pi, playerIndex, true, p };
14        } else {
15          if (verbose) {
16            Utilities.wrForce(className + ": p is null!
              Deactivating...");
17          }
18          p = null;
19          return new object[] { pi, playerIndex, false, p };
20        }
```

```
21          } else {
22              if (verbose) {
23                  Utilities.wrForce(className + ": pi is null!
                    Deactivating...");
24              }
25              pi = null;
26              playerIndex = -1;
27              p = null;
28              return new object[] { pi, playerIndex, false, p };
29          }
30      } else {
31          if (verbose) {
32              Utilities.wrForce(className + ": g is null! Deactivating...");
33          }
34          pi = null;
35          playerIndex = -1;
36          p = null;
37          return new object[] { pi, playerIndex, false, p };
38      }
39 }
```

The three methods listed previously are very important utility methods used in various places throughout the game's code base. The first entry, LoadStartingSet, is used by the BaseScript class' Prep method. This means that it's used in a lot of classes that extend the BaseScript class. The main purpose of this method is to locate the GameState game object and find the associated GameState script component. The method returns an array of results with the last entry in the array being a Boolean value that indicates the success of the operation.

The next method listed, LoadStartingSetAndLocalPlayerInfo, is similar to the one we just reviewed except that it goes one step further, and after loading the game state, it will look for a local PlayerInfo component. This component is used to indicate which player a certain game object belongs to. The method then tries to load the player state data associated with that player. The code on lines 24–38 locates the associated PlayerState object if the GameState has been properly loaded. Take a look at these two methods and make sure you understand them well. Most of the code in either method is there to safely exit if an issue has been encountered.

The last method listed in this group is the LoadPlayerInfo method. This method is used to load player state data associated with a game object. Notice that the code is very similar to the second half of the previously reviewed method. Essentially, this process uses the player's index from a PlayerInfo object instance to locate the player's PlayerState instance that is stored in the GameState class. Any issues encountered in looking up the Unity components result in a response that indicates an error. Take a look at the arguments used in these methods. Pay special attention to the use of out arguments to update certain object references without relying on the method's return object. Next up, let's take a look at the class in action.

Demonstration: Utilities

Because the Utilities class is a plain C# class, we won't use a demonstration scene. Instead, we'll review some pertinent code that uses some of the methods we've just reviewed. For this particular demo, we'll take a look at a snippet of code that shows the Utilities class in action. The following code is from the BaseScript's Start method.

Listing 6-31. Utilities Demonstration 1

```
1 public bool Prep(string sName) {
2     scriptName = sName;
3     scriptActive = (bool)Utilities.LoadStartingSet(scriptName, out
      gameState)[2];
4     MarkScriptActive(scriptName, scriptActive);
5     return scriptActive;
6 }
```

```
1 public bool PrepPlayerInfo(string sName) {
2     scriptName = sName;
3     scriptActive = (bool)Utilities.LoadStartingSetAndLocalPlayerInfo(scri
      ptName, out gameState, out PlayerInfo pi, out int playerIndex, out p,
      gameObject, true)[2];
4     MarkScriptActive(scriptName, scriptActive);
5     return scriptActive;
6 }
```

The first method listed is the Prep method. This method is called by most of the classes that extend the BaseScript class. Take special notice of the method call on line 3. Three things are going on here. The scriptActive field is updated with the value in index 2 of the array returned by a call to the LoadStartingSet method. Also, note that the gameState method argument is adorned with the out keyword. This means that the local object can be updated by the method call. In this way, we can update a number of important class fields and reference the Boolean result, returned array index 2, of the operation. Not too shabby.

The second method listed previously, PrepPlayerInfo, is very similar to the method we just reviewed. It uses the LoadStartingSetAndLocalPlayerInfo class preparation method. Note that the gameState, playerInfo, playerIndex, and playerState arguments are all out method arguments, meaning they can all be updated by the method call. This lets us get a lot of configuration steps done in a minimal amount of space. I think it's powerful and it works but look at how less clear the code is. Something longer but descriptive would be more to my liking. Make sure you understand this class before moving on. It is very important and used throughout the code base. Next, we'll take a look at the code behind the blimp camera.

Class Review: CameraFollowXz

The CameraFollowXz class is a MonoBehaviour designed to follow the movements of the current player's car as it traverses the track. The class is fairly concise, but there is enough complexity that we should use the standard class review steps listed in the following group:

1. Static/Constants/Read-Only Class Members

2. Class Fields

3. Pertinent Method Outline/Class Headers

4. Support Method Details

5. Main Method Details

6. Demonstration

This class doesn't have any enumerations or support methods to speak of, so we'll omit those sections. Let's start the review process by taking a look at the class' static members.

Static/Constants/Read-Only Class Members: CameraFollowXz

The CameraFollowXz class has a few static fields for us to discuss. Let's get to it.

Listing 6-32. CameraFollowXz Static/Constants/Read-Only Class Members 1

```
public static readonly float BLIMP_FLY_HEIGHT = 110f;
public static readonly float BLIMP_FLY_MIN = 30f;
```

The first static field, listed previously, is the BLIMP_FLY_HEIGHT static field. This field represents the height the blimp camera has as it follows the hover racer. The height is modified by the speed of the hover racer. This means that the camera is lower at slower speeds and higher at faster speeds. The next field is the BLIMP_FLY_MIN field. This field sets a minimum height that the camera will use to follow the player. That wraps up the class' static fields. Next, let's review the class' remaining fields.

Class Fields: CameraFollowXz

This class has three fields for us to review, listed as follows.

Listing 6-33. CameraFollowXz Class Fields 1

```
private float x = 0.0f;
private float y = 0.0f;
private float z = 0.0f;
```

The set of class fields matches the component values of a Vector3 object. These fields are used to calculate the blimp camera's position based on the current player's position and speed.

Pertinent Method Outline/Class Headers: CameraFollowXz

The CameraFollowXz class has the following method outline.

Listing 6-34. CameraFollowXz Pertinent Method Outline/Class Headers 1

```
//Main
void Start();
void Update();
```

Subsequently, I'll list the class' import statements and declaration.

Listing 6-35. CameraFollowXz Pertinent Method Outline/Class Headers 2

```
using UnityEngine;

public class CameraFollowXz : BaseScript {}
```

In the next review section, we'll take a look at the class' main methods.

Main Method Details: CameraFollowXz

The two main methods listed in the following group are the class' Start and Update methods. Let's have a look.

Listing 6-36. CameraFollowXz Main Method Details 1

```
01 void Start() {
02     base.Prep(this.GetType().Name);
03     if (BaseScript.IsActive(scriptName) == false) {
04         Utilities.wrForce(scriptName + ": Is Deactivating...");
05         return;
06     }
07 }

01 void Update() {
02     if (BaseScript.IsActive(scriptName) == false) {
03         return;
04     }
05
```

```
06    if (gameState != null) {
07        p = gameState.GetCurrentPlayer();
08        if (p != null) {
09            if (p.player != null && p.player.transform != null) {
10                x = p.player.transform.position.x;
11                y = (p.player.transform.position.y + ((BLIMP_FLY_HEIGHT *
                      p.speedPrct) + BLIMP_FLY_MIN));
12                z = p.player.transform.position.z;
13                transform.position = new Vector3(x, y, z);
14            }
15        }
16    }
17 }
```

The Start method is called as part of the MonoBehaviour's life cycle. It's called in the component's initialization phase. Line 2 of the method calls the base class' Prep method. This method is used to configure the class and register the result. A check to see if the class configuration was successful is made on line 3. This is the standard initialization for classes that extend the BaseScript class and don't need player state data.

The second method listed is the class' Update method. This method is called each game frame by the Unity game engine if the component is active. On lines 2–4, we have the standard safety check. If the class has not been configured correctly, then the method exits without doing any work. If the gameState field is not null, then we store a reference to the current player state on line 7. If the current player state is defined, line 8, and the player's game object and transform are defined, then we set the x, y, and z class fields based on the current player's position lines 10-13.

Notice that the vertical axis, y, is based on the current player's y coordinate plus a value determined by the hover racer's current speedPrct. This causes the blimp camera to follow the current player's hover racer at a greater height when the car is moving faster. The camera won't go below the minimum height, however. On line 13, the blimp camera's position is updated. This line will actually set the position of the game object that the CameraFollowXz script is attached to. We only attach it to a Camera object, but it would also work with other game objects. In the next section, we'll take a look at a demonstration of the CameraFollowXz class.

Demonstration: CameraFollowXz

The demonstration of the CameraFollowXz class is a scene named
"DemoCameraFollowXz". The scene is located in the "Project" panel, in the "Scenes"
folder. Before you run the scene, let me explain how it works. This demo is actually very
similar to the "DemoCollideScript" scene we checked out earlier. The main difference
here is that this scene has a full set of menu screens and an in-game HUD.

As such, the scene will start with a menu screen visible. In order to start the scene,
you'll need to click the "Track1" or "Track2" buttons. You can also click the restart
button in the lower left-hand corner of the game screen. You'll notice that when this
demo scene starts, we can see a full in-game HUD including a blimp camera. The blimp
camera will follow the current player around the board at a height dependent on the
hover racer's speed. Take the car for a spin and check out how the blimp camera works.
We'll wrap up this chapter with a look at the WaypointCompare class.

Class Review: WaypointCompare

The WaypointCompare class is used to order the array of waypoint markers loaded from
the current track. The class is fairly short and direct, so we'll list the class directly, as
follows, and review it. Let's take a look at some code!

Listing 6-37. CameraFollowXz Class Review 1

```
01 public class WaypointCompare : IComparer {
02     private WaypointCheck obj1 = null;
03     private WaypointCheck obj2 = null;
04
05     public int Compare(object o1, object o2) {
06         obj1 = (WaypointCheck)o1;
07         obj2 = (WaypointCheck)o2;
08         if (obj1.waypointIndex > obj2.waypointIndex) {
09             return 1;
10         } else if (obj1.waypointIndex < obj2.waypointIndex) {
11             return -1;
```

```
12        } else {
13            return 0;
14        }
15    }
16 }
```

Notice that the WaypointCompare class doesn't extend Unity's MonoBehaviour or our BaseScript class. Instead, because it is used for class comparisons, the WaypointCompare class extends the IComparer interface. On lines 2–3, the class fields obj1 and obj2 are listed. They are used to hold the comparison objects cast to the proper class type. On line 5, the Compare method is defined. It takes two generic objects as arguments for comparison, and it's called automatically by the array sorting method.

Notice that on lines 6–7, the method arguments are cast to WaypointCheck object instances. Note that private class fields are used as local variables to circumvent the garbage collector. Lines 8–14 determine the relationship between the two WaypointCheck objects. Comparison is done against the WaypointCheck's waypointIndex. Based on the relationship between them, a 1, -1, or 0 is returned by the method indicating order. Let's take a look at a demonstration of this class.

Demonstration: WaypointCompare

Because the WaypointCompare class isn't an extension of the MonoBehaviour class, we won't demonstrate it using a scene. Instead, we'll take a look at the class in action. The following code snippet is from the GameState class' FindWaypoints method.

Listing 6-38. CameraFollowXz Demonstration 1

```
1 public WaypointCompare wpc = new WaypointCompare();
...
2 object[] ar = row.ToArray();
3 System.Array.Sort(ar, wpc);
```

This example is very simple. Line 1 shows the declaration of the wpc class field used in line 3. It takes an array of objects that are WaypointCheck instances loaded from the track's game objects, line 2. Next, the array sort method is called, line 3, with the array of waypoints and an instance of the WaypointCompare class as arguments.

Chapter Conclusion

In this chapter, we took a moment to review the "other" classes in the Hover Racers game. This introduced us to a number of interesting topics. I'll list some potential items as follows. Take a moment to ponder them.

1. Cleanup Scripts: Ensures that game objects are managed if they fall off of the board or track. Also, they can be used in water hazards and other track features to reset the player.

2. Programmatically Adjust Sound: Engine sound control is used to add realism to the game and is a useful effect to add to your toolbox.

3. C# Support Classes: Use of plain C# classes to add functionality to the game in the form of quick, easy-to-use utilities.

4. Centralized Control Code: The `Utilities` class acts as a centralization point for game settings and important, core, configuration functionality.

5. Camera Tricks: We created a blimp camera effect with a simple `MonoBehaviour` attached to a Unity `Camera` object.

There are a number of useful applications of the Unity engine in this chapter. Take it to the next level and create some of your own. In the next chapter, we'll take a look at the input classes. You should be aware of the notion that different components, mainly, script components (`MonoBehaviours`), can alter game objects - each frame - via their `Update` method. Be aware that changes to a `GameObject` or script component can be made from many different places in the code. I find that centralized design models, think of the `Utilities` class, work better for me, but, perhaps, a larger team would benefit more from a distributed model. You'll have to find what works best for your situation.

CHAPTER 7

Input Classes

In this chapter, we'll review, in detail, the input classes used to power the game controls. I should mention that Hover Racers is set up to support keyboard, mouse, controller, and touch input. The classes we'll look at in this chapter are as follows:

1. Character Motor

2. FPS Input Controller

3. MouseLookNew

4. GameState (Touch Input Snippet Only)

The `CharacterMotor` class is perhaps the most complicated of the classes listed. It contains the following subclasses:

1. CharacterMotorMovement

2. CharacterMotorSliding

3. CharacterMotorJumping

These classes are used to manage different components of the hover racer's movement. The remaining classes, `FPSInputController` and `MouseLookNew`, are less complex and do not define any subclasses. Let's start the review with the `CharacterMotor`'s subclasses. The classes we're looking at in this chapter can be found in either of the two locations listed here:

1. \Standard Assets\Character Controllers\Sources\Scripts\

2. \Standard Assets\mmg_scripts\

If you run into trouble finding a particular class, just search for it in the Unity editor using the "Project" panel's search bar or look for it in Visual Studio in the "Solution Explorer" panel.

© Victor G Brusca 2022
V. G Brusca, *Advanced Unity Game Development*, https://doi.org/10.1007/978-1-4842-7851-2_7

Class Review: CharacterMotorMovement

The CharacterMotorMovement class is used to control the character motor for the purpose of moving an object. The class is concise, so we'll forego the more verbose class review process and just list the class here.

Listing 7-1. CharacterMotorMovement Class Review 1

```
01 [System.Serializable]
02 public class CharacterMotorMovement {
03     public float maxForwardSpeed = 3.0f;
04     public float maxSidewaysSpeed = 10.0f;
05     public float maxBackwardsSpeed = 10.0f;
06     public AnimationCurve slopeSpeedMultiplier = new AnimationCurve(new
       Keyframe(-90, 1), new Keyframe(0, 1), new Keyframe(90, 0.70f));
07
08     public float maxGroundAcceleration = 30.0f;
09     public float maxAirAcceleration = 20.0f;
10     public float gravity = 10.0f;
11     public float maxFallSpeed = 22.0f;
12
13     [System.NonSerialized]
14     public CollisionFlags collisionFlags;
15
16     [System.NonSerialized]
17     public Vector3 velocity;
18
19     [System.NonSerialized]
20     public Vector3 frameVelocity = Vector3.zero;
21
22     [System.NonSerialized]
23     public Vector3 hitPoint = Vector3.zero;
24
25     [System.NonSerialized]
26     public Vector3 lastHitPoint = new Vector3(Mathf.Infinity, 0, 0);
27 }
```

Before I delve into the code review, I'd like to take a moment to mention some of the code attributes used in the previously listed class. The `System.Serializable` attribute is used to explicitly tell Unity that the values of certain class fields should be serialized and used to drive the "Inspector" panel values. The flip side of that coin is the `System.NonSerialized` attribute. This attribute is used to escape a field, which would otherwise normally be serialized, from the serialization and display process. In short, fields with the nonserialized attribute are not displayed by the "Inspector" panel even if they normally would.

Onto the class review. The `CharactorMotor` class consists of a series of public class fields. The first three fields are used to set a maximum speed for the forward, backward, and sideways speeds that affect the hover racers' movement. Keep in mind these values are refined in other parts of the code as part of the game initialization process. The `slopeSpeedMultiplier` field is an instance of Unity's `AnimationCurve` class. It's used to modify the hover racer's speed when it encounters a slope or incline in the ground's surface.

The `maxGroundAcceleration` class field is used to control the car's horizontal accelerations. The next field, `maxAirAcceleration`, acts in the same way except it's applied when the hover racer is off the ground. The `gravity` field is used to apply a downward force to bring the hover racer back down to the ground. The `maxFallSpeed` field controls how fast the car can fall back down to the ground as gravity takes effect. Next, the `collisionFlag` field is used to report information about the hover racer's collisions.

The `velocity` vector keeps track of the hover racer's current velocity. The `frameVelocity` field is similar but is used internally, presumably to track velocity per game frame. The last two fields listed, `hitPoint` and `lastHitPoint`, are used to track collision points during movement for internal velocity control in the `CharacterMotor` class. We'll take a look at the `CharacterMotorJumping` class next.

Class Review: CharacterMotorJumping

The `CharacterMotorJumping` is used to help manage character movement during jumps. Let me list the class here for us to review.

Listing 7-2. CharacterMotorJumping Class Review 1

```
01 [System.Serializable]
02 public class CharacterMotorJumping {
03     public bool enabled = true;
04     public float baseHeight = 1.0f;
05     public float extraHeight = 4.1f;
06     public float perpAmount = 0.0f;
07
08     public float steepPerpAmount = 0.5f;
09
10     [System.NonSerialized]
11     public bool jumping = false;
12
13     [System.NonSerialized]
14     public bool holdingJumpButton = false;
15
16     [System.NonSerialized]
17     public float lastStartTime = 0.0f;
18
19     [System.NonSerialized]
20     public float lastButtonDownTime = -100.0f;
21
22     [System.NonSerialized]
23     public Vector3 jumpDir = Vector3.up;
24 }
```

It's important to note that the class we're reviewing is not actively used by the game. I want to cover it just the same so you can add different kinds of jump in your next game. The first field, enabled, indicates the jump capability is active. The following two class fields, baseHeight and extraHeight, set the jump base height and an extra jump height value. Subsequently, the perpAmount and steepPerpAmount are used in calculations to determine how the character jumps on inclines and steep surfaces. The jumping flag is used to indicate if the character is marked as jumping.

Other classes in the game track the player state and record if the hover racer is jumping or not. In our case, a collision with a jump marker dictates if the hover racer is jumping. Because the racers don't jump on a button press, that would be interesting though, the game doesn't use the default jump modifier code. As such, this class may not accurately describe the character's jump state. The next field, holdingJumpButton, is a Boolean value indicating that the jump button is being held down. Last but not least, the jumpDir field indicates the direction of the jump. The next class we'll look at models the hover racer's sliding or side-to-side motion.

Class Review: CharacterMotorSliding

The CharacterMotorSliding class is similar to the subclasses we've just reviewed. Let's take a look.

Listing 7-3. CharacterMotorSliding Class Review 1

```
1 [System.Serializable]
2 public class CharacterMotorSliding {
3     public bool enabled = true;
4     public float slidingSpeed = 15.0f;
5     public float sidewaysControl = 1.0f;
6     public float speedControl = 0.4f;
7 }
```

This class, as I mentioned earlier, is used to control a hover racer's side-to-side motion. The first field indicates if sliding is enabled. The second entry, slidingSpeed, indicates the velocity of the sliding movement while the sidewaysControl field is used to track how much control the player has over lateral movement. Lastly, the speedControl field is used to control how much the player can influence the hover racer's sliding speed. That wraps up the subclass review. Next, we'll take a close look at the CharacterMotor class.

Class Review: CharacterMotor

The CharacterMotor class is responsible for the basic movement of the hover racers. Jumping and gravity, as managed by this class, are actually disabled by the game. Sliding and horizontal movements are enabled. There is a code attribute listed at the top of this class:

```
[RequireComponent(typeof(CharacterController))]
```

This code attribute indicates that this MonoBehaviour component requires the presence of a CharacterController component attached to the same GameObject. This is handled through the Unity editor. If the character motor seems to have knowledge of the hover racer's collision state that's because it gets that information from the CharacterController class, which we'll cover in just a bit. I should also mention that the FPSInputController script drives the CharacterContoller. In this way, input vectors are updated by the FPSInputController.

The input and movement setup in the game is kind of complicated, so we'll outline it here.

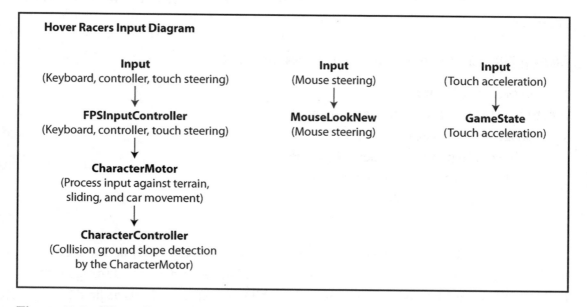

Figure 7-1. *Hover Racers Input Diagram*

Not too bad. If we wrote our own controllers from scratch, this would probably look a bit different. But in this case, we're using some legacy controller classes from Unity, so this is what we've got. With that being said, let's outline our class review.

1. Class Fields

2. Pertinent Method Outline/Class Headers

3. Support Method Details

4. Main Method Details

5. Demonstration

There are no static class members or enumerations to speak of, so we'll skip those sections of the review process. We have some work to do; let's get to it.

Class Fields: CharacterMotor

The first of the `CharacterMotor` class' fields is as follows.

Listing 7-4. CharacterMotor Class Fields 1

```
public bool aiOn = false;
bool canControl = true;
bool useFixedUpdate = true;
```

The `aiOn` field is a Boolean flag that indicates if AI control is active for the current hover racer. The `canControl` field is another Boolean flag used to indicate if the player can control the hover racer. The last entry in the set is the `useFixedUpdate` Boolean. If this field is set to true, the class will use fixed update calls. Fixed update calls are just that, fixed rate update calls. This differs from the standard `Update` methods we've seen thus far. The standard `Update` method is called once per game frame. This can, however, be variable in its rate due to fluctuations in the game frame rate. For important physics calculations, we use the `FixedUpdate` callback method because it is more stable and reliable.

Listing 7-5. CharacterMotor Class Fields 2

```
public Vector3 inputMoveDirection = Vector3.zero;
public bool inputJump = false;
public CharacterMotorMovement movement = new CharacterMotorMovement();

public CharacterMotorJumping jumping = new CharacterMotorJumping();

public CharacterMotorSliding sliding = new CharacterMotorSliding();

public bool grounded = true;
```

The `inputMoveDirection` vector represents the direction of movement as set by the `FPSInputController`. The `inputJump` field is a Boolean flag that is used to indicate the jump button has been pressed. Normally this input would come from the `FPSInputController`, but we've altered the default functionality of that script to use an input mapping more suitable for a racing game, disabling button press–based jumping. Following the inputJump field are the three fields used to model the character's movement. We've just reviewed them, so I'll assume you have a solid idea of what they're about. Lastly, we have the grounded field that is used to indicate the character is grounded.

Listing 7-6. CharacterMotor Class Fields 3

```
public Vector3 groundNormal = Vector3.zero;
private Vector3 lastGroundNormal = Vector3.zero;
private Transform tr;
private CharacterController controller;
```

The last set of class fields for us to review starts off with the groundNormal vector. This field is a Vector3 instance that intersects the plane of the ground perpendicularly and is used to determine things like ground slope. Following that field is the lastGroundNormal field that tracks the previous ground normal vector. The Transform, tr, is used to hold a reference to a Unity Transform object during calculations. Transform objects are used to position and scale Unity GameObjects.

The CharacterController field, controller, is a reference to the required CharacterController component. It's ultimately the controller that is moved by this class, and it's the source of collision data indicating the character is grounded or encountering a slope or steep incline. The last two fields are part of the standard class initialization steps we've encountered time and time again. Next up, we'll check out the class' pertinent methods.

Pertinent Method Outline/Class Headers: CharacterMotor

The CharacterMotor class has a number of methods for us to look at, listed as follows.

Listing 7-7. CharacterMotor Pertinent Method Outline/Class Headers 1

```
//Main Methods
void Awake();
private void UpdateFunction();
void FixedUpdate();
void Update();
void OnControllerColliderHit(ControllerColliderHit hit);
```

```
//Support Methods
private Vector3 ApplyInputVelocityChange(Vector3 velocity);

private Vector3 ApplyGravityAndJumping(Vector3 velocity);

private Vector3 GetDesiredHorizontalVelocity();
private Vector3 AdjustGroundVelocityToNormal(Vector3 hVelocity, Vector3
groundNormal);

private bool IsGroundedTest();
float GetMaxAcceleration(bool grounded);
float CalculateJumpVerticalSpeed(float targetJumpHeight);

bool TooSteep();
float MaxSpeedInDirection(Vector3 desiredMovementDirection);
```

The class' import statements and headers are as follows.

Listing 7-8. CharacterMotor Pertinent Method Outline/Class Headers 2

```
using UnityEngine;

//Require a character controller to be attached to the same game object
[RequireComponent(typeof(CharacterController))]
[AddComponentMenu("Character/Character Motor")]

public class CharacterMotor : BaseScript {}
```

Notice the RequireComponent entry we discussed earlier. Below that entry is a Unity-specific code attribute that is used to customize the "Inspector" panel when viewing the GameObject that the CharacterMotor component is attached to. In this case, it simply adds a menu header with the name listed. In the next section, we'll take a look at the class' support methods. Also take note of the fact that this class extends the BaseScript class and as such is a MonoBehaviour instance with all the default functionality provided by the BaseScript class.

Support Method Details: CharacterMotor

The CharacterMotor class' support methods are rather complex. There are a number of vector operations that would take a lot of explanation both with regard to the code and the mathematics involved. I'm not prepared to cover the material to that depth

163

in this text. We'll review the methods from a higher level and try to focus on what the methods actually do, and not so much how the math works. I invite you to break down any complex calculations and make a determination about the mathematics involved on your own.

Our first method up for review is the `ArrayInputVelocityChange` method. This method takes a `Vector3` velocity argument that should represent the input-driven velocity vector. This method takes into consideration the ground slope, sliding direction, and speed. It enforces the maximum velocity change and checks to see if the character is jumping. Now, direct your attention to the `ApplyGravityAndJumping` method and take a quick look at the code. The `ApplyGravityAndJumping` method is responsible for handling the vertical axis adjustments regarding jumping, ground slope, max fall speed, and gravity. Keep in mind this method is not in use by the game and is designed to work with button press–based jumping. The Hover Racers game, as is, uses collision-based jump markers as opposed to button press jump controls.

The `GetDesiredHorizontalVelocity` method is responsible for taking the `inputMoveDirection` and determining the character's maximum speed for the given direction. This method will modify the car's max speed on slopes based on the slope speed multiplier curve, a `CharacterMotorMovement` class field we reviewed previously. The following method, `AdjustGroundVelocityToNormal`, is used to adjust the ground velocity vector using a series of cross-product vector operations. This establishes a clean, properly directed vector for ground movement based on input.

Following this entry is the `IsGroundedTest` method. This method returns a Boolean value indicating if the character is touching the ground. Subsequently, the `GetMaxAcceleration` method returns the movement class' maximum ground or air acceleration depending on the state of the car. The `CalculateJumpVerticalSpeed` method is calculated from the `targetJumpHeight` and the current gravity. The `TooSteep` method uses the `groundNormal` vector and the controller field's `slopeLimit` to determine if the ground slope is too steep for the racer.

`MaxSpeedInDirection` is a method used to determine the maximum speed the character can travel in the given direction taking into account sideways and backwards speeds. Again, we covered the support methods in less detail than we normally would to avoid lengthy discussions about mathematics. Focus on the described usage of the listed support methods as you review their code. That brings us to the conclusion of the `CharacterMotor` class' support methods. In the next review section, we'll take a look at the class' main methods.

Main Method Details: CharacterMotor

The first main method for us to review is the Awake method. The Awake method is a Unity component life cycle callback method similar to the Start method. The difference between the Awake and Start methods is that the Start method is called only when a script is enabled and after all objects are initialized so you can connect to them while the Awake is called when the script instance is being loaded. These two functions are called before the first Update method, and there is no performance difference between them.

Listing 7-9. CharacterMotor Main Method Details 1

```
01 void Awake() {
02    controller = GetComponent<CharacterController>();
03    tr = transform;
04    base.PrepPlayerInfo(this.GetType().Name);
05    if (BaseScript.IsActive(scriptName) == false) {
06        Utilities.wrForce(scriptName + ": Is Deactivating...");
07        return;
08    } else {
09        aiOn = p.aiOn;
10    }
11 }
```

The first two lines of code set the controller and tr class fields based on the attached, and required, CharacterController component and the transform of the current game object. The code on line 4 prepares the class by loading GameState and PlayerState data. The snippet of code on lines 5–10 is responsible for checking if the class' initialization was successful. If not, the class prints some logs and returns, lines 6 and 7. If the initialization was successful, then the aiOn field is updated to match the current player's state on line 9. The next main method up for review is the UpdateFunction method.

This method handles the class' updates and is called by either the FixedUpdate or Update method depending on the value of the useFixedUpdate field. In this way, we've abstracted the actual update code one level so that it could be accessed by two different callback methods. This cuts down on redundancy. Let's jump into some code.

Listing 7-10. CharacterMotor Main Method Details 2

```
01 private void UpdateFunction() {
02    if (BaseScript.IsActive(scriptName) == false) {
03       return;
04    }
05
06    // We copy the actual velocity into a temporary variable that we can
       manipulate.
07    Vector3 velocity = movement.velocity;
08
09    // Update velocity based on input
10    velocity = ApplyInputVelocityChange(velocity);
11
12    // Apply gravity and jumping force
13    velocity = ApplyGravityAndJumping(velocity);
14
15    // Save lastPosition for velocity calculation.
16    Vector3 lastPosition = tr.position;
17
18    // We always want the movement to be framerate
       independent.  Multiplying by Time.deltaTime does this.
19    Vector3 currentMovementOffset = velocity * Time.deltaTime;
20
21    // Find out how much we need to push towards the ground to avoid
       losing grounding
22    // when walking down a step or over a sharp change in slope.
23    float pushDownOffset = Mathf.Max(controller.stepOffset, new Vector3
       (currentMovementOffset.x, 0, currentMovementOffset.z).magnitude);
24    if (grounded) {
25       currentMovementOffset -= pushDownOffset * Vector3.up;
26    }
27
28    // Reset variables that will be set by collision function
29    //movingPlatform.hitPlatform = null;
30    groundNormal = Vector3.zero;
```

```
31
32    // Move our character!
33    movement.collisionFlags = controller.Move(currentMovementOffset);
34
35    movement.lastHitPoint = movement.hitPoint;
36    lastGroundNormal = groundNormal;
37
38    // Calculate the velocity based on the current and previous position.
39    // This means our velocity will only be the amount the character
      actually moved as a result of collisions.
40    Vector3 oldHVelocity = new Vector3(velocity.x, 0, velocity.z);
41    movement.velocity = (tr.position - lastPosition) / Time.deltaTime;
42    Vector3 newHVelocity = new Vector3(movement.velocity.x, 0, movement.
      velocity.z);
43
44    // The CharacterController can be moved in unwanted directions when
      colliding with things.
45    // We want to prevent this from influencing the recorded velocity.
46    if (oldHVelocity == Vector3.zero) {
47       movement.velocity = new Vector3(0, movement.velocity.y, 0);
48    } else {
49       float projectedNewVelocity = Vector3.Dot(newHVelocity,
         oldHVelocity) / oldHVelocity.sqrMagnitude;
50       movement.velocity = oldHVelocity * Mathf.
         Clamp01(projectedNewVelocity) + movement.velocity.y * Vector3.up;
51    }
52
53    if (movement.velocity.y < velocity.y - 0.001) {
54       if (movement.velocity.y < 0) {
55          // Something is forcing the CharacterController down faster
            than it should.
56          // Ignore this
57          movement.velocity.y = velocity.y;
58       } else {
```

```
59          // The upwards movement of the CharacterController has been
            blocked.
60          // This is treated like a ceiling collision - stop further
            jumping here.
61          jumping.holdingJumpButton = false;
62      }
63   }
64
65   // We were grounded but just lost grounding
66   if (grounded && !IsGroundedTest()) {
67      grounded = false;
68
69      // We pushed the character down to ensure it would stay on the
        ground if there was any.
70      // But there wasn't so now we cancel the downwards offset to make
        the fall smoother.
71      tr.position += pushDownOffset * Vector3.up;
72   }
73   // We were not grounded but just landed on something
74   else if (!grounded && IsGroundedTest()) {
75      grounded = true;
76   }
77 }
```

The method is escaped without doing any work if the class is marked as inactive, lines 2–4. On line 2, we copy the movement field's velocity, CharacterMotorMovement instance, to a local variable, velocity. The movement vector can be adjusted by any number of MonoBehaviours. As such, it's copied to a local variable at the start of the method. In this case, it's safe to think of the velocity vector as being determined by player input. On line 10, we pass the velocity vector through the ApplyInputVelocityChange method. This method adjusts the component values of the vector to account for direction, sliding, jumping, and ground slope.

Subsequently, the velocity vector is further adjusted by the ApplyGravityAndJumping method. Although the game doesn't use this method, if enabled, it will apply jumping, gravity, and steep slope detection to the velocity vector. Remember we're altering this vector starting from the player's desired input and then applying adjustments based on terrain, sliding, jumping, and gravity. Ultimately this vector will be applied to the hover racer to adjust its position as the game runs.

Recall that we're not using this class' jumping capabilities opting instead to use a collision detection–based jump. Next, the lastPosition variable is set on line 16. On line 19, the velocity is converted to a frame rate independent value by multiplying it against the value of Time.deltaTime. When you multiply the velocity vector by the value of Time.deltaTime, you're effectively changing the value of the vector's components to a rate, per second. Downward sloping terrain is handled on lines 23–26 by pushing the hover racer down toward the ground.

On line 30, we reset the groundNormal class field to a zero vector in preparation for processing new collision information. The hover racer is moved on line 33 by applying the frame-independent movement vector. The collision results are stored in the movement object's collisionFlags field. Following this, the lastHitPoint and lastGroundNormal fields are updated with the current set of values.

The old and new horizontal velocities are calculated on lines 40-42. The old velocity is based on the velocity field's value. The new velocity is calculated based on the hover racer's current position when compared to its previous position, line 41. Notice that we divide by the value of Time.deltaTime to expand the component values from frame rate independent to full values. The newHVelocity is set on line 42 from the X and Z component values of the updated movement velocity vector.

The code on lines 46–63 is responsible for refining the car's velocity taking into account unwanted movement directions due to object collisions, including ceiling detection, that's used by the class' jump implementation but not by the game at large. The last snippet of code, lines 65–76, is used to detect changes in the ground state including losing the ground, taking off, and gaining the ground, landing. We'll take a look at the remaining main methods next.

Listing 7-11. CharacterMotor Main Method Details 3

```
01 void FixedUpdate() {
02     if (useFixedUpdate) {
03         UpdateFunction();
04     }
05 }
```

```
01 void Update() {
02     if (!useFixedUpdate) {
03         UpdateFunction();
04     }
05 }
```

```
01 void OnControllerColliderHit(ControllerColliderHit hit) {
02     if (BaseScript.IsActive(scriptName) == false) {
03         return;
04     }
05
06     if (hit.normal.y > 0 && hit.normal.y > groundNormal.y && hit.
       moveDirection.y < 0) {
07         if ((hit.point - movement.lastHitPoint).sqrMagnitude > 0.001 ||
           lastGroundNormal == Vector3.zero) {
08             groundNormal = hit.normal;
09         } else {
10             groundNormal = lastGroundNormal;
11         }
12
13         movement.hitPoint = hit.point;
14         movement.frameVelocity = Vector3.zero;
15     }
16 }
```

The first two methods listed in this set are the Unity callback methods
FixedUpdate and Update. Depending on the value of the useFixedUpdate field,
one or the other method is used. The last method in the class for us to review is the
OnControllerColliderHit method. This method is used to determine the value of the
groundNormal Vector3 field. Note that the hitPoint and frameVelocity fields of the
movement object are set at the end of the method.

Many of the calculations in this class are complex, difficult to visualize, and
downright scary. Fear not! You can approach any calculation or field value by adding
debugging and running the game to see how the values correspond to the actual
movements of the hover racer. Use that information to get a foothold in determining how
the field is used and what kind of data it holds. Up next, we'll detail how to demonstrate
the CharacterMotor class.

Demonstration: CharacterMotor

The best way to demonstrate the CharacterMotor class is to play any of the demo scenes we've looked at thus far or the actual game, scene "Main13" or "Main14". While the game is running in the "Game" panel, you can look at the "Hierarchy" panel and expand the StartingSet entry. Select the HoverCar0 child entry. Find the "Character Motor" entry in the "Inspector'" panel and expand it. Watch the field values change as the car moves on the track.

A very good way to perform this demonstration is to run the actual game and let the computer mode run while you peruse the "Character Motor" component's values in the "Inspector" panel. Try to see how certain values change while the AI player races around the track. The next class we'll look at is the FPSInputController class.

Class Review: FPSInputController

The FPSInputController class is responsible for responding to user input. Based on inputs, certain values in the CharacterMotor are set, which in turn causes the CharacterController to move the character. We'll use the following review steps to cover this class:

1. Class Fields

2. Pertinent Method Outline/Class Headers

3. Main Method Details

4. Demonstration

The first review section we'll look at is the class fields. Remember the location of this class is in the following folder: "\Standard Assets\Character Controllers\Sources\Scripts\".

Class Fields: FPSInputController

The FPSInputController class has a number of fields that help it manage the user input it takes into consideration when controlling the CharacterMotor.

Listing 7-12. FPSInputController Class Fields 1

```
private CharacterMotor motor;
public bool aiOn = false;
public Vector3 directionVector = Vector3.zero;
public float directionLength = 0.0f;
public Vector3 inputMoveDirection = Vector3.zero;
public float touchSpeed = 0.0f;
public float touchSpeedDie = 0.065f;
```

The CharacterMotor field, as we've seen previously, takes the FPS input controller's movement vector and uses it in various calculations ultimately ending in moving the character, in this case, a hover racer model. The Boolean flag aiOn is responsible for turning AI control on and off in conjunction with the other input classes. The next field, directionVector, indicates the direction of movement. Subsequently, the directionLength field represents the magnitude of the movement vector. The inputMoveDirection field is a Vector3 instance that indicates the input move direction. The last two entries are used to manage acceleration when touch input is used. The touchSpeed field, used to accelerate the car, and the touchSpeedDie field, that is used to slow down the touch-based acceleration after touch input is removed. Next, we'll look at the class' pertinent method outline.

Pertinent Method Outline/Class Headers: FPSInputController

The class has only two main methods for us to review.

Listing 7-13. FPSInputController Pertinent Method Outline/Class Headers 1

```
//Main Methods
void Awake();
void Update();
```

The class' import statements and declaration are as follows.

Listing 7-14. FPSInputController Pertinent Method Outline/Class Headers 2

```
using UnityEngine;

// Require a character controller to be attached to the same game object
[RequireComponent(typeof(CharacterMotor))]
[AddComponentMenu("Character/FPS Input Controller")]

public class FPSInputController : BaseScript {}
```

Notice that the class declaration uses the "RequireComponent" code attribute to require the CharacterMotor component be attached to the parent game object. Also note that the class extends the BaseScript class, which in turn extends the MonoBehaviour class as we've seen previously. In the next section, we'll take a look at the class' main methods.

Main Methods Details: FPSInputController

This section contains two methods we'll review in detail, listed as follows.

Listing 7-15. FPSInputController Main Method Details 1

```
01 void Awake() {
02     motor = GetComponent<CharacterMotor>();
03     base.PrepPlayerInfo(this.GetType().Name);
04     if (BaseScript.IsActive(scriptName) == false) {
05        Utilities.wrForce(scriptName + ": Is Deactivating...");
06        return;
07     } else {
08        aiOn = p.aiOn;
09     }
10 }

01 void Update() {
02     if (BaseScript.IsActive(scriptName) == false) {
03        return;
04     }
05
```

```
06    // Get the input vector from keyboard or analog stick
07    directionVector = Vector3.zero;
08    if (gameState.gamePaused == true) {
09       return;
10    } else if (gameState.gameRunning == false) {
11       return;
12    }
13
14    if (aiOn == true && p != null) {
15       if (p.pause == true) {
16          return;
17       }
18       directionVector = p.UpdateAiFpsController();
19    } else {
20       if (Input.touchSupported == true && gameState.accelOn == true) {
21          if (Input.touchSupported == true) {
22             if (gameState.accelOn == true) {
23                touchSpeed = 1.0f;
24                directionVector = new Vector3(Input.
                  GetAxis("Horizontal"), 0, touchSpeed);
25             } else {
26                touchSpeed -= (touchSpeed * touchSpeedDie);
27                if (touchSpeed < 0.0) {
28                   touchSpeed = 0.0f;
29                }
30                directionVector = new Vector3(Input.
                  GetAxis("Horizontal"), 0, touchSpeed);
31             }
32          }
33       } else {
34          if (Input.GetAxis("Turn") < 0.0f) {
35             if (Input.GetAxis("Horizontal") < 0.0f) {
36                transform.Rotate(0, -1.75f, 0);
```

```
37              } else {
38                  transform.Rotate(0, -1.25f, 0);
39              }
40          }
41
42          if (Input.GetAxis("Turn") > 0.0f) {
43              if (Input.GetAxis("Horizontal") > 0.0f) {
44                  transform.Rotate(0, 1.75f, 0);
45              } else {
46                  transform.Rotate(0, 1.25f, 0);
47              }
48          }
49
50          if (Input.GetAxis("Vertical") > 0.0f) {
51              touchSpeed = 1.0f;
52              directionVector = new Vector3(Input.GetAxis("Horizontal"),
                0, touchSpeed);
53          } else if (Input.GetAxis("Vertical") < 0.0f) {
54              touchSpeed = -0.65f;
55              directionVector = new Vector3(Input.GetAxis("Horizontal"),
                0, touchSpeed);
56          } else {
57              touchSpeed -= (touchSpeed * touchSpeedDie);
58              if (touchSpeed < 0.0f) {
59                  touchSpeed = 0.0f;
60              }
61              directionVector = new Vector3(Input.GetAxis("Horizontal"),
                0, touchSpeed);
62          }
63      }
64  }
65
```

```
66      if (directionVector != Vector3.zero) {
67          // Get the length of the direction vector and then normalize it
68          // Dividing by the length is cheaper than normalizing when we
            already have the length anyway
69          directionLength = directionVector.magnitude;
70          directionVector = directionVector / directionLength;
71
72          // Make sure the length is no bigger than 1
73          directionLength = Mathf.Min(1.0f, directionLength);
74
75          // Make the input vector more sensitive towards the extremes and
            less sensitive in the middle
76          // This makes it easier to control slow speeds when using analog sticks
77          directionLength = directionLength * directionLength;
78
79          // Multiply the normalized direction vector by the modified length
80          directionVector = directionVector * directionLength;
81      }
82
83      // Apply the direction to the CharacterMotor
84      inputMoveDirection = transform.rotation * directionVector;
85      motor.inputMoveDirection = inputMoveDirection;
86 }
```

The first method for us to look at is the Awake class initialization method. The motor field is set on line 2. Next, on line 3, we call the player info version of the base class' preparation methods. This takes care of setting up our standard fields, game, and player state data while also registering the result of the operation. On line 4, we check if the class was configured correctly. If not, we write some logs and exit. If so, we update the aiOn field with the current value from the PlayerState instance, base class field, p, line 8.

The next method for us to review is the Unity engine callback method, Update. This method is called once per game frame. Lines 2–4 should be very familiar by now. The code is there to escape the method in case the class configuration fails for some reason. On lines 7–12, the directionVector is reset to the zero vector, and the method is escaped if the game is paused or otherwise not running. AI control is handled on lines 14–19 with a call to the `UpdateAIFpsController` method, line 18, doing most of the work to calculate the next movement vector.

Next, let's look at a little block of code on lines 20–33. This code is responsible for handling touch input. In this case, the acceleration is controlled by the presence of touch input, and the direction is handled by processing the horizontal change of the touch input. Direct your attention to the code on lines 34–48. This block of code is responsible for turning the hover racer left or right.

From lines 50–64, we determine if the input is moving the hover racer forward or backward. Notice that in the same process for touch input, we don't let the car go in reverse, line 28. When using keyboard or controller input however, we can go in reverse, line 54. Take a look at the code from lines 56 to 62. Can you figure out what this code does? It slowly lowers the car's velocity down to zero when no touch is detected. The remaining block of code on lines 66-85 cleans up the direction vector with the final application to the player taking place on lines 84-85. That brings us to the conclusion of this review step.

Demonstration: FPSInputController

Much like the `CharacterMotor` class, the `FPSInputController` class doesn't have a dedicated demonstration scene. Rather, any scene will do. When you run the scene, take a moment to find and expand the "Starting Set" entry in the Unity editor's "Hierarchy" panel. Select the child entry, `HoverCar0`, and look for the "FPS Input Controller" script component entry in the "Inspector" panel and expand it.

Now go back and play the game and/or demo scene while watching the attributes of the class change in the inspector panel. This is a great way to get an idea of how the actual input translates to values in the class and movement to the hover racer. That brings us to the end of the `FPSInputController` class' review. Next, we'll take a look at the mouse input handler.

Class Review: MouseLookNew

The `MouseLookNew` class is used to process mouse input and convert it to rotation data so the user can steer the hover racer with the mouse. We'll use the following steps to review this class:

1. Enumerations

2. Class Fields

3.   Pertinent Method Outline/Class Headers

4.   Main Method Details

5.   Demonstration

This class is short and sweet. We'll be done with the review in no time. We'll start things off with a look at the class' enumerations.

Enumerations: MouseLookNew

The MouseLookNew class has one enumeration for use to discuss. The enumeration in question is as follows.

Listing 7-16. MouseLookNew Enumerations 1

```
1 public enum RotationAxes {
2     MouseXAndY = 0,
3     MouseX = 1,
4     MouseY = 2
5 }
```

The enumeration is used to describe the available types of input-driven rotation. I should mention that just because they're listed here doesn't mean that all the options are supported by the game. In any case, the RotationAxes enumeration is a convenient way to describe a rotation of some kind in terms of mouse input. Next, we'll see how the class fields model mouse input in more detail.

Class Fields: MouseLookNew

The MouseLookNew class mainly has fields that help model a sensitivity-filtered mouse input. Let's have a look at the class fields listed as follows.

Listing 7-17. MouseLookNew Class Fields 1

```
public RotationAxes axes = RotationAxes.MouseXAndY;
public float sensitivityX = 12.0f;
public float sensitivityY = 12.0f;
public float minimumX = -360.0f;
public float maximumX = 360.0f;
```

The first field listed, axes, is used to describe what axis data should be retrieved. This is a descriptive field. It doesn't drive functionality; it reflects the current configuration. Subsequently, there are two fields, minimumX and maximumX, used to describe the sensitivity applied to the input for the X and Y axes. The next two fields can be used to constrain X axis values. I'll list the remaining fields here.

Listing 7-18. MouseLookNew Class Fields 2

```
public float minimumY = -60.0f;
public float maximumY = 60.0f;
public float mouseX = 0f;
public float mouseY = 0f;
public bool aiOn = false;
```

The first two fields listed, minimumY and maximumY, can be used to constrain the calculated Y axis value. Next up, the mouseX and mouseY fields are used to hold raw mouse input data for the X and Y axes. The aiOn field is a Boolean flag used to toggle AI control of the mouse. Lastly, the rigidBodyTmp field is used to reference the current player's rigid body component.

Pertinent Method Outline/Class Headers: MouseLookNew

This class has only two methods for us to worry about, but we'll complete the pertinent method review section to be thorough.

Listing 7-19. MouseLookNew Pertinent Method Outline/Class Headers 1

```
//Main Methods
void Start();
void Update();
```

The class' import statements and declaration are as follows.

Listing 7-20. MouseLookNew Pertinent Method Outline/Class Headers 2

```
using UnityEngine;

public class MouseLookNew : BaseScript {}
```

Note that this class extends the BaseScript class, which means that it's a MonoBehaviour with a standard set of base fields used to plug into the game's game state objects. In the next section, we'll take a look at the main methods in detail.

Main Method Details: MouseLookNew

The class' main methods are listed in the next group. I should mention that touch screen input such as dragging one finger across the screen is interpreted as mouse steering input if the device has touch enabled. Let's jump into some code!

Listing 7-21. MouseLookNew Main Method Details 1

```
01 void Start() {
02    base.PrepPlayerInfo(this.GetType().Name);
03    if (BaseScript.IsActive(scriptName) == false) {
04       Utilities.wrForce(scriptName + ": Is Deactivating...");
05       return;
06    } else {
07       aiOn = p.aiOn;
08    }
09
10    // Make the rigid body not change rotation
11    rigidBodyTmp = GetComponent<Rigidbody>();
12    if (rigidBodyTmp != null) {
13       rigidBodyTmp.freezeRotation = true;
14    }
15
16    if (Input.touchSupported == true) {
17       sensitivityX = 5.0f;
18       sensitivityY = 5.0f;
19    }
20 }

01 void Update() {
02    if (BaseScript.IsActive(scriptName) == false) {
03       return;
04    }
```

```
05
06    if (gameState.gamePaused == true) {
07        return;
08    } else if (gameState.gameRunning == false) {
09        return;
10    }
11
12    if (aiOn == true && p != null) {
13        if (p.pause == true) {
14            return;
15        }
16        p.UpdateAiMouseLook();
17    } else {
18        if (gameState.newTouch == false) {
19            mouseX = Input.GetAxis("Mouse X");
20            transform.Rotate(0, mouseX * sensitivityX, 0);
21        }
22    }
23 }
```

The class' Start method has a few points for us to discuss. On lines 2–6, we have the standard initialization for a MonoBehaviour, by extending the BaseScript class, that needs game state and player state data, line 2. If there are any issues with the class' configuration, we exit the method. Otherwise, we toggle the class' aiOn field to match that of the player's state object, line 7. Next, on lines 11–14, we freeze the rotation of the game object's Rigidbody if it's available. In general, in this game, we don't let the player rotate on an axis other than the Y axis. Lastly, on lines 16–19, if the current device supports touch, we drop the sensitivity on the X and Y axes from 12.0f to 5.0f.

Demonstration: MouseLookNew

The best demonstration of the MouseLookNew class is to play the game or run any demonstration while monitoring the current player's MouseLookNew component in the "Inspector" panel. To do so, start the game or demo scene and then go to the "Hierarchy" panel and find the entry named StartingSet. Expand it and select the HoverCar0 child entry. Select it and then take a look at the "Inspector" panel.

Now, find the "Mouse Look New" component entry and expand it. Return to the game and keep playing. Notice that the class' values change as you use the mouse while playing the game. Keep an eye out for what kind of values is shown in the inspector. That brings us to the conclusion of this class review. Next, we'll take a look at some touch input code that resides in the GameState class to wrap up the chapter.

Class Review: GameState (Touch Input Snippet Only)

The GameState class is the main control class for the game. As such, it provides a centralization point for the exchange of data about players, the HUD, the menu system, and more. Because we want the touch input data to be centralized, we made the decision to include the touch input code in the GameState class' Update method. Let's see how it works.

Listing 7-22. GameState Touch Input Snippet 1

```
01 if (Input.touchCount == 1) {
02    touchScreen = true;
03
04    if (Input.GetTouch(0).phase == TouchPhase.Began) {
05       newTouch = true;
06       accelOn = true;
07    } else if (Input.GetTouch(0).phase == TouchPhase.Moved) {
08       newTouch = false;
09    } else if (Input.GetTouch(0).phase == TouchPhase.Stationary) {
10       newTouch = false;
11    } else if ((Input.GetTouch(0).phase == TouchPhase.Ended || Input.
      GetTouch(0).phase == TouchPhase.Canceled)) {
12       newTouch = false;
13       accelOn = false;
14    }
15 } else {
16    newTouch = false;
17    accelOn = false;
18 }
```

182

The first line of code is used to detect if there is one finger on the touch screen. Hover Racers is designed to work with one finger by accelerating the car when the screen is touched and slowing it down when it is not. Furthermore, while the screen is being touched, moving the finger left or right will steer the car left or right. On line 2, the touchScreen Boolean field is set to true to indicate an active touch screen.

On lines 4–6, if a new touch has begun, the newTouch and accelOn Boolean fields are set to true. If the finger has moved, line 7, the new touch Boolean is set to false. This indicates that touch steering input should be processed. Similarly, if the touch doesn't move, the newTouch field is set to false. When the touch interaction ends, line 11, then the newTouch and accelOn fields are set to false. The last bit of code on lines 16–17 is there to turn touch input off if no input is detected.

Chapter Conclusion

We've covered a lot of material in this chapter; specifically we reviewed the classes behind the game's input handling. These classes take touch, mouse, keyboard, and controller input and use it to move, turn, and strafe the hover racer. If you look carefully, you'll notice that all the input was looked up using string constants that describe a certain mapping. For instance, in the MouseLookNew class, we used "Mouse X" for mouse X axis input. More information on the input mapping used by the game will be provided later on in the text. The input handler classes we've covered in this chapter are as follows:

1. CharacterMotor: This class is driven by the FPSInputController and drives the CharacterContoller component. This class is mainly used to control basic movement over the ground taking into account ground slope. In our case, sliding is also a part of the calculations, but jumping and gravity are disabled.

2. FPSInputController: This class, in conjunction with its subclasses, takes user input from different sources and passes it on to the CharacterMotor class to ultimately drive the CharacterController and the hover racer model.

3. MouseLookNew: This class, as the name suggests, uses mouse input to steer the car. It's also able to process touch screen input to steer the hover racer if touch screen input is active on the device.

4. GameState (touch input): The GameState class, due to its centralization, is a great place to store data that needs to be shared. As such, the class is used to detect touch input, setting a few class fields to indicate touch input is active among other things.

Some of the math and vector calculations used by these classes are complex. If you plan to make changes to it, take the time to add logging and other code to monitor and understand how the code you're changing works. Also keep in mind that you can, and should, monitor script components while you play the game in the Unity editor. Be aware that value changes made using the "Inspector" panel will be lost when the game is stopped. Keep that in mind while fine-tuning input control class fields. In the next chapter, we'll take a look at the game's menu system classes.

CHAPTER 8

Menu System Classes

In this chapter, we'll review the game's menu system classes, but before we do, I want to go over the structure of the game's classes. In this chapter, we're going to introduce a new base class that provides core menu screen support for other menu screen classes. Since things are getting a bit more complicated, it's best that we go over the game's class structure here.

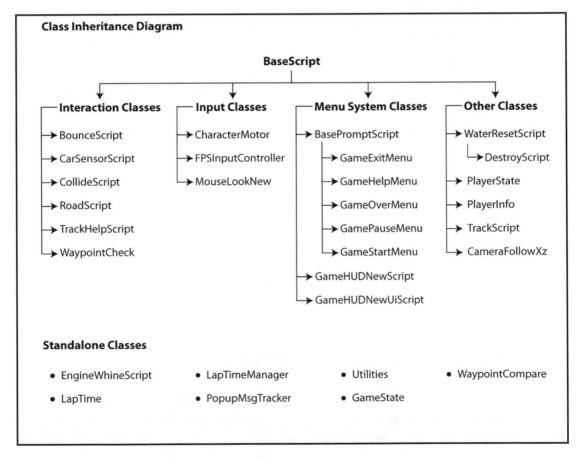

Figure 8-1. *Hover Racers Class Inheritance Diagram 1*

A Hover Racers class diagram showing extension of base classes and stand-alone classes

© Victor G Brusca 2022
V. G Brusca, *Advanced Unity Game Development*, https://doi.org/10.1007/978-1-4842-7851-2_8

As you can see in the previously listed diagram, most of the classes in the Hover Racers code base extend the `BaseScript` class and by extension the `MonoBehaviour` class. That means that all of those classes listed in the tree structure under the `BaseScript` class entry are script components that can be attached to Unity game objects. You can see this in any of the demo scenes you've reviewed thus far. Notice that there are a few menu system classes that extend a new second-order base class, the `BasePromptScript` class. In the preceding diagram, there are two second-order base classes: the `BasePromptScript` and the `WaterResetScript` classes.

We won't cover any Unity editor menu system details here, but we will cover them later on in the text. There are actually three classes that are more alike than other menu system classes. We'll be looking over these classes in detail. I'll list them here.

1. GamePauseMenu

2. GameOverMenu

3. GameExitMenu

There are a few other menu system classes used by the game, some of which we'll discuss a bit in this chapter.

1. GameHelpMenu

2. GameHUDNewScript

3. GameHUDNewUiScript

4. GameStartMenu

We'll start our review with the base class that is extended by the first group of classes previously listed, the `BasePromptScript` class. This script is concise, so we'll skip the more complex class review and just list the class in its entirety.

Class Review: BasePromptScript

As shown in the previously listed diagram, the `BasePromptScript` class is the base class for the `GameExitMenu`, `GameHelpMenu`, `GameOverMenu`, `GamePauseMenu`, and `GameStartMenu` classes. This base class extends the other base class we know all too well, `BaseScript`. As such, any extending classes are `MonoBehaviours`, by inheritance, that have functionality defined in both base classes available to them. Because the "prompt" menu screens all have similar features, two buttons, a sound effect, and a text prompt, etc., it makes sense to centralize the functionality, fields and methods, into one base class. We'll use the following review steps to cover this class.

1. Class Fields

2. Pertinent Method Outline/Class Headers

3. Support Method Details

4. Main Method Details

5. Demonstration

And with that, let's get to it, shall we? The first section up is the class fields.

Class Fields: BasePromptScript

The BasePromptScript class has a number of class fields that are used to track interactions with the menu screen from keyboard, mouse, controller, or touch input. It sounds like we're doing a lot here, but let's think about it for a minute. The Unity game engine has mouse support which means all the UI buttons will respond to mouse click events. Also, Unity supports touch input, so touch screen devices will support button click interactions natively. So we get that much for free. Not bad. The input we have to concern ourselves with is keyboard and controller input, and you'll see this reflected in the class' fields and methods.

Listing 8-1. BasePromptScript Class Fields 1

```
public bool keyBrdInput = false;
public int keyBrdInputIdx = 0;
public int keyBrdInputPrevIdx = -1;
public int keyBrdInputIdxMax = 2;
public int keyBrdInputIdxMin = 0;
public Text txt = null;
public bool btnPressed = false;
public Button btnOne;
public Button btnTwo;
```

The keyBrdInput field is used to determine if the input mappings, "MenuSelectUp" or "MenuSelectDown," are being used. In this way, controller input and keyboard input can be mapped to the keywords listed previously to create a seamless abstraction for different input sources. What this means is that we have the game configured to route certain keyboard keys, up and down arrow, to the same input mapping as the controller directional pad's up and down arrow for menu input. The next field in the list, keyBrdInputIdx, is used to track which UI element is currently highlighted by the class. The keyBrdInputPrevIdx is used to track what the previously highlighted UI element. In relation to these fields are the next two class fields, keyBrdInputIdxMin and keyBrdInputIdxMax. These fields are used to dictate the minimum and maximum indexes of UI elements available on the current menu screen.

The screens that extend the BasePromptScript class are mainly yes or no menu screens with a text prompt. In this case, the maximum index is set to 2. Following these fields is the Unity UI Text class instance, txt. This class is used to display the text prompt on the menu screen. The Boolean flag btnPressed is used to track if a menu button has been pressed. Finally, the btnOne and btnTwo fields are instances of the Unity UI class Button and are used to display the menu screen's button options. That concludes this review section. Next, we'll take a look at the class' pertinent method outline.

Pertinent Method Outline/Class Headers: BasePromptScript

The BasePromptScript class has a few main and support methods for us to review, listed here.

Listing 8-2. BasePromptScript Pertinent Method Outline/Class Headers 1

```
//Main Methods
public void Update();
public void InvokeClick(int current);

//Support Methods
public void SetBtnTextColor(int prev, int current);
```

The class' import statements and headers are as follows. Note that the BasePromptScript class extends the BaseScript class as we've mentioned previously. Also, take a moment to notice the import statements, specifically the UnityEngine.UI namespace.

Listing 8-3. BasePromptScript Pertinent Method Outline/Class Headers 2

```
using UnityEngine;
using UnityEngine.UI;

public class BasePromptScript : BaseScript {}
```

This brings us to the end of this section. Let's begin the method review next with the class' support methods.

Support Method Details: BasePromptScript

This class has only one support method for us to discuss, listed here.

Listing 8-4. BasePromptScript Support Method Details 1

```
01 public void SetBtnTextColor(int prev, int current) {
02     if (prev == 0) {
03         txt = btnOne.transform.GetChild(0).GetComponent<Text>();
04         txt.color = Color.white;
05     } else if (prev == 1) {
06         txt = btnTwo.transform.GetChild(0).GetComponent<Text>();
07         txt.color = Color.white;
08     }
09
10     if (current == 0) {
11         txt = btnOne.transform.GetChild(0).GetComponent<Text>();
12         txt.color = Color.red;
13     } else if (current == 1) {
14         txt = btnTwo.transform.GetChild(0).GetComponent<Text>();
15         txt.color = Color.red;
16     }
17 }
```

The SetBtnTextColor method is used to alter the menu screen's button text color to indicate which button has been highlighted by using the keyboard or controller input. In this method, on lines 2–8, we reset the text color to white for the previously highlighted UI element. Notice that we grab a reference to the Text component and then adjust its color field, lines 4 and 7. Similarly, we need to adjust the currently highlighted UI element to indicate it is the selected element. The code on lines 10–16 is the same as in the previous block of code except that in this case, we change the text to red. The red color indicates a highlighted UI element. In the next section, we'll cover the class' main methods.

Main Method Details: BasePromptScript

The BasePromptScript class has two main methods for us to review. We'll detail both in the subsequent listing.

Listing 8-5. BasePromptScript Main Method Details 1

```
01 public void Update() {
02     if (BaseScript.IsActive(scriptName) == false) {
03         return;
04     }
05
06     if (keyBrdInput == false) {
07         if (Input.GetButtonUp("MenuSelectUp")) {
08             keyBrdInput = true;
09             keyBrdInputIdx = 0;
10             keyBrdInputPrevIdx = -1;
11             SetBtnTextColor(keyBrdInputPrevIdx, keyBrdInputIdx);
12         } else if (Input.GetButtonDown("MenuSelectDown")) {
13             keyBrdInput = true;
14             keyBrdInputIdx = (keyBrdInputIdxMax - 1);
15             keyBrdInputPrevIdx = -1;
16             SetBtnTextColor(keyBrdInputPrevIdx, keyBrdInputIdx);
17         }
18     } else {
19         if (Input.GetButtonUp("MenuSelectUp")) {
20             if (keyBrdInputIdx + 1 < keyBrdInputIdxMax) {
21                 keyBrdInputPrevIdx = keyBrdInputIdx;
22                 keyBrdInputIdx++;
23             } else {
```

```
24          keyBrdInputPrevIdx = (keyBrdInputIdxMax - 1);
25          keyBrdInputIdx = 0;
26        }
27        SetBtnTextColor(keyBrdInputPrevIdx, keyBrdInputIdx);
28      } else if (Input.GetButtonDown("MenuSelectDown")) {
29        if (keyBrdInputIdx - 1 >= keyBrdInputIdxMin) {
30          keyBrdInputPrevIdx = keyBrdInputIdx;
31          keyBrdInputIdx--;
32        } else {
33          keyBrdInputPrevIdx = keyBrdInputIdx;
34          keyBrdInputIdx = (keyBrdInputIdxMax - 1);
35        }
36        SetBtnTextColor(keyBrdInputPrevIdx, keyBrdInputIdx);
37      } else if (Input.GetButtonDown("Submit")) {
38        InvokeClick(keyBrdInputIdx);
39      }
40    }
41 }
```

```
01 public void InvokeClick(int current) {
02    if (current == 0) {
03      btnOne.onClick.Invoke();
04    } else if (current == 1) {
05      btnTwo.onClick.Invoke();
06    }
07 }
```

The first method we'll look at is the class' Update method. This method is called every game frame and is responsible for adjusting the state of the menu screen in response to user input. On lines 2–4, as you might have expected, the method is escaped without doing any work if the class configuration fails. Let me describe what's going on with the menu screen and how it handles the keyboard and controller input. It'll make reviewing the next block of code more effective. When the menu screen first displays, there is no selected UI element. If the proper keyboard or controller input is detected, arrow keys and directional pad buttons, then the menu reacts by selecting the first UI element, highlighting it. From this point on, further input of this kind will change the selected UI element. If the highlighted element is the last element in the menu, the first UI element is then highlighted and vice versa.

With that in mind, let's look at the method that is responsible for implementing the functionality we just described. The code on lines 6–18 is used to handle the initial keyboard or controller input and select a UI element. If "MenuSelectUp" input is detected, then the keyBrdInput flag is set to true, and the first menu button is highlighted, lines 8–11. Alternatively, if "MenuSelectDown" is detected, then the keyBrdInput flag is also set to true, but we select the last menu button, lines 13–16. The next block of code on lines 18–40 executes if the keyBrdInput flag is true. In this case, if "MenuSelectUp" input is detected, we move the selected UI element up one and cycle it back to the first element if we move past the last UI element, lines 20–27. In a similar fashion, if "MenuSelectDown" input is detected, we move the selected UI element down one and cycle back to the last element if we move past the first UI element, lines 29–36.

Lastly, on lines 37–39, if "Submit" input is detected, we submit the menu screen by invoking a click event on the currently selected button with a call to the InvokeClick method on line 38. The last method in the set is the Invoke method. This method is used to provide a way to programmatically induce a click event on either of the menu screen's two buttons. That concludes this review section. In the next section, we'll look at how to demonstrate this class' functionality.

Demonstration: BasePromptScript

It's a little bit difficult to clearly demonstrate the BasePromptScript class in action because it's a base class used by a few of the game's menu screens. That being said, we can certainly view some of those menu screens in action. Our best bet is to run the full game. If you open up the project in the Unity editor and direct your attention to the "Project" panel, you should see an entry named "Scenes". Open this folder and find the scene named "Main13" or "Main14". These two scenes will start the full game. Once the game is running, start a race and then click the exit button in the lower left-hand corner of the game after the countdown completes. You should be greeted with the GameExitMenu screen. Interact with it using the keyboard or controller to visualize the code we just reviewed. We'll take a look at some specific menu screens next.

Class Review: GamePauseMenu

The GamePauseMenu class is an example of a two-button prompt screen that extends the BasePromptScript class we've just reviewed. As such, it gets a lot of its functionality from the BasePromptScript and BaseScript base classes. We'll use the following review steps to cover this class.

1. Pertinent Method Outline/Class Headers

2. Support Method Details

3. Main Method Details

4. Demonstration

The reason why we have only four review steps is because we've extended multiple base classes and inherited their functionality simplifying the class' implementation. Let's look at the class' outline next.

Pertinent Method Outline/Class Headers: GamePauseMenu

This class has one main method and a few support methods for us to check out and not much else. Let's have a look, shall we?

Listing 8-6. GamePauseMenu Pertinent Method Outline/Class Headers 1

```
//Main Methods
void Start();

//Support Methods
public void PerformResumeGameUI();
public void PerformResumeGame();
public void PerformEndGameUI();
public void PerformEndGame();
```

The class' import statements and declaration are as follows.

193

Listing 8-7. GamePauseMenu Pertinent Method Outline/Class Headers 2

```
using UnityEngine;
using UnityEngine.SceneManagement;
using static GameState;

public class GamePauseMenu : BasePromptScript {}
```

Note that the GamePauseMenu class extends the BasePrompScript class as we've noted previously. Also, note that the class had some more imports than we've previously seen, specifically the UnityEngine.SceneManager namespace and GameState imports. The "using static GameState" line allows this class to access enumerations from the GameState class. You'll see them used in the class' methods, for example, use of the GameStateIndex.NONE value in the PerformEndGame method.

Support Method Details: GamePauseMenu

The GamePauseMenu class has a number of support methods for us to review. Let's jump into some code!

Listing 8-8. GamePauseMenu Support Method Details 1

```
01 public void PerformResumeGameUI() {
02     PerformResumeGame();
03 }

01 public void PerformResumeGame() {
02     if (BaseScript.IsActive(scriptName) == false) {
03         return;
04     }
05     gameState.PlayMenuSound();
06     gameState.HidePauseMenu();
07 }

01 public void PerformEndGameUI() {
02     PerformEndGame();
03 }
```

```
01 public void PerformEndGame() {
02    if (BaseScript.IsActive(scriptName) == false) {
03       return;
04    }
05    PlayerPrefs.SetInt("GameStateIndex", (int)GameStateIndex.NONE);
06    PlayerPrefs.Save();
07    gameState.PlayMenuSound();
08    gameState.ResetGame();
09    SceneManager.LoadScene(gameState.sceneName);
10 }
```

The set of support methods for us to review is responsible for handling click input events, because the UI system was designed to allow for different inputs to activate the button click events. To support this, the functionality of the buttons is abstracted from the input event handlers by one level as we'll soon see. The first method for us to peruse is the PerformResumeGameUI method. This method is directly wired to the GamePauseMenu screen's buttons. When the menu screen button is clicked, the PerformResumeGameUI method calls the PerformResumeGame method to do the actual work of resuming the game.

This allows us to call the PerformResumeGame method directly to accomplish the same task in response to keyboard and controller inputs. The next method listed, PerformResumeGame, is responsible for resuming the game after it's been paused. On lines 2–4, we have the standard escape code that prevents the method from doing any work if there has been an issue configuring the class. On line 5, we play a menu sound, from the GameState class instance, to indicate that user input has been received, and on line 6, we hide the pause menu resuming the game. Note that the menu screens rely heavily on the centralized functionality provided by the GameState class.

Following this entry is the PerformEndGameUi method. This method is directly connected to a button on the menu screen and is called in response to user input. It calls the PerformEndGame method to do the actual work of ending the game. Notice that in both cases, the direct user input event handler has to make one more method call to perform the work necessary. This is the one level of abstraction I mentioned earlier.

The standard escape code is on lines 2–4 of the PerformEndGame method. To end the game properly, we need to reset the game's "GameStateIndex" player preference and save the change, lines 5–6. Next, we play a menu sound effect to indicate the user input was received, line 7, and reset the game on line 8. The last thing we need to do is reset the entire scene which is done with the method call on line 9. This call will ask the scene manager to reload the current scene for us. In the next section, we'll look at this class' main methods.

Main Method Details: GamePauseMenu

The GamePauseMenu class has one main method for us to review. It should look very familiar by this point in the text. We'll cover it just the same though. Best to be thorough.

Listing 8-9. GamePauseMenu Main Method Details 1

```
01 void Start() {
02     base.Prep(this.GetType().Name);
03     if (BaseScript.IsActive(scriptName) == false) {
04         Utilities.wrForce(scriptName + ": Is Deactivating...");
05         return;
06     }
07 }
```

This is an example of a simple Start method. The class is prepped on line 2, and if anything has gone wrong, the method writes some logs and exits, lines 4–5. There's not much more to it than that. Let's see if we can't come up with a decent demonstration of this class in the next review section.

Demonstration: GamePauseMenu

The best way to demonstrate the GamePauseMenu in action is to run the main game. Locate the "Project" panel and find the "Scenes" folder, and open it. Look for the scenes named "Main13" or "Main14". Open the scene and run it. You'll need to start a player-controlled race by clicking the "Track 1" or "Track 2" button. Once the race countdown starts, click on another application other than the Unity editor. Notice that the game pause menu screen pops up and the game stops.

Return to the Unity editor and use the up and down keyboard buttons to change the selected pause menu button. Notice that you can click the buttons using the mouse or the enter key. This is our abstraction layer at work. The GameOverMenu and GameExitMenu classes are very similar to the class we've just reviewed. I'll leave you to look at them on your own. Make sure you understand the classes well before you move on.

Class Review: GameHelpMenu

The GameHelpMenu is used to show a series of help screens that describe different details about the Hover Racers game. This menu screen is a bit more complicated than the one we reviewed previously. We'll use the following steps to review this class.

1. Class Fields

2. Pertinent Method Outline/Class Headers

3. Support Method Details

4. Main Method Details

5. Demonstration

We'll see some similar code with regard to the UI interactions, selecting, clicking, etc, as we've seen before but with a little bit more complexity to it.

Class Fields: GameHelpMenu

The GameHelpMenu has a number of class fields used to control user interaction with the help menu. The different help menu screens are used to show different images that provide information about how to play the game.

Listing 8-10. GameHelpMenu Class Fields 1

```
//***** Class Fields: Images *****
public Image help1 = null;
public Image help2 = null;
public Image help3 = null;
public Image help4 = null;
public Image help5 = null;
public Image help6 = null;
public Image help7 = null;
public Image help8 = null;

//***** Internal Variables *****
private Image img = null;
private int idx = 0;
private int MAX_INDEX = 8;
```

```
//***** Class Fields *****
public Button btnPrev = null;
public Button btnNext = null;
public Button btnThree = null;
```

The first eight entries are all Unity Image instances that are used to display different help screens with information about how to play the game. These images are configured in the Unity editor using the "Inspector" panel and not programmatically. The following entry, img, is used as a temporary place holder to help change the text color of the menu's different buttons. The MAX_INDEX field is used to indicate the maximum number of help images displayed by this menu screen. The remaining class fields are buttons used to navigate the help menu screens. We'll view the pertinent method outline next.

Pertinent Method Outline/Class Headers: GameHelpMenu

The GameHelpMenu class' pertinent method outline is as follows.

Listing 8-11. GameHelpMenu Pertinent Method Outline/Class Headers 1

```
//Main Methods
void Start();
new void Update();
public new void InvokeClick(int current);
public new void SetBtnTextColor(int prev, int current);

//Support Methods
public void EnablePrev();
public void DisablePrev();
public void EnableNext();
public void DisableNext();
private void ShowHelpScreen(int i);

//Support Methods: Input Handlers
public void PerformMainMenuUI();
public void PerformMainMenu()
public void PerformNextUI();
```

```
public void PerformNext();
public void PerformPrevUI();
public void PerformPrev();
```

There are actually a few important points I'd like to discuss at this juncture. For one, notice that there are method entries adorned with the new keyword. The reason for this is because these methods are defined by one of the base classes that the GameHelpMenu class extends. The new keyword is used to tell the compiler that the method is being redefined. The other thing I wanted to mention is that we have a new section of methods, the "Support Methods: Input Handlers". The reason for this is that there are a bunch of input handlers and I thought we should separate them since their functionality and use are similar. Next, we'll take a look at the class' imports and declaration detailed in the following listing.

Listing 8-12. GameHelpMenu Pertinent Method Outline/Class Headers 2

```
using UnityEngine;
using UnityEngine.UI;

public class GameHelpMenu : BasePromptScript {}
```

This class uses imports from the UnityEngine and UnityEngine.UI namespaces. Note that the GameHelpMenu class extends the BasePromptScript base class. We've seen this class in use before. It adds some default fields and functionality to the menu classes that extend it.

Support Method Details: GameHelpMenu

The GameHelpMenu class has a number of support methods. These methods come in two flavors: support methods and the input handler methods. We'll start off with the standard support methods listed as follows.

Listing 8-13. GameHelpMenu Support Method Details 1

```
01 public void EnablePrev() {
02    if (btnPrev != null) {
03       btnPrev.interactable = true;
04    }
05 }
```

```
01 public void DisablePrev() {
02     if (btnPrev != null) {
03         btnPrev.interactable = false;
04     }
05 }
```

```
01 public void EnableNext() {
02     if (btnNext != null) {
03         btnNext.interactable = true;
04     }
05 }
```

```
01 public void DisableNext() {
02     if (btnNext != null) {
03         btnNext.interactable = false;
04     }
05 }
```

```
01 private void ShowHelpScreen(int i) {
02     if (help1 != null) {
03         help1.gameObject.SetActive(false);
04     }
05
06     if (help2 != null) {
07         help2.gameObject.SetActive(false);
08     }
09
10     if (help3 != null) {
11         help3.gameObject.SetActive(false);
12     }
13
14     if (help4 != null) {
15         help4.gameObject.SetActive(false);
16     }
17
```

```
18      if (help5 != null) {
19          help5.gameObject.SetActive(false);
20      }
21
22      if (help6 != null) {
23          help6.gameObject.SetActive(false);
24      }
25
26      if (help7 != null) {
27          help7.gameObject.SetActive(false);
28      }
29
30      if (help8 != null) {
31          help8.gameObject.SetActive(false);
32      }
33
34      if (i == 0) {
35          help1.gameObject.SetActive(true);
36          DisablePrev();
37          EnableNext();
38      } else if (i == 1) {
39          help2.gameObject.SetActive(true);
40          EnablePrev();
41          EnableNext();
42      } else if (i == 2) {
43          help3.gameObject.SetActive(true);
44          EnablePrev();
45          EnableNext();
46      } else if (i == 3) {
47          help4.gameObject.SetActive(true);
48          EnablePrev();
49          EnableNext();
50      } else if (i == 4) {
51          help5.gameObject.SetActive(true);
52          EnablePrev();
53          EnableNext();
```

```
54    } else if (i == 5) {
55       help6.gameObject.SetActive(true);
56       EnablePrev();
57       EnableNext();
58    } else if (i == 6) {
59       help7.gameObject.SetActive(true);
60       EnablePrev();
61       EnableNext();
62    } else if (i == 7) {
63       help8.gameObject.SetActive(true);
64       EnablePrev();
65       DisableNext();
66    }
67 }
```

The first few methods are used to enable or disable some of the form's UI elements. In this case, we have methods to control enabling or disabling the next and prev buttons. These methods are very simple and similar in nature. Take a moment to look them over and make sure you understand them before moving on. The next method we'll look at is the ShowHelpScreen method.

The ShowHelpScreen method is similar to the enable/disable methods we just looked at except it's designed to work with all the menu's help images and it's responsible for disabling all images and then enabling only the specified image. In the method's first block of code, lines 2–32, each image field is checked for null values and, if defined, is subsequently disabled. The next code block on lines 34–66 is used to enable the specified image and the associated previous and next buttons depending on the current position in the list of images. The first and last images disable the previous and next buttons, respectively. That wraps up the class' basic support methods. In the next section, we'll take a look at the class' input handler support methods.

Input Handler Support Method Details: GameHelpMenu

The second set of support methods for us to cover is the input handler support methods. These methods follow a similar pattern to that which we've seen before in the two button prompt menu screens. An example is the GamePauseMenu class. I'll detail the methods here.

Listing 8-14. GameHelpMenu Input Handler Support Method Details 1

```
01 public void PerformMainMenuUI() {
02     PerformMainMenu();
03 }

01 public void PerformMainMenu() {
02     if (BaseScript.IsActive(scriptName) == false) {
03         return;
04     }
05     gameState.PlayMenuSound();
06     gameState.ShowStartMenu();
07     gameState.HideHelpMenu();
08 }

01 public void PerformNextUI() {
02     PerformNext();
03 }

01 public void PerformNext() {
02     if (BaseScript.IsActive(scriptName) == false) {
03         return;
04     }
05     gameState.PlayMenuSound();
06     if ((idx + 1) < MAX_INDEX) {
07         idx++;
08     }
09     ShowHelpScreen(idx);
10 }

01 public void PerformPrevUI() {
02   PerformPrev();
03 }

01 public void PerformPrev() {
02     if (BaseScript.IsActive(scriptName) == false) {
03         return;
04     }
```

```
05    gameState.PlayMenuSound();
06    if ((idx - 1) >= 0) {
07        idx--;
08    }
09    ShowHelpScreen(idx);
10 }
```

The GameHelpMenu menu has three buttons, so we'll have three sets of two methods each following the same abstraction we saw in the GamePauseMenu class' input handler. In this case, we have the main menu, previous, and next buttons. Notice that in each case, the actual work is done by a local class method and each such method is protected from doing any work unless the class is properly configured. Look over these methods and make sure they make sense to you before moving on.

Main Method Details: GameHelpMenu

The GameHelpMenu class has four methods for us to peruse. There are two MonoBehaviour life cycle callback methods, Start and Update, as well as two UI management methods, InvokeClick and SetBtnTextColor.

Listing 8-15. GameHelpMenu Main Method Details 1

```
01 void Start() {
02    keyBrdInputIdxMax = 3;
03    base.Prep(this.GetType().Name);
04    if (BaseScript.IsActive(scriptName) == false) {
05        Utilities.wrForce(scriptName + ": Is Deactivating...");
06        return;
07    }
08 }
```

```
01 new void Update() {
02    if (BaseScript.IsActive(scriptName) == false) {
03        return;
04    }
05
```

```
06    if (keyBrdInput == false) {
07       if (Input.GetButtonUp("MenuSelectUp")) {
08          keyBrdInput = true;
09          if (idx == 0) {
10             keyBrdInputIdx = 1;
11             keyBrdInputPrevIdx = -1;
12          } else {
13             keyBrdInputIdx = 0;
14             keyBrdInputPrevIdx = -1;
15          }
16          SetBtnTextColor(keyBrdInputPrevIdx, keyBrdInputIdx);
17       } else if (Input.GetButtonDown("MenuSelectDown")) {
18          keyBrdInput = true;
19          if (idx == MAX_INDEX - 1) {
20             keyBrdInputIdx = (keyBrdInputIdxMax - 1);
21             keyBrdInputPrevIdx = -1;
22          } else {
23             keyBrdInputIdx = 1;
24             keyBrdInputPrevIdx = -1;
25          }
26          SetBtnTextColor(keyBrdInputPrevIdx, keyBrdInputIdx);
27       }
28    } else {
29       if (Input.GetButtonDown("MenuSelectUp")) {
30          if (keyBrdInputIdx + 1 < keyBrdInputIdxMax) {
31             keyBrdInputPrevIdx = keyBrdInputIdx;
32             keyBrdInputIdx++;
33          } else {
34             keyBrdInputPrevIdx = (keyBrdInputIdxMax - 1);
35             keyBrdInputIdx = 0;
36          }
37
```

```
38              if (idx == 0 && keyBrdInputIdx == 0) {
39                  keyBrdInputIdx++;
40              } else if (idx == (MAX_INDEX - 1) && keyBrdInputIdx ==
                (keyBrdInputIdxMax - 1)) {
41                  keyBrdInputIdx = 0;
42              }
43
44              SetBtnTextColor(keyBrdInputPrevIdx, keyBrdInputIdx);
45          } else if (Input.GetButtonDown("MenuSelectDown")) {
46              if (keyBrdInputIdx - 1 >= keyBrdInputIdxMin) {
47                  keyBrdInputPrevIdx = keyBrdInputIdx;
48                  keyBrdInputIdx--;
49              } else {
50                  keyBrdInputPrevIdx = keyBrdInputIdx;
51                  keyBrdInputIdx = (keyBrdInputIdxMax - 1);
52              }
53
54              if (idx == 0 && keyBrdInputIdx == 0) {
55                  keyBrdInputIdx = (keyBrdInputIdxMax - 1);
56              } else if (idx == (MAX_INDEX - 1) && keyBrdInputIdx ==
                (keyBrdInputIdxMax - 1)) {
57                  keyBrdInputIdx--;
58              }
59
60              SetBtnTextColor(keyBrdInputPrevIdx, keyBrdInputIdx);
61          } else if (Input.GetButtonDown("Submit")) {
62              InvokeClick(keyBrdInputIdx);
63          }
64      }
65 }
```

The first method for us to look at is the Start method. The first line of code, line 2, is used to set the menu's maximum selection index to control highlighted UI elements when using the keyboard or controller to navigate the help menu's buttons. The remaining lines of code, 3–7, perform the standard class configuration we've seen time and time again. The next method for us to look at is the class' Update method.

As expected, the code on lines 2–4 is used to prevent the method from executing if the class' configuration encountered an issue. The first branch of the if statement on line 6 that runs from lines 7 to 27 is meant to set the menu's highlighted UI element from an initial state where the keyBrdInput field is false. User input from the keyboard or controller will result in either the first or last selectable UI element being highlighted. The second branch of the main if statement that runs from lines 29 to 63 is used to process keyboard or controller input after the initial UI element is selected. This code supports cycling through the selectable UI elements either forward or backward. Lastly, on lines 61–63, the "Submit" input is detected, and the InvokeClick method is called with the currently selected menu item index as an argument. This method will invoke a click event on the target button.

Listing 8-16. GameHelpMenu Main Method Details 2

```
01 public new void InvokeClick(int current) {
02     if (current == 0) {
03         if (idx > 0) {
04             btnOne.onClick.Invoke();
05         }
06     } else if (current == 1) {
07         btnTwo.onClick.Invoke();
08     } else if (current == 2) {
09         if (idx < MAX_INDEX - 1) {
10             btnThree.onClick.Invoke();
11         }
12     }
13 }
```

```
01 public new void SetBtnTextColor(int prev, int current) {
02     if (prev == 0) {
03         img = btnOne.GetComponent<Image>();
04         img.color = Color.white;
05     } else if (prev == 1) {
06         txt = btnTwo.transform.GetChild(0).GetComponent<Text>();
07         txt.color = Color.black;
```

```
08    } else if (prev == 2) {
09        img = btnThree.GetComponent<Image>();
10        img.color = Color.white;
11    }
12
13    if (current == 0) {
14        img = btnOne.GetComponent<Image>();
15        img.color = Color.red;
16    } else if (current == 1) {
17        txt = btnTwo.transform.GetChild(0).GetComponent<Text>();
18        txt.color = Color.red;
19    } else if (current == 2) {
20        img = btnThree.GetComponent<Image>();
21        img.color = Color.red;
22    }
23 }
```

The second set of main methods for us to look at, listed previously, contains two methods. These methods are used to invoke button click events and set the text color of the menu's buttons to indicate a selected UI element. The first method we'll look into is the InvokeClick method. We've seen this method before in the BasePromptScript and GamePauseMenu classes. Note the new keyword in the method declaration. This indicates to the compiler that this method, inherited from the BasePromptScript class, is being redefined here. If we are asked to click the first button, line 2 of the method, this corresponds to the "Previous" button. Notice that we only invoke the click event if the help menu screen index is greater than 0. This means that we are not on the first screen so we can go back.

On lines 6–8, if the currently selected button index is 1, which corresponds to the "Main Menu" button, we process the click event without discretion. The last snippet of code on lines 8–12 performs a "Next" button click if there are more help menu screens to view. The next method, SetBtnTextColor, is responsible for setting the button text color on the specified button. It also resets the previous button's text color. The change in text color is used to highlight a menu button, indicating it's selected. The little code block on lines 2–11 is used to restore the text color on the previously selected button, while the block of code on lines 13–22 is used to set the text color of the currently selected button. That brings us to the conclusion of this review section. In the next section, we'll take a look at the class' demonstration.

Demonstration: GameHelpMenu

To demonstrate the GameHelpMenu class in action, the best thing for us to do is run the full game, scene "Main13" or "Main14", and launch the help menu by clicking the "Help" button on the start menu. Open the game project in the Unity editor, direct your attention to the "Project" panel and find the "Scenes" folder. Open one of the main scenes and run the game by pressing the Unity editor's play button. When the game starts, click the "Help" button as mentioned and launch the help menu screen. Try using the keyboard, controller, or mouse to interact with the menu's UI elements. Keep the code you just reviewed in mind as you do so.

Remaining Menu Classes

The remaining menu system classes are listed as follows:

1. GameStartMenu

2. GameHUDNewScript

3. GameHUDNewUiScript

I won't be reviewing these classes in detail here. The three remaining classes are very similar to the classes we've just reviewed. There isn't really any new general knowledge to gain from reviewing them; however, you should look them over and make sure you're familiar with them. Please be sure to do so. Try and view each menu screen in the actual game by using the approaches outlined in the demonstration sections of this chapter.

We didn't cover setting up a menu screen, as far as the objects and components in the Unity editor are concerned, but we will a little later on in the text. That brings us to the conclusion of this chapter. I want to recap what we've covered before we move on.

Chapter Conclusion

In this chapter, we managed to cover the main aspects of the game's menu system. And we knocked a few more points off of the game specification list in the process. Let's summarize the material we've covered in this chapter.

1. BasePromptScript: The base class used by most of the game's menu system. The class contains core, shared, functionality to simplify the implementation of the extending classes.

2. GamePauseMenu: This class is a concrete implementation of a two-option menu screen that uses the `BasePromptScript` as a base class. We also reviewed UI event abstraction as demonstrated by the class' ability to invoke click events on the menu screen's buttons.

3. GameHelpMenu: This class is an example of a more complex menu screen implementation. While this class also extends the `BasePromptScript` class, it overwrites much of the base class' functionality to support a three-button menu screen.

While we didn't cover every menu screen in the game, we covered a core set of examples that took us through the key common aspects of the menu system's implementation. Make sure you take a look at the classes we didn't cover here. Read through them carefully and follow along with the actual menu screen from the full game scenes, "Main13" or "Main14". We're almost done with the code portion of the text, but we have a lot of important ground to cover, so hang in there. In the next chapter, we'll begin our review of the heart of the game, the classes that manage the player and game states.

CHAPTER 9

Player and Game State Classes Part 1

In this chapter, we're going to take a look at the classes that are responsible for tracking the player and game states. There is a lot of code for us to review, so I've separated the review into two chapters. The classes involved with this two-chapter review are listed as follows:

1. PlayerInfo   (Chapter 09: Part 1)

2. TrackScript (Chapter 09: Part 1)

3. PlayerState (Chapter 09: Part 1)

4. GameState   (Chapter 10: Part 2)

The first two classes listed, PlayerInfo and TrackScript, are ancillary to the subsequent two classes, PlayerState and GameState. Because the first two classes are very simple and direct, we'll start with them. Let's get to it!

Class Review: PlayerInfo

The PlayerInfo class, as we've seen a few times before, is responsible for loosely associating a Unity game object with a player. To do so, this class holds the index of the associated player, in the array of available players stored in the GameState class. This class is short, so I'll just list it here.

Listing 9-1. PlayerInfo Class Review 1

```
01 using UnityEngine;
02
```

© Victor G Brusca 2022
V. G Brusca, *Advanced Unity Game Development*, https://doi.org/10.1007/978-1-4842-7851-2_9

```
03 public class PlayerInfo : MonoBehaviour {
04     public int playerIndex = 0;
05 }
```

Yup, it's that simple. It's actually deviously simple. Because the PlayerInfo class extends the MonoBehaviour class, it's a script component and can be attached to Unity game objects. When assigned to a game object in the Unity editor, you can set the value of the playerIndex field. This information can be found from the parent game object and used to look up the player's PlayerState object stored in the game's main class, the GameState class. We've seen this use case before during our review of the interaction classes. Next up, we'll take a look at the TrackScript class. This class is another MonoBehaviour used to hold information related to the state of the game, more specifically settings that are associated with the current racetrack.

Class Review: TrackScript

The TrackScript class is another simple state class that is used to hold basic configuration information about the current racetrack. This class is short and sweet, so we'll just list it here in its entirety.

Listing 9-2. TrackScript Class Review 1

```
1 using UnityEngine;
2
3 public class TrackScript : MonoBehaviour {
4     public int index = 0;
5     public bool headLightsOn = false;
6     public int laps = 3;
7     public string sceneName = "";
8 }
```

The TrackScript is expected to reside on the GameState Unity game object next to instances of the GameState and PlayerState components as shown here.

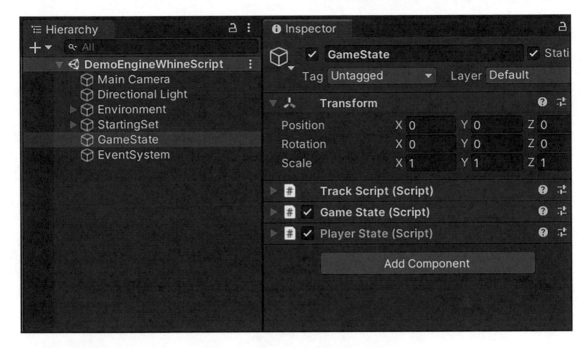

Figure 9-1. *GameState Unity Game Object Configuration*

A screenshot depicting the setup of the GameState game object. It shows the GameState, PlayerState, and TrackScript MonoBehaviours, script components, attached to the same parent game object as required

The GameState class is responsible for loading and processing the data stored in the associated TrackScript component. The class' first field, index, is not currently being used by the game. Feel free to implement some index specific code like atmospheric effects or different background music. The next field listed, headLightsOn, is a Boolean flag used to indicate if the hover racer's headlights should be turned on for the current track. Subsequently, the laps field is used to suggest the number of laps that the current track has. I say suggest because the track difficulty and mode will also affect the number of laps for a given racetrack. Lastly, the sceneName field can be used to provide a name for the current track/scene. The next class we'll look at is the PlayerState class. This class is a monster, so be prepared for a lengthy class view.

Class Review: PlayerState

The PlayerState class is a MonoBehaviour class through extension of the BaseScript class. It is used to track the state of a player throughout the game. Because of this, the class has a large number of fields tracking all manner of values related to the car's movement and state. Because the PlayerState class is so complex, we'll use the more structured review process and follow these steps to review it:

1. Static/Constants/Read-Only Class Members

2. Class Fields

3. Pertinent Method Outline/Class Headers

4. Support Method Details

5. Main Method Details

6. Demonstration

There are no pertinent enumerations to speak of, so we'll omit that section. I should take a moment to mention that there are a lot, like almost too many, class fields to review. Don't get overwhelmed by this, we'll cover everything slowly and in detail. Don't think you have to have it all in your brain after the first reading. You'll most likely have to reference this class review a few times while working with the game's code. For the most part, you won't have to adjust these fields at all, so just think of it as us being thorough. And with that, let's get started.

Static/Constants/Read-Only Class Members: PlayerState

The PlayerState class has a number of static and read-only class fields. These fields are used for finding resources, tracking certain modifiers, and values that define the type of race that's running.

Listing 9-3. PlayerState Static/Constants/Read-Only Class Members 1

```
public static bool SHOW_AI_LOGIC = true;
public static readonly int TYPE_SPEED_SLOW = 0;
public static readonly int TYPE_SPEED_NORM = 1;
public static readonly int TYPE_SPEED_BOOST = 2;
public static readonly int TYPE_PLAYER_HUMAN = 0;
```

```
public static readonly int TYPE_PLAYER_COMPUTER = 1;
public static readonly int TYPE_CAR_HOVER_GREEN = 0;
public static readonly int TYPE_CAR_HOVER_BLACK = 3;
public static readonly int TYPE_CAR_HOVER_RED = 4;
public static readonly int TYPE_CAR_HOVER_PURPLE = 5;
public static readonly int DEFAULT_POSITION = 0;
public static readonly float DEFAULT_MAX_SPEED = 200.0f;

public static readonly float DEFAULT_GRAVITY = 11.0f;
public static float LIMIT_MAX_SPEED = 300.0f;
```

The first set of static class fields for us to look at is listed previously. The first entry, SHOW_AI_LOGIC, is used to control the display of the AI-controlled car's driving calculations. This is actually a really cool feature. Set this field's value to true before running the full version of the game, scene "Main13" or "Main14". Open the scene and run it. While the AI hover racers run the track, change to the Unity editor's "Scene" panel. Make sure that you have a top-down view of the racetrack and are zoomed out so that you can see a large portion of the track. Follow the hover racers as they make their way around the track, and you should notice little green lines directed from the cars to the next few waypoints. These lines are part of the car's AI driving logic calculations.

Now that we've gone over that, let's get back to the class' fields. Up next are three entries that are used to represent slow, normal, or boost speeds. The following two entries, those starting with "TYPE_PLAYER_", are used to indicate the type of the current player, AI or human controlled. Subsequently, there are four entries that are used to indicate the type of race car used for the given player. The DEFAULT_POSITION field is used to provide a default position value for the current player. The next two entries, DEFAULT_MAX_SPEED and DEFAULT_GRAVITY, are used to provide default values for the hover racer's gravity and max speed values. The last entry listed in this set is used to represent the limit on a player's maximum speed. Let's move on to the next set of fields to review.

Listing 9-4. PlayerState Static/Constants/Read-Only Class Members 2

```
public readonly int MAX_IS_MISS_TIME = 2;
public readonly int MAX_IS_SHOT_TIME = 2;
public readonly int MAX_IS_HIT_TIME = 2;
public readonly int MAX_IS_LAP_COMPLETE_TIME = 6;
public static readonly int DEFAULT_LIFE_AMOUNT = 3;
```

```
public readonly int INVINC_SECONDS = 10;
public static readonly int DEFAULT_DAMAGE_AMOUNT = 0;
public readonly float MIN_STUCK_DISTANCE = 30.0f;
public readonly float MIN_STUCK_TIME = 3.0f;
public readonly float MIN_WAYPOINT_DISTANCE = 30.0f;
public readonly int MAX_SPEED_BONUS_DRAFTING = 4;
public readonly int MAX_SPEED_BONUS_PASSING = 20;
public readonly float MAX_SMOKE_TIME = 1000.0f;
public readonly int MAX_GAINED_LIFE_TIME = 2;
public static readonly string AUDIO_CLIP_CAR_SOUND1 = "CarAirNonGapless";

public static readonly string AUDIO_CLIP_CAR_SOUND2 = "car_idle_lp_01";

public static readonly string AUDIO_CLIP_GUN_SHOT = "explosion_short_blip_
rnd_01";
```

The previously listed set of static/read-only class fields starts with four maximum timing values. These fields begin with the text "MAX_IS_". These fields hold maximum timing values for battle mode notifications miss, shot, hit, and the lap complete time notification. Next up, we have the DEFAULT_LIFE AMOUNT field that sets the starting life point total for players. The INVINC_SECONDS field is used to set a maximum limit on how long the invincibility modifier is active. Following this field is the DEFAULT_DAMAGE_ AMOUNT field that is used to prepare each player's damage points.

Subsequently, we have a set of minimum value read-only fields. The MIN_STUCK_ DISTANCE field represents a distance value used to determine if the current player's hover racer has not moved a sufficient distance and is now stuck. Similarly, the MIN_STUCK_ TIME field is used to set a minimum time the player's hover racer hasn't moved to be marked as stuck. Both fields are used to determine if the player is stuck or not. The last min value entry, MIN_WAYPOINT_DISTANCE, is the minimum distance you can be from a waypoint before it's considered to be the "next" waypoint on the track.

The next four fields for us to look at are maximum values used to set limits on a few of the hover racer's behaviors. The first two of these entries are used to set a limit on the speed bonus received from drafting and passing another hover racer. The next of the max fields, MAX_SMOKE_TIME, is used to set a limit on how long the gunshot smoke effect will last. This particle effect has been commented out and is left for the reader to implement. Similarly, the MAX_GAINED_LIFE_TIME field is used to set a limit on how long the gained life notification will last.

The last three entries in this set of static fields are used to locate AudioSource components with the specified name. That brings us to the conclusion of the static class members review section. In the next section, we'll start the review of the class' remaining fields.

Class Fields: PlayerState

The PlayerState class has a number of fields left for us to review. There are a ton of them. They are used to control, track, and model all aspects of the hover racer's behavior for both AI and human-controlled players. Let's get to it!

Listing 9-5. PlayerState Class Fields 1

```
//***** Class Fields *****
public int index = 0;
public GameObject player;
public bool active = true;
public float offTrackSeconds = 6.0f;
public float wrongDirectionSeconds = 6.0f;

//***** Input Class Fields *****
public CharacterController controller;
public CharacterMotor cm;
public MouseLookNew mouseInput;
public FPSInputController fpsInput;
public Transform home;
private bool hasSetHome = false;
public bool pause = false;

//***** Car Descriptor Class Fields *****
//0 = slow, 1 = norm, 2 = boost
public int speedType = TYPE_SPEED_SLOW;

//0 = human, 1 = computer
public int playerType = TYPE_PLAYER_HUMAN;
```

```
//0 = green hover, 1 = red hover, 2 = black hover,
//3 = black hover, 4 = red hover, 5 = purple hover
public int carType = TYPE_CAR_HOVER_GREEN;

//***** Speed Class Fields *****
public float speed = 0.0f;
public float speedPrct = 0.0f;
public float speedPrctLimit = 0.0f;
public float maxSpeed = DEFAULT_MAX_SPEED;
public int position = DEFAULT_POSITION;
public float gravity = DEFAULT_GRAVITY;
```

The first set of fields for us to review starts with a group of general class fields. The first field is the all-important index field. This field is used to indicate which player, in the array of available players, this player state instance is associated with. The next field, a GameObject instance, player, is used to hold a reference to the Unity game object representing the player. In this case, this is the hover racer model.

The Boolean flag active is used to indicate if the player is active. Following that field is the offTrackSeconds field. This field describes the number of seconds a car has been off track before the off-track notification is shown. Subsequently, wrongDirectionSeconds represents the number of seconds a car has to be going the wrong direction before the wrong direction notification is displayed.

The next group of fields we'll look at are the input class fields. The controller field is a CharacterController instance for the current player. Next, there is a CharacterMotor instance, cm. We also have instances of MouseLookNew, mouseInput, and FPSInputController, fpsInput, to round out our control classes. The home field, a Transform instance, is used to record the player's home or starting position.

The Boolean flag hasSetHome is used to indicate if the home position has been set. Next, the pause field is a Boolean flag indicating if the player is paused. The following group of class fields is the car descriptor class fields. The first such field is the speedType field. This field has a value of 0, 1, or 2, which represents speeds slow, norm, or boost. Similarly, the playerType field is an integer value with 0 representing a human player and 1 representing a computer player.

The last field in this group is the carType field. This field is used to describe the type of car the player is racing. In our case, it describes the color of the hover racer. The values are noted in the comments by the field definition listed previously. The last group of fields we have to look at in this set are the speed class fields. These fields are used to represent different speed-related characteristics, values, and limits. The speed field represents the speed of the player's car. The speedPrct field is used to represent what percentage of the hover racer's maximum speed the car is currently traveling. The speedPrctLimit field is similar except it represents the percentage of the LIMIT_MAX_SPEED value the car is currently traveling.

The maxSpeed field is used to hold the car's current maximum speed. Next, the position field represents the car's current position in the race, and the gravity field is used to represent the car's gravity. That brings us to the next set of class fields to review. I'll list them here.

Listing 9-6. PlayerState Class Fields 2

```
//***** Time Class Fields *****
public string time;
public int timeNum;
public float totalTime = 0;
public float hour = 0;
public float min = 0;
public float s = 0;
public float ms = 0;

//***** Off Track Class Fields *****
public bool offTrack = false;
public float offTrackTime = 0.0f;

//***** Wrong Direction Class Fields *****
public bool wrongDirection = false;
public float wrongDirectionTime = 0.0f;

//***** Skipped Waypoint Class Fields *****
public bool skippedWaypoint = false;
public float skippedWaypointTime = 0.0f;

//***** Cameras and Objects Class Fields *****
public GameObject gun;
public GameObject gunBase;
public new Camera camera;
```

```
public Camera rearCamera;
public GameObject car;
public GameObject carSensor;
```

The next set of class fields for us to look at is used track the time the current player has been racing on the track. The first entry, `time`, is a string representation of the player's lap time. The following field, `timeNum`, is a single large integer representation of the player's lap time. Next, the `totalTime` field represents the total duration of time, in milliseconds, on the given lap. The individual components of the current track time are subsequently listed. The first entry, `hour`, indicates the number of hours spent on the current track. Hopefully not too many.

Following that, the `min` class field tracks the number of minutes spent on the current track, while the next two fields, `s` and `ms`, are used to indicate the second and millisecond components of the time spent racing the current track. The next three groups of fields are used to track the player's off-track, wrong direction, and skipped waypoint states. The off-track class fields are up for review next. The first entry in this group is the `offTrack` field. This field is a Boolean flag used to indicate the player is off of the racetrack. The second field in this group indicates the amount of time the current player has been off the track.

Following this group of fields are the wrong direction class fields. In a similar pattern to that of the off-track fields, the wrong direction fields consist of a Boolean flag and a timing value, `wrongDirection` and `wrongDirectionTime` fields. The next group of fields, the skipped waypoint class fields, also consists of a Boolean flag and a time tracking field. This group contains the `wrongDirection` and `wrongDirectionTime` fields. The next group of fields, the skipped waypoint class fields, similarly, also consists of a Boolean flag and a time tracking field. These are the `skippedWaypoint` and `skippedWaypointTime` class fields. This pattern is used frequently to measure the duration of some functionality then toggle a Boolean field to turn that functionality on or off.

Next up is a group of fields that represent the cameras and objects associated with the player's hover racer. The first such field is the `GameObject` instance, gun. This field is a reference to the car's gun object. This object comes into play during the game's battle mode. The next field is the `GameObject` instance, gunBase. This is also a reference to a game object, in this case, the base model that the gun rests on. We have a particularly important field listed next, `camera`. This camera is positioned inside the hover racer's cockpit. It's used as the main camera during game play.

The next field is the `rearCamera` field. This camera is used as the hover racer's rear-view camera. Next, we have the ever-important `car` field. This field references the game object that represents the player in the race. Their hover racer. The next and last field in this group is the `carSensor` game object that represents the car's forward-looking sensor. We've looked at this earlier during advanced interaction classes review, Chapter 5. Let's move on to the next set of class fields.

Listing 9-7. PlayerState Class Fields 3

```
//***** Car Status Class Fields *****
public int ammo = 0;
public bool gunOn = false;
public bool isBouncing = false;
public bool isJumping = false;
public bool isDrafting = false;
public bool isShot = false;
public float isShotTime = 0.0f;
public bool isHit = false;
public float isHitTime = 0.0f;
public bool isMiss = false;
public float isMissTime = 0.0f;

public bool lapComplete = false;
public float lapCompleteTime = 0.0f;
public bool armorOn = false;
public bool boostOn = false;
public bool invincOn = false;
public float invincTime = 0.0f;
public int lifeTotal = DEFAULT_LIFE_AMOUNT;
public int damage = DEFAULT_DAMAGE_AMOUNT;
public int points = 0;
public bool alive = true;
```

This group of class fields has to do with the hover racer's current state. The first field indicates the amount of ammo the player has. The next field, gunOn, is used to indicate if the gun modifier is active or not. The next three fields (isBouncing, isJumping, and isDrafting) are used in the same manner as the gunOn field we just reviewed. The next six fields in the group follow the same pattern we've previously seen regarding track and waypoint indicators.

In each case, there is a Boolean flag and a time tracking field for shooting, hit, and miss events. Please note that these events are only available in the game's battle mode. The next two fields, lapComplete and lapCompleteTime, follow the same exact pattern we've just seen. The next field, lapComplete, indicates that the lap has been completed, while the following, lapCompleteTime, tracks the duration of the lap. The armorOn and boostOn fields are Boolean flags used to indicate that the given modifier is active or inactive. The invinvOn and invincTime fields follow the same pattern we've seen and include a Boolean flag and a timing field.

The lifeTotal field indicates the player's life point total. The damage field is an integer value that indicates the amount of damage the current car has received. The points field is not actively used by the game but is available for you to use as you see fit. Similarly, the Boolean flag alive is intended to be used to indicate if the current player is still alive, but it's not actively used by the game. The next set of class fields we'll take a look at is the speed and waypoint-related fields. I'll list them here.

Listing 9-8. PlayerState Class Fields 4

```
//***** Speed Class Fields *****
public int maxForwardSpeedSlow = 50;
public int maxSidewaysSpeedSlow = 12;
public int maxBackwardsSpeedSlow = 5;
public int maxGroundAccelerationSlow = 25;
public int maxForwardSpeedNorm = 200;
public int maxSidewaysSpeedNorm = 50;
public int maxBackwardsSpeedNorm = 20;
public int maxGroundAccelerationNorm = 100;
public int maxForwardSpeedBoost = 250;
public int maxSidewaysSpeedBoost = 60;
public int maxBackwardsSpeedBoost = 30;
public int maxGroundAccelerationBoost = 120;

//***** Waypoint Class Fields *****
public ArrayList waypoints = null;
public float waypointDistance = 0.0f;
public float waypointDistancePrev = 0.0f;
```

The next set of class fields for us to review, listed previously, contains two groups of fields. These fields are used in tracking the player's speed and waypoint interactions. The different speed fields fall into three categories: slow, norm, and boost. Each category has four entries. Regarding the slow speed, we have the maxForwardSpeedSlow field that holds a value used for the forward slow speed. Following this we have sideways and backwards speeds for the slow speed category. The last field in this category is the ground acceleration speed slow field.

The same exact entries exist for the norm and boost speed categories. The norm speeds are used for on-track movement. The slow speeds are used for off-track movement. And lastly, the boost speeds are used for movement when the car has an active boost modifier. The next three fields are associated with the waypoint system of the track. The first entry is an ArrayList instance used to hold references to all of the track's waypoints.

The following two fields are used to track the distance between the car and the next waypoint, waypointDistance and waypointDistancePrev. The previous waypoint distance calculation is stored in the waypointDistancePrev field as you might have guessed. These calculations are used as part of the waypoint calculation and AI system, which brings us to the next group of class fields for us to review, the AI fields.

Listing 9-9. PlayerState Class Fields 5

```
//***** AI Class Fields Part 1 *****
public bool aiOn = false;
public int aiWaypointTime = 0;
public int aiWaypointLastIndex = -1;
public int aiWaypointIndex = 0; //0 = first node
public int aiWaypointRoute = 0;
public float aiTurnStrength = 1.0f;

public float aiSpeedStrength = 1.0f;
public float aiStrafeStrength = 0.0f;
public float aiSlide = 0.0f;

//0 = looking, 1 = testing, 2 = acting
public int aiIsStuckMode = 0;
public bool aiIsStuck = false;
public float aiWaypointDistance = 0f;
```

```
public Vector3 aiRelativePoint = Vector3.zero;
public float aiTime1 = 0.0f;
public float aiTime2 = 0.0f;
public float aiSlowDownTime = 0.0f;
public float aiSlowDown = 0.0f;
public bool aiSlowDownOn = false;
```

The next group of fields for us to review are the first set of AI class fields. These fields are used by the game's AI system to move, calculate the move of, or report the status of AI-controlled hover racers. The first entry, aiOn, is a Boolean flag indicating if the hover racer's AI mode is on. The aiWaypointTime field holds an integer representation that's a copy of the current player's current timeNum field. The next two fields, aiWaypointpointLastIndex and aiWaypointIndex, are used to track the player's previous and current waypoint index. These are triggered by the player's hover racer, interacting with waypoint objects. I should note that although I'm saying "player's," this also means an AI opponent player and not just a human player.

The aiWaypointRoute field is used to load waypoints for the specified route. This feature is not really used in the game as implemented; rather, the route is always set to zero. Feel free to expand on this functionality if you'd like. The next field, aiTurnStrength, is not implemented by the game currently but could be used as part of the AI steering calculations. The following field, aiSpeedStrength, is used by the game's AI calculations to control the hover racer's speed vector.

Similarly, the aiStrafeStrength field is used to control the strafe component of the AI-controlled hover racer's calculated speed vector. The aiSlide field provides the AI with a sliding component to use in velocity calculations. In handling "stuck" hover racers, we run through some checks over time to indicate that the car is stuck. The aiIsStuckMode field helps keep track of the is-stuck check that's being performed.

Ultimately, the result of the "is-stuck" calculation is stored in the aiIsStuck field. Next, we have the aiWaypointDistance field that is used to track distance to the next waypoint in AI mode. The aiRelativePoint field is used to determine what aiStrafeStrength should be used when the AI is steering the hover racer. The next two fields, aiTime1 and aiTime2, are used in tracking time intervals, for instance, when checking the different aiIsStuckModes. The last two fields in this group are the aiSlowDownTime and aiSlowDown fields. These fields are used to control the hover racer's speed on turns. The aiSlowDownTime field measures the duration of the current slowdown. The next field, aiSlowDown, is a value indicating how much the car should slow down. The value is driven by the track's waypoint markers. Lastly, the `aiSlowDownOn` field is used to indicate that the slowdown modifier is currently on. We have a few more AI fields to review. I'll list the next set here.

Listing 9-10. PlayerState Class Fields 6

```
//***** AI Class Fields Part 2 *****
public float aiSlowDownDuration = 100.0f;
public bool aiIsPassing = false;
public float aiPassingTime = 0.0f;
public int aiPassingMode = 0;
public bool aiHasTarget = false;
public float aiHasTargetTime = 0.0f;

public bool aiIsReloading = false;
public float aiIsReloadingTime = 0.0f;
public bool aiHasGainedLife = false;
public float aiHasGainedLifeTime = 0.0f;
public bool aiIsLargeTurn = false;
public float aiIsLargeTurnSpeed = 0.0f;

public float aiLastLookAngle = 0.0f;
public float aiNextLookAngle = 0.0f;
public float aiNext2LookAngle = 0.0f;
public float aiMidLookAngle = 0.0f;
public float aiMid2LookAngle = 0.0f;
public bool aiCanFire = false;

public float aiBoostTime = 0.0f;
public int aiBoostMode = 0;
public int aiWaypointJumpCount = 0;
public int aiWaypointPassCount = 0;
```

We've covered a ton of class fields and we're almost done, so hang in there. We still have two more sets of fields to review. The remaining AI fields are listed previously. The first entry brings us back to the slowdown fields. The `aiSlowDownDuration` field is used to track the hover racer's slowdown. This value is set on AI-controlled cars by the track's waypoint markers. The next three entries are fields that have to do with the AI hover racer's passing modifier. The aiIsPassing field is a Boolean flag indicating that the AI car is in passing mode. The aiPassingTime field is then used to measure the duration of time spent passing the hover racer in front of the current car. Related to these two fields is the aiPassingMode field that sets the mode of the passing attempt.

The next two variables follow a pattern we've seen before. The aiHasTarget field indicates a target has been set, while the aiHasTargetTime field is used to measure the duration that target has been active. Following this pair are two more Boolean flag and time duration field sets. Take a look at them, reloading and life gain. Large turns are detected from the AI-controlled car's turning angles. The angle determines the value of the aiLargeTurnSpeed field. This mechanism is used to help control the car's speed on certain turns with large angles.

Look over the next five fields. These are all float values designed to hold angles based on the calculations between the hover racer's direction and the distance to the next waypoints. The aiCanFire Boolean is used to indicate if the car is able to fire a shot. This is only available in the game's battle mode variation. The next pair of fields, aiBoostMode and aiBoostTime, follows a similar structure to the Boolean flag, time duration field sets seen previously. In this case, the mode determines the behavior, and the time field tracks the duration. The aiWaypointPassCount field tracks the number of waypoints passed in a somewhat dumb way. It doesn't track repeats and jumps well, but it can be used to make determinations based on how its value changes. There is one remaining set of class fields for use to review.

Listing 9-11. PlayerState Class Fields 7

```
//***** Other Class Fields *****
public GameObject gunExplosion = null;
public GameObject gunHitSmoke = null;
public bool gunSmokeOn = false;
public float gunSmokeTime = 0.0f;
//public ParticleEmitter gunExplosionParticleSystem = null;

//public ParticleEmitter gunHitSmokeParticleSystem = null;

public GameObject flame = null;
public int totalLaps = 3;
public int currentLap = 0;
```

```
public bool prepped = false;
public GameObject lightHeadLight = null;

public AudioListener audioListener = null;
public AudioSource audioGunHit = null;
public AudioSource audioCarSound1 = null;
public AudioSource audioCarSound2 = null;
```

The last set of class fields we'll review are the "other" class fields. The gunExplosion and gunHitSmoke fields are game object references that point to objects in the player's hover racer, specifically the car's hierarchy of Unity GameObjects. The next two fields should look familiar. They follow the same pattern we've seen before. This pair of fields, gunSmokeOn and gunSmokeTime, is used to control the gun's smoke effect. This feature is currently disabled in the game. I'll explain. This feature was implemented in a legacy way that has since gone away. We've left the code that powers it in place but commented out so that you can use it to add new up-to-date particle effects to the game and supporting code. The next field is the GameObject flame that references part of the hover racer's model structure. The totalLaps field has a value indicating the number of laps the current race has.

Similarly, the currentLap field indicates what lap the current player is on. The Boolean flag prepped is used to indicate that the player has been prepped and is ready to go. As you may have imagined, the lightHeadLight field is used to turn the car's headlamp on or off. Wrapping up this set of fields, and the field review section, are the audio listener and sound resource fields used by the player's hover racer. Congratulations, you've made it to the end of this review section. In the next section, we'll take a look at the class' pertinent method outline.

Pertinent Method Outline/Class Header: PlayerState

The PlayerState class has few methods for us to review. I'll list them here.

Listing 9-12. PlayerState Pertinent Method Outline/Class Headers 1

```
//Main Methods
void Start();
public bool PerformGunShotHit();
public Vector3 UpdateAiFpsController();
```

```
public void MoveToCurrentWaypoint();
public void MoveToWaypoint(int index);
public void UpdateAiMouseLook();
public void Update();
public void Reset();

//Support Methods
public void LoadAudio();
public void PauseSound();
public void UnPauseSound();
public bool IsValidWaypointIndex(int index);
public void StampWaypointTime();
public void PlayGunShotHitAudio();
public WaypointCheck GetCurrentWaypointCheck();
public void PerformLookAt(WaypointCheck wc);
public void ResetTime();
public int GetLife();
public int GetLifeHUD();
public int GetLapsLeft();
public void SetDraftingBonusOn();
public void SetDraftingBonusOff();
public void SetBoostOn();
public void SetBoostOff();
public void SetCurrentSpeed();
public void ShowInvinc();
public void HideInvinc();
public void ShowGun();
public void HideGun();
public void SetSlow();
public void SetNorm();
public void SetBoost();
private int GetPastWaypointIndex(int wpIdx);
```

There are certainly a lot of support methods for us to review, but since most of them are really simple and direct, we'll get through them quickly.

Listing 9-13. PlayerState Pertinent Method Outline/Class Headers 2

```
using System.Collections;
using UnityEngine;

public class PlayerState : BaseScript {}
```

Note that the PlayerState class extends the BaseScript class inheriting some standard functionality that we've seen before during previous class reviews. In the next review section, we'll take a look at the class' support methods.

Support Method Details: PlayerState

The PlayerState class has a number of support methods for us to look at. A couple of these methods are very simple, so I'll list them here, but we won't do an in-depth review on them due to their simplicity. Please take the time to review them carefully. Don't move on unless you understand what these methods do and how they are used.

Listing 9-14. PlayerState Support Method Details 1

```
01 public void PauseSound() {
02     if (audioCarSound1 != null) {
03         audioCarSound1.Stop();
04     }
05
06     if (audioCarSound2 != null) {
07         audioCarSound2.Stop();
08     }
09 }
```

```
01 public void UnPauseSound() {
02     if (audioCarSound1 != null) {
03         audioCarSound1.Play();
04     }
05
06     if (audioCarSound2 != null) {
07         audioCarSound2.Play();
08     }
09 }
```

```
01 public bool IsValidWaypointIndex(int index) {
02     if (waypoints == null) {
03         waypoints = gameState.GetWaypoints(aiWaypointRoute);
04     }
05
06     if (waypoints != null && index >= 0 && index <= (waypoints.Count - 1)) {
07         return true;
08     } else {
09         return false;
10     }
11 }
```

```
01 public void StampWaypointTime() {
02     aiWaypointTime = timeNum;
03 }
```

```
01 public void PlayGunShotHitAudio() {
02     if (audioGunHit != null) {
03         if (audioGunHit.isPlaying == false) {
04             audioGunHit.Play();
05         }
06     }
07 }
```

```
01 public WaypointCheck GetCurrentWaypointCheck() {
02     if (waypoints != null) {
03         return (WaypointCheck)waypoints[aiWaypointIndex];
04     } else {
05         return null;
06     }
07 }
```

```
01 public void PerformLookAt(WaypointCheck wc) {
02     wcVpla = wc.transform.position;
03     wcVpla.y = player.transform.position.y;
04     player.transform.LookAt(wcVpla);
05 }
```

```
01 public void ResetTime() {
02     totalTime = 0f;
03 }
```

```
01 public int GetLife() {
02     return (lifeTotal - damage);
03 }
```

```
01 public int GetLifeHUD() {
02     return (lifeTotal - damage);
03 }
```

```
01 public int GetLapsLeft() {
02     return (totalLaps - currentLap);
03 }
```

```
01 public void SetDraftingBonusOn() {
02     isDrafting = true;
03     SetCurrentSpeed();
04 }
```

```
01 public void SetDraftingBonusOff() {
02     isDrafting = false;
03     SetCurrentSpeed();
04 }
```

```
01 public void SetBoostOn() {
02     boostOn = true;
03     SetBoost();
04 }
```

```
01 public void SetBoostOff() {
02     boostOn = false;
03     SetNorm();
04 }
```

```
01 public void SetCurrentSpeed() {
02     if (speedType == 0) {
03         SetSlow();
```

```
04      } else if (speedType == 1) {
05          SetNorm();
06      } else if (speedType == 2) {
07          SetBoost();
08      }
09  }
```

```
01  public void ShowInvinc() {
02      invincOn = true;
03      invincTime = 0f;
04  }
```

```
01  public void HideInvinc() {
02      invincOn = false;
03      invincTime = 0f;
04  }
```

```
01  public void ShowGun() {
02      gunOn = true;
03      if (gun != null) {
04          gun.SetActive(true);
05      }
06
07      if (gunBase != null) {
08          gunBase.SetActive(true);
09      }
10  }
```

```
01  public void HideGun() {
02      gunOn = false;
03      if (gun != null) {
04          gun.SetActive(false);
05      }
06
07      if (gunBase != null) {
08          gunBase.SetActive(false);
09      }
10  }
```

These support methods are simple in their nature. Most are only a few lines of code. I won't review them in any detail here. Please read them over and make sure you understand them and that they make sense to you before you move on. We'll move on to the more complex support methods. Let's take a look!

Listing 9-15. PlayerState Support Method Details 2

```
01 public void LoadAudio() {
02     audioSetLa = player.GetComponents<AudioSource>();
03     if (audioSetLa != null) {
04         lLa = audioSetLa.Length;
05         for (iLa = 0; iLa < lLa; iLa++) {
06             aSLa = (AudioSource)audioSetLa[iLa];
07             if (aSLa != null) {
08                 if (aSLa.clip.name == AUDIO_CLIP_GUN_SHOT) {
09                     audioGunHit = aSLa;
10                 } else if (aSLa.clip.name == AUDIO_CLIP_CAR_SOUND1) {
11                     audioCarSound1 = aSLa;
12                 } else if (aSLa.clip.name == AUDIO_CLIP_CAR_SOUND2) {
13                     audioCarSound2 = aSLa;
14                 }
15             }
16         }
17     }
18 }
```

```
01 public void SetSlow() {
02     if (BaseScript.IsActive(scriptName) == false) {
03         return;
04     }
05
06     if (cm == null) {
07         return;
08     }
09
```

```
10    speedType = 0;
11    cm.movement.maxForwardSpeed = maxForwardSpeedSlow;
12    if (isDrafting == true) {
13       cm.movement.maxForwardSpeed += MAX_SPEED_BONUS_DRAFTING;
14    }
15
16    if (aiIsPassing == true) {
17       cm.movement.maxForwardSpeed += MAX_SPEED_BONUS_PASSING;
18    }
19    cm.movement.maxSidewaysSpeed = maxSidewaysSpeedSlow;
20    cm.movement.maxBackwardsSpeed = maxBackwardsSpeedSlow;
21    cm.movement.maxGroundAcceleration = maxGroundAccelerationSlow;
22 }

01 public void SetNorm() {
02    if (BaseScript.IsActive(scriptName) == false) {
03       return;
04    }
05
06    if (cm == null) {
07       return;
08    }
09
10    speedType = 1;
11    cm.movement.maxForwardSpeed = maxForwardSpeedNorm;
12    if (isDrafting == true) {
13       cm.movement.maxForwardSpeed += MAX_SPEED_BONUS_DRAFTING;
14    }
15
16    if (aiIsPassing == true) {
17       cm.movement.maxForwardSpeed += MAX_SPEED_BONUS_PASSING;
18    }
19    cm.movement.maxSidewaysSpeed = maxSidewaysSpeedNorm;
20    cm.movement.maxBackwardsSpeed = maxBackwardsSpeedNorm;
21    cm.movement.maxGroundAcceleration = maxGroundAccelerationNorm;
22 }
```

```
01 public void SetBoost() {
02     if (BaseScript.IsActive(scriptName) == false) {
03         return;
04     }
05
06     if (cm == null) {
07         return;
08     }
09
10     speedType = 2;
11     cm.movement.maxForwardSpeed = maxForwardSpeedBoost;
12     if (isDrafting == true) {
13         cm.movement.maxForwardSpeed += MAX_SPEED_BONUS_DRAFTING;
14     }
15
16     if (aiIsPassing == true) {
17         cm.movement.maxForwardSpeed += MAX_SPEED_BONUS_PASSING;
18     }
19     cm.movement.maxSidewaysSpeed = maxSidewaysSpeedBoost;
20     cm.movement.maxBackwardsSpeed = maxBackwardsSpeedBoost;
21     cm.movement.maxGroundAcceleration = maxGroundAccelerationBoost;
22 }
```

```
01 private int GetPastWaypointIndex(int wpIdx) {
02     if (wpIdx - 5 >= 0) {
03         wpIdx -= 5;
04     } else if (wpIdx - 4 >= 0) {
05         wpIdx -= 4;
06     } else if (wpIdx - 3 >= 0) {
07         wpIdx -= 3;
08     } else if (wpIdx - 2 >= 0) {
09         wpIdx -= 2;
10     } else if (wpIdx - 1 >= 0) {
11         wpIdx -= 1;
```

```
12     } else {
13         wpIdx = 0;
14     }
15     return wpIdx;
16 }
```

The first of our more complex support methods, listed previously, is the LoadAudio method. This method is used to load audio resources for use as certain of the hover racer's sound effects. On line 2 of the method, we get a list of AudioSource components attached to the player object. Looping over the resulting array, we look for three specific sound files and store the reference in class fields, lines 9, 11, and 13.

The next three methods, listed previously, are used to update the speed of the current player's car. The first entry, SetSlow, is used to set the hover racer to a slow speed when it goes off the track. The very familiar, or should be, code on lines 2–4 prevents this method from doing any work if the class has not been configured properly. On lines 6–8, we exit the method if the character motor field, cm, is undefined.

Next, the speedType field is updated with a value representing the slow, normal, or boost speed on line 10. The new forward speed is calculated taking into account drafting and passing on lines 11–18. The remaining of the hover racer's speed-related fields are updated on lines 19–21 at the end of the method. I've listed the SetNorm and SetBoost methods following the SetSlow method. These methods are nearly identical to the SetSlow method, so we won't review them here. Instead, we'll leave their review up to you. Please make sure you understand the method before moving on.

The last method listed in this section is the GetPastWaypointIndex method. This method is responsible for finding past waypoints. It tries to find a valid waypoint five indexes behind the player's current waypoint index. If the determined index value is not valid, then a waypoint four indexes behind the player's current waypoint index is checked and so on. That brings us to the conclusion of this review section. Up next, we'll take a look at the class' main methods.

Main Method Details: PlayerState

The PlayerState class has a few main methods that are responsible for configuring and updating class fields among other things. Let's take a look at the first group of main methods up for review.

Listing 9-16. PlayerState Main Method Details 1

```
01 void Start() {
02    base.Prep(this.GetType().Name);
03    if (BaseScript.IsActive(scriptName) == false) {
04        Utilities.wrForce(scriptName + ": Is Deactivating...");
05        return;
06    }
07 }

01 public bool PerformGunShotHit() {
02    if (armorOn == true) {
03        armorOn = false;
04        isShot = true;
05        gunSmokeOn = true;
06        gunSmokeTime = 0.0f;
07        gunHitSmoke.SetActive(true);
08        //gunHitSmokeParticleSystem.Emit();
09        return true;
10    } else {
11        if (invincOn == true) {
12            return false;
13        } else {
14            damage++;
15            isShot = true;
16            gunSmokeOn = true;
17            gunSmokeTime = 0.0f;
18            gunHitSmoke.SetActive(true);
19            //gunHitSmokeParticleSystem.Emit();
20            PlayGunShotHitAudio();
21
22            if (GetLife() <= 0) {
23                aiWaypointIndex = GetPastWaypointIndex(aiWaypointIndex);
24                damage = 0;
```

```
25              if (aiWaypointIndex >= 0 && aiWaypointIndex < waypoints.
                Count) {
26                  MoveToCurrentWaypoint();
27              }
28          }
29          return true;
30      }
31   }
32 }
```

```
01 public void MoveToWaypoint(int index) {
02     aiWaypointIndex = index;
03     MoveToCurrentWaypoint();
04 }
```

```
01 public void MoveToCurrentWaypoint() {
02     if (BaseScript.IsActive(scriptName) == false) {
03         return;
04     }
05
06     pause = true;
07     WaypointCheck wc = (WaypointCheck)waypoints[aiWaypointIndex];
08     Vector3 wcV = wc.transform.position;
09     wcV.y = wc.waypointStartY;
10
11     cm.movement.velocity = Vector3.zero;
12     player.transform.position = wcV;
13     isDrafting = false;
14     isJumping = false;
15     isBouncing = false;
16     SetNorm();
17     ShowInvinc();
18
19     if (aiWaypointIndex + 1 >= 0 && aiWaypointIndex + 1 < waypoints.Count) {
20         wc = (WaypointCheck)waypoints[aiWaypointIndex + 1];
21     }
```

```
22      aiWaypointJumpCount++;
23      PerformLookAt(wc);
24      pause = false;
25 }
```

The first main method we'll look at is the Start method. The implementation of this method follows the standard process we've seen many times before. The call to the Prep method loads the standard set of variables followed by a test to see if the class initialized correctly. The following method listed, PerformGunShotHit, is used to apply a gunshot hit result to the current player.

The first block of code on lines 2–9 handles the hit when the current player has an active armor modifier. Note that the armor modifier is set to false, the isShot flag is set to true, and some effect fields are reset to show a gunshot hit with a puff of smoke. I should mention, again, that these particle effects have been disabled and left for you to implement. In the next large block of code from lines 11 to 30, the method handles processing gunshot hits when no armor modifier is active.

The first section of this large code block, lines 11–13, handles a gunshot hit when the current player has their invincibility modifier set to true. The second part of this large block of code runs from lines 14 to 29. This code snippet handles the gunshot hit. The current player's damage and isShot flag are adjusted on lines 14–15. The gunshot hit effect is prepared on lines 16–19. On line 20, the audio sound effect, signaling a valid, damaging hit, is played.

If the player has no more hit points, line 22, then the player is reset on the track in the same way a player who hits a water hazard is reset. This is handled on lines 23–27. The first step in this process is to find a previous waypoint to move the player back to, as a penalty for taking a lethal hit. I should mention these features of the game are only available in battle mode.

A call to the GetPastWaypointIndex method determines how far back we can move the current player. On line 24, the current player's damage is set to zero, and the hover racer is repositioned with a call to the MoveToCurrentWaypoint method, on line 26. The next method listed, MoveToWaypoint, is the first player repositioning method in the method set. This is a pass-through method that updates the aiWaypointIndex field, line 2, and then actually moves the player with a call to the MoveToCurrentWaypoint method. We'll look at that method now.

The second player repositioning method listed, MoveToCurrentWaypoint, does the actual work of moving the player's hover racer. The first few lines of code, 2–4, prevent the method from doing any work if the class has not been configured correctly. The code on lines 6–24 does the work of repositioning the player. First, the player is paused, line 6; then the new player's position is determined by the current waypoint and the value of the waypointStartY field of the waypoint object on line 9.

The code on lines 11–17 sets the player's speed, position, and modifier values. Notice that the player receives the invincibility modifier on line 17. We need to figure out what direction the player should face in given the player's new position. To do so, we find the next waypoint, determined on lines 19–21. The player's jump count field is incremented, and the player's direction is adjusted on lines 22–23. Last but not least, the player is unpaused on line 24. In the next set of main methods to review, we'll look at the Update and Reset methods.

Listing 9-17. PlayerState Main Method Details 2

```
001 public void Update() {
002     if (BaseScript.IsActive(scriptName) == false) {
003         return;
004     }
005
006     if (prepped == false || cm == null) {
007         return;
008     } else if (hasSetHome == false && player != null) {
009         home = player.transform;
010         hasSetHome = true;
011     }
012
013     //speed calculations
014     speed = cm.movement.velocity.magnitude;
015     if (boostOn == true || aiIsPassing == true) {
016         speed = LIMIT_MAX_SPEED;
017     }
018     speedPrct = (speed / maxSpeed);
019     speedPrctLimit = (speed / LIMIT_MAX_SPEED);
020
```

```
021      position = gameState.GetPosition(index, position);
022
023      //timing values
024      totalTime += Time.deltaTime;
025      ms = Mathf.RoundToInt((totalTime % 1) * 1000);
026      s = Mathf.RoundToInt(Mathf.Floor(totalTime));
027      min = Mathf.RoundToInt(Mathf.Floor((s * 1f) / 60f));
028      s -= (min * 60f);
029      hour = Mathf.RoundToInt(Mathf.Floor((min * 1f) / 60f));
030      min -= (hour * 60f);
031      time = string.Format("{0:00}:{1:00}:{2:000}", min, s, ms);
032      timeNum = int.Parse(string.Format("{0:00}{1:00}{2:00}{3:000}", hour,
         min, s, ms));
033
034      //waypoint distance calculations
035      if (waypoints != null && waypoints.Count > 0) {
036        wc = (WaypointCheck)waypoints[aiWaypointIndex];
037        if (wc != null) {
038          wcV = wc.transform.position;
039          wcV.y = player.transform.position.y;
040          waypointDistancePrev = waypointDistance;
041          waypointDistance = Vector3.Distance(wcV, player.transform.
             position);
042        }
043      }
044
045      //invincibility modifier
046      if (invincOn == true) {
047        invincTime += Time.deltaTime;
048      } else {
049        invincTime = 0f;
050      }
051
```

```
052    if (invincOn == true && invincTime >= INVINC_SECONDS) {
053        invincOn = false;
054    }
055
056    //has gained life
057    if (aiHasGainedLife == true) {
058        aiHasGainedLifeTime += Time.deltaTime;
059    } else {
060        aiHasGainedLifeTime = 0f;
061    }
062
063    if (aiHasGainedLife == true && aiHasGainedLifeTime >= MAX_GAINED_
       LIFE_TIME) {
064        aiHasGainedLife = false;
065    }
066
067    //gun smoke effect
068    if (gunSmokeOn == true) {
069        gunSmokeTime += Time.deltaTime * 100f;
070    } else {
071        gunSmokeTime = 0f;
072    }
073
074    if (gunSmokeOn == true && gunSmokeTime >= MAX_SMOKE_TIME) {
075        gunSmokeOn = false;
076        gunSmokeTime = 0f;
077        gunHitSmoke.SetActive(false);
078        //gunHitSmokeParticleSystem.emit = false;
079    }
080
081    //is shot time
082    if (isShot == true) {
083        isShotTime += Time.deltaTime;
084    } else {
085        isShotTime = 0f;
086    }
```

```
087
088    if (isShot == true && isShotTime >= MAX_IS_SHOT_TIME) {
089       isShot = false;
090    }
091
092    //is hit time
093    if (isHit == true) {
094       isHitTime += Time.deltaTime;
095    } else {
096       isHitTime = 0f;
097    }
098
099    if (isHit == true && isHitTime >= MAX_IS_SHOT_TIME) {
100       isHit = false;
101    }
102
103    //is miss time
104    if (isMiss == true) {
105       isMissTime += Time.deltaTime;
106    } else {
107       isMissTime = 0f;
108    }
109
110    if (isMiss == true && isMissTime >= MAX_IS_SHOT_TIME) {
111       isMiss = false;
112    }
113
114    //lap complete time
115    if (lapComplete == true) {
116       lapCompleteTime += Time.deltaTime;
117    } else {
118       lapCompleteTime = 0f;
119    }
120
```

```
121     if (lapComplete == true && lapCompleteTime >= MAX_IS_LAP_COMPLETE_
        TIME) {
122         lapComplete = false;
123     }
124
125     //off track checks
126     if (offTrack == true) {
127         offTrackTime += Time.deltaTime;
128     } else {
129         offTrackTime = 0f;
130     }
131
132     if (offTrack == true && offTrackTime >= offTrackSeconds) {
133         if (waypoints != null && waypoints.Count > 0) {
134             //move car to waypoint center
135             aiWaypointIndex = GetPastWaypointIndex(aiWaypointIndex);
136             if (aiWaypointIndex >= 0 && aiWaypointIndex < waypoints.Count) {
137                 MoveToCurrentWaypoint();
138             }
139             offTrack = false;
140             offTrackTime = 0f;
141         }
142     }
143
144     //wrong direction checks
145     if (wrongDirection == true) {
146         wrongDirectionTime += Time.deltaTime;
147     } else {
148         wrongDirectionTime = 0f;
149     }
150
151     if (wrongDirection == true && wrongDirectionTime >=
        wrongDirectionSeconds) {
152         if (waypoints != null && waypoints.Count > 0) {
153             //move car to waypoint center
154             aiWaypointIndex = GetPastWaypointIndex(aiWaypointIndex);
```

```
155        if (aiWaypointIndex >= 0 && aiWaypointIndex < waypoints.Count) {
156            MoveToCurrentWaypoint();
157        }
158        wrongDirection = false;
159        wrongDirectionTime = 0;
160      }
161    }
162 }
```

```
001 public void Reset() {
002    totalTime = 0f;
003    min = 0f;
004    s = 0f;
005    ms = 0f;
006    hour = 0f;
007    ammo = 0;
008    damage = 0;
009    points = 0;
010
011    boostOn = false;
012    invincOn = false;
013    invincTime = 0.0f;
014    gunOn = false;
015    armorOn = false;
016    offTrack = true;
017    gunSmokeOn = false;
018    gunSmokeTime = 0f;
019
020    prepped = false;
021    offTrack = false;
022    offTrackTime = 0.0f;
023    wrongDirection = false;
024    wrongDirectionTime = 0.0f;
025    skippedWaypoint = false;
026    skippedWaypointTime = 0.0f;
027    position = 6;
```

```
028    currentLap = 0;
029    waypointDistance = 0.0f;
030    waypointDistancePrev = 0.0f;
031    alive = true;
032
033    isBouncing = false;
034    isJumping = false;
035    isDrafting = false;
036    isShot = false;
037    isShotTime = 0.0f;
038    isHit = false;
039    isHitTime = 0.0f;
040    isMiss = false;
041    isMissTime = 0.0f;
042
043    aiIsStuck = false;
044    aiIsPassing = false;
045    aiPassingTime = 0.0f;
046    aiPassingMode = 0;
047    aiHasTarget = false;
048    aiHasTargetTime = 0.0f;
049    aiIsReloading = false;
050    aiIsReloadingTime = 0.0f;
051
052    aiIsLargeTurn = false;
053    aiIsLargeTurnSpeed = 0.0f;
054    aiCanFire = false;
055    aiBoostTime = 0.0f;
056    aiBoostMode = 0;
057    aiWaypointTime = 0;
058    aiWaypointLastIndex = -1;
059    aiWaypointIndex = 0;
060    aiWaypointJumpCount = 0;
061    aiWaypointPassCount = 0;
062 }
```

The next set of main methods to review, listed previously, has two important methods that we'll look at now. The first method we'll look into is the ever-important Update method. This method handles a few different responsibilities for us. It takes care of calculating current speeds, distances to waypoints, and tracking the duration of different modifiers. It's important to note that the PlayerState class is doing the same work for both human and AI-controlled players.

The main purpose of the Update method is to track the state of the hover racer and monitor the timing durations involved with different modifiers. The modifiers are set through the hover racer's interaction with other cars and track features like jump and boost markers. Note that this class doesn't plug into or drive the game's HUD. That process is handled by the GameState class as we'll see in just a bit. Let's go over the details of the Update method now.

The first few lines of code protect the method from executing if the class has not been properly configured, lines 2–4. Next, on lines 6–7, the method returns if the class has not been marked as having been initialized correctly or doesn't have the character motor field, cm, properly defined. The code on lines 8–11 sets the hover racer's home position based on its initial position. Speed calculations are performed on lines 14–19.

The hover racer's speed is set equal to the magnitude of the car's velocity vector. If the car is in boost mode or the aiIsPassing flag is true, then the car's speed is set to the LIMIT_MAX_SPEED value. On lines 18–19, the speed percentage values are updated. Total lap time is incremented on line 24, and the car's current position in the race is updated on line 21. The next block of code in the Update method handles the lap timing values, lines 25–32. Milliseconds, seconds, and minutes are determined from the totalTime field. Notice that on line 28, we subtract all the seconds that can be represented as minutes. A similar calculation is performed on line 30 to subtract all the minutes that can be represented by hours.

Two important class fields, time and timeNum, are updated on lines 31 and 32. The time field is a string representation of the current lap time. The timeNum field is a special encoding that holds the current lap time as a single integer. The next block of code are the waypoint distance calculations on lines 35–43. This code is responsible for getting the current waypoint's center position and recommended Y position.

The current and previous waypoint distances are set on lines 40–41. While these values aren't used by the human player, they are used by the AI players to control the hover racer. Following this block of code we have the invincibility modifier code, lines 46–54. This code follows a simple pattern we'll see a few more times in this method.

If the invincibility modifier is active, line 46, then we increment the modifier's timing value, line 47. If not, the modifier time is set to zero, line 49. The last bit of code on lines 52–54 resets the invincibility modifier if it was active for more than the allotted time.

The next block of code, lines 57–65, the "has gained life" section, functions in the same way as the code we've just reviewed. Take a look at it and make sure you understand it before moving on. Including this block of code, the remaining code blocks are very similar, and you should quickly review it on your own. The blocks of code are as follows:

- Gun Smoke Effect: 68–79

- Is Shot Time: 82–90

- Is Hit Time: 93–101

- Is Miss Time: 104–112

- Lap Complete Time: 115–123

The code is very direct. You'll have no trouble following it. Still, take the time to look it over. The two remaining responsibilities of this method are the off-track checks and the wrong direction checks. These two code blocks follow the same pattern, so I'll review one first and leave the second block of code for you to review. Direct your attention to the "off-track checks" section of code on lines 126–142. The if statement on lines 126–130 follows the same pattern we've seen before. If the Boolean flag is true, we increment the off-track time; otherwise, we set its value to zero.

On line 132, if the off-track flag is set to true and we've reached the offTrackSeconds time, then we have to adjust the position of the hover racer because we're off the track. If there are waypoints to process, line 133, then we move the car to the waypoint determined by the method call on line 135. If the determined index is valid, we move the car and reset the off-track flag and timing fields.

The last block of code in the Update method, "wrong direction checks," follows, very closely, the code we've just reviewed, so I'll leave it up to you to look it over. The last method in this set of main methods is the Reset method. This method simply resets class fields to default values. There's not much more to discuss about it. Give it a quick review and let's move on to the last two main methods left to peruse, the AI control methods.

Listing 9-18. PlayerState Main Method Details 3

```
001 public Vector3 UpdateAiFpsController() {
002     if (player == null || prepped == false || cm == null) {
003         return Vector3.zero;
004     }
005
006     if (waypoints == null) {
007         waypoints = gameState.GetWaypoints(aiWaypointRoute);
008     }
009
010     if (waypoints == null) {
011         return Vector3.zero;
012     }
013
014     //calculate strafe strength
015     aiStrafeStrength = 0.0f;
016     aiSpeedStrength = 1.0f;
017
018     if (waypoints != null) {
019         fpsWc = (WaypointCheck)waypoints[aiWaypointIndex];
020         aiRelativePoint = player.transform.InverseTransformPoint(fpsWc.
         transform.position);
021
022         if (aiRelativePoint.x <= -30.0f) {
023             aiStrafeStrength = -0.30f;
024         } else if (aiRelativePoint.x >= 30.0f) {
025             aiStrafeStrength = 0.30f;
026         } else if (aiRelativePoint.x <= -20.0f) {
027             aiStrafeStrength = -0.20f;
028         } else if (aiRelativePoint.x >= 20.0f) {
029             aiStrafeStrength = 0.20f;
030         } else if (aiRelativePoint.x <= -15.0f) {
031             aiStrafeStrength = -0.15f;
032         } else if (aiRelativePoint.x >= 15.0f) {
033             aiStrafeStrength = 0.15f;
```

```
034        } else if (aiRelativePoint.x <= -10.0f) {
035          aiStrafeStrength = -0.10f;
036        } else if (aiRelativePoint.x >= 10.0f) {
037          aiStrafeStrength = 0.10f;
038        } else if (aiRelativePoint.x <= -5.0f) {
039          aiStrafeStrength = -0.05f;
040        } else if (aiRelativePoint.x >= 5.0f) {
041          aiStrafeStrength = 0.05f;
042        } else if (aiRelativePoint.x <= -1.0f) {
043          aiStrafeStrength = -0.01f;
044        } else if (aiRelativePoint.x >= 1.0f) {
045          aiStrafeStrength = 0.01f;
046        }
047      }
048
049      //calculate side, above, collisions
050      sidesUfp = (int)(cm.movement.collisionFlags & CollisionFlags.Sides);
051      aboveUfp = (int)(cm.movement.collisionFlags & CollisionFlags.Above);
052
053      if (sidesUfp == 0) {
054        collSidesUfp = false;
055      } else {
056        collSidesUfp = true;
057      }
058
059      if (aboveUfp == 0) {
060        collAboveUfp = false;
061      } else {
062        collAboveUfp = true;
063      }
064
065      //calculate is stuck data
066      if (aiTime2 > 1 && cm.movement.collisionFlags == CollisionFlags.None) {
067        aiTime2 = 0;
068        aiIsStuckMode = 0;
```

```
069        aiTime1 = 0;
070        aiIsStuck = false;
071    } else if (aiTime2 > 1 && Mathf.Abs(waypointDistance -
       aiWaypointDistance) > MIN_STUCK_DISTANCE && !(collAboveUfp ||
       collSidesUfp)) {
072        aiTime2 = 0;
073        aiIsStuckMode = 0;
074        aiTime1 = 0;
075        aiIsStuck = false;
076    } else if (collAboveUfp || collSidesUfp) {
077        aiTime2 = 0;
078        aiIsStuckMode = 1;
079        aiWaypointDistance = waypointDistance;
080        aiIsStuck = true;
081    }
082
083    //test and apply is stuck data
084    if (aiIsStuckMode == 1 && aiTime1 >= MIN_STUCK_TIME && cm.movement.
       velocity.magnitude <= 30 && Mathf.Abs(waypointDistance -
       aiWaypointDistance) <= MIN_STUCK_DISTANCE) {
085        aiIsStuckMode = 2;
086        aiTime2 = 0f;
087        aiTime1 = 0f;
088        aiIsStuck = true;
089    } else if (aiIsStuckMode == 1 && aiTime1 > MIN_STUCK_TIME) {
090        aiIsStuckMode = 0;
091        aiTime2 = 0f;
092        aiTime1 = 0f;
093        aiIsStuck = false;
094    }
095
096    //process aiIsStuckMode
097    if (aiIsStuckMode == 1) {
098        aiTime1 += Time.deltaTime;
099    } else if (aiIsStuckMode == 2) {
```

```
100        if (waypoints != null && waypoints.Count > 0) {
101            //move car to waypoint center
102            aiWaypointIndex = GetPastWaypointIndex(aiWaypointIndex);
103            if (!(aiWaypointIndex >= 0 && aiWaypointIndex < waypoints.
               Count)) {
104                fpsV = new Vector3(0, 0, 0);
105                return fpsV;
106            }
107            MoveToCurrentWaypoint();
108            aiIsStuckMode = 0;
109            aiIsStuck = false;
110            aiTime2 = 0f;
111            aiTime1 = 0f;
112            aiStrafeStrength = 0f;
113        }
114
115        fpsV = new Vector3(0, 0, 0);
116        return fpsV;
117    }
118
119    if (aiIsStuckMode != 0) {
120        aiTime2 += Time.deltaTime;
121    }
122
123    //apply waypoint slow down
124    if ((aiSlowDownOn == true && aiSlowDown < 1.0f && speedPrct > 0.3f)
       || (aiSlowDown >= 1.0f)) {
125        aiSlowDownTime += (Time.deltaTime * 100);
126        aiSpeedStrength = aiSlowDown;
127        if (aiSlowDownTime > aiSlowDownDuration) {
128            aiSlowDownOn = false;
129            aiSlowDownTime = 0.0f;
130        }
131    }
132
```

```
133    //handle large turn
134    if (aiIsLargeTurn == true) {
135       if (aiSpeedStrength > aiIsLargeTurnSpeed) {
136          aiSpeedStrength = aiIsLargeTurnSpeed;
137       }
138    }
139
140    fpsV = new Vector3(aiStrafeStrength, 0, aiSpeedStrength);
141    return fpsV;
142 }

001 public void UpdateAiMouseLook() {
002    if (BaseScript.IsActive(scriptName) == false) {
003       return;
004    }
005
006    if (waypoints == null) {
007       waypoints = gameState.GetWaypoints(aiWaypointRoute);
008    }
009
010    if (waypoints == null || player == null || prepped == false ||
       !(aiWaypointIndex >= 0 && aiWaypointIndex < waypoints.Count)) {
011       return;
012    }
013
014    wc1 = (WaypointCheck)waypoints[aiWaypointIndex];
015    if (SHOW_AI_LOGIC) {
016       Debug.DrawRay(player.transform.position, (wc1.transform.
          position - player.transform.position), Color.green);
017    }
018
019    umlA = 0.0f;
020    umlForward = (player.transform.TransformDirection(Vector3.forward) * 20);
021
```

```
022    if (SHOW_AI_LOGIC) {
023        Debug.DrawRay(player.transform.position, umlForward, Color.
           magenta);
024    }
025
026    if (waypointDistance >= MIN_WAYPOINT_DISTANCE) {
027        wcV1 = wc1.transform.position;
028        wcV1.y = player.transform.position.y;
029        umlA = Vector3.Angle(umlForward, (wcV1 - player.transform.
           position));
030        aiLastLookAngle = umlA;
031
032        umlTmpIdx = 0;
033        if (aiWaypointIndex + 1 >= 0 && aiWaypointIndex + 1 < waypoints.
           Count) {
034            umlTmpIdx = (aiWaypointIndex + 1);
035        } else {
036            umlTmpIdx = 0;
037        }
038
039        wc2 = (WaypointCheck)waypoints[umlTmpIdx];
040        wcV2 = wc2.transform.position;
041        wcV2.y = player.transform.position.y;
042        umlA = Vector3.Angle(umlForward, (wcV2 - player.transform.
           position));
043        aiNextLookAngle = umlA;
044
045        if (SHOW_AI_LOGIC) {
046            Debug.DrawRay(player.transform.position, (wc2.transform.
               position - player.transform.position), Color.green);
047        }
048
049        umlTmpIdx = 0;
050        if (aiWaypointIndex + 2 >= 0 && aiWaypointIndex + 2 < waypoints.
           Count) {
```

```
051          umlTmpIdx = (aiWaypointIndex + 2);
052      } else {
053          umlTmpIdx = 0;
054      }
055
056      wc5 = (WaypointCheck)waypoints[umlTmpIdx];
057      wcV5 = wc5.transform.position;
058      wcV5.y = player.transform.position.y;
059      umlA = Vector3.Angle(umlForward, (wcV5 - player.transform.position));
060      aiNext2LookAngle = umlA;
061
062      if (SHOW_AI_LOGIC) {
063          Debug.DrawRay(player.transform.position, (wc5.transform.
             position - player.transform.position), Color.green);
064      }
065
066      if (speedPrct > 0.2f) {
067          umlAngle = Mathf.Abs(aiNextLookAngle);
068
069          if (umlAngle > 80) {
070              aiIsLargeTurn = true;
071              aiIsLargeTurnSpeed = 0.65f;
072
073          } else if (umlAngle >= 65 && umlAngle <= 80) {
074              aiIsLargeTurn = true;
075
076              if (speedPrct >= 0.95f) {
077                  aiIsLargeTurnSpeed = 0.05f;
078              } else if (speedPrct >= 0.85f) {
079                  aiIsLargeTurnSpeed = 0.10f;
080              } else {
081                  aiIsLargeTurnSpeed = 0.15f;
082              }
083
```

```
084              } else if (umlAngle >= 60) {
085                  aiIsLargeTurn = true;
086
087                  if (speedPrct >= 0.95f) {
088                      aiIsLargeTurnSpeed = 0.10f;
089                  } else if (speedPrct >= 0.85f) {
090                      aiIsLargeTurnSpeed = 0.15f;
091                  } else {
092                      aiIsLargeTurnSpeed = 0.25f;
093                  }
094
095              } else if (umlAngle >= 45) {
096                  aiIsLargeTurn = true;
097
098                  if (speedPrct >= 0.95f) {
099                      aiIsLargeTurnSpeed = 0.20f;
100                  } else if (speedPrct >= 0.85f) {
101                      aiIsLargeTurnSpeed = 0.25f;
102                  } else {
103                      aiIsLargeTurnSpeed = 0.35f;
104                  }
105
106              } else if (umlAngle >= 30) {
107                  aiIsLargeTurn = true;
108
109                  if (speedPrct >= 0.95f) {
110                      aiIsLargeTurnSpeed = 0.40f;
111                  } else if (speedPrct >= 0.85f) {
112                      aiIsLargeTurnSpeed = 0.45f;
113                  } else {
114                      aiIsLargeTurnSpeed = 0.55f;
115                  }
116
117              } else if (umlAngle >= 15) {
118                  aiIsLargeTurn = true;
119
```

```
120             if (speedPrct >= 0.95f) {
121                 aiIsLargeTurnSpeed = 0.60f;
122             } else if (speedPrct >= 0.85f) {
123                 aiIsLargeTurnSpeed = 0.65f;
124             } else {
125                 aiIsLargeTurnSpeed = 0.75f;
126             }
127
128         } else {
129             aiIsLargeTurn = false;
130         }
131     } else {
132         aiIsLargeTurn = false;
133     }
134
135     tr = Quaternion.LookRotation(wcV1 - player.transform.position);
136     player.transform.rotation = Quaternion.Slerp(player.transform.
        rotation, tr, Time.deltaTime * 5.0f);
137 } else {
138     aiLastLookAngle = 0.0f;
139     aiNextLookAngle = 0.0f;
140     aiMidLookAngle = 0.0f;
141 }
142 }
```

The first AI method we'll look at is the UpdateAiFpsController method. This method is responsible for controlling the hover racer's horizontal velocity vectors. In other words, it controls the X and Z axis velocities. The first few lines of code form the standard protection code we've seen many times before, lines 2–4. Next, the code on lines 6–12 are there to make sure the class waypoints are properly set. Notice that the method returns an empty Vector3 instance when escaped.

The first snippet of code we'll look at is a fairly large snippet of code, lines 15–47. It is responsible for determining the hover racer's strafe, side-to-side movement, strength. On lines 15–16, the components of the new velocity vector, aiStrafeStrength and aiSpeedStrength, are defaulted to 0 and 1, respectively. This corresponds to full forward speed and no side-to-side speed. If the waypoints are defined, line 18, then we get a reference to the current waypoint, and we use a call to the InverseTransformPoint method to determine the relative point, aiRelativePoint, from the car's current position. This lets us know if we need to apply a strafe velocity to the hover racer. On lines 22–46, the value of the aiStrafeStrength field is set based on the distance of the relative point.

The next responsibility of the method is to calculate the side and above collisions with regard to the hover racer. On lines 50 and 51, the side and above collisions are determined by checking the character motor movement field's collisions flags. A simple check results in setting the values of the class fields, collSidesUfp and collAboveUfp, lines 53–57 and 59–63. The next calculation this method is responsible for is handled by the "calculate is stuck data" section on lines 66–81.

The first two conditions checked, lines 66–71 and 71–76, reset the is-stuck data. In the first case, no collisions are detected. In the second case, the hover racer is far away from the waypoint, and no side or above collisions are detected. The third condition checked starts the is-stuck AI modifier if either a side or above collision is found. Setting the class field aiIsStuckMode to 1 begins the process, line 78.

The next calculation in the AI-driven is-stuck process will escalate the is-stuck mode to 2 if the current mode is 1 and the hover racer's velocity is slow. It also takes into consideration if the car is still near the current waypoint and the MIN_STUCK_TIME duration has expired, lines 84–89. In the next condition checked, if the is-stuck mode is 1 and value of aiTime1 has passed the MIN_STUCK_TIME duration, we reset the AI stuck mode process by setting the value of aiIsStuckMode to 0 on line 90. The last lines of code associated with the is-stuck AI modifier, "process aiIsStuckMode," run from lines 97 to 117.

In the first case, we check if the is-stuck mode has a value of 1, then the aiTime1 field is incremented by the frame time, line 98. This part of the process gives the car a little bit of time to get unstuck if possible. We saw previously that if enough time passes, the field aiIsStuckMode is set to a value of 2. The condition where aiIsStuckMode has a value of 2 is handled on lines 99–117. In this snippet of code, the hover racer is moved if possible, and all is-stuck modifier fields are reset, lines 107–112. Notice that if certain values don't make sense, the method returns a zero Vector3 value, lines 105 and 116.

The code on lines 119–121 takes care of incrementing the value of the aiTime2 class field. We have a few more responsibilities to cover before we're done with this method. The next code snippet runs from lines 124 to 131 and is responsible for applying waypoint slowdowns. These are slowdown hints that are set on AI-controlled player's hover racers as they pass through certain waypoints. If the waypoint's `aiSlowDownOn` field is set to true, handled by the `WaypointCheck` class, and certain slowdown and speed values exist, the AI slowdown modifier is applied.

On line 125, the slowdown time tracker is incremented, while on line 126, the `aiSpeedStrength` value is set according to the current slowdown value. On lines 127–130, if enough time has passed, the slowdown fields are reset. Last but not least, we have one last responsibility to consider, the "handle large turn" calculation. The code for this runs from lines 134 to 138. If the `aiLongTurn` flag is set to true, then the hover racer's calculated speed strength is set to the current value of the `aiIsLargeTurnSpeed` field, line 136. The last bit of code in this method creates a new `Vector3` instance based on the value of the `aiStrafeStength` and `aiSpeedStrength` fields, lines 140–141, and returns it.

That brings us to the last method up for review in the `PlayerState` class' set of main methods, the `UpdateAiMouseLook` method. The first lines of this method, 2–4, are the standard class config checks we've seen time and time again. On lines 6–8, the class' `waypoints` field is initialized if it's null. Next, we check to make sure all required fields and values are properly set, lines 10–12. The method variable `wc1` is set based on the current waypoint index, line 14, and the `umlA` and `umlForward` fields are initialized on lines 19 and 20. Note that the `umlForward` field is a vector that points forward from the hover racer.

The debugging code on lines 15–17 is responsible for drawing an arrow from the center of the car to the center of the next waypoint. If the `SHOW_AI_LOGIC` field is set to true, then a green arrow will be displayed in the "Scene" panel while the game is run in the Unity editor. The forward indicating vector, `umlForward`, is drawn on lines 22–24 as a magenta line, if the AI logic debugging is turned on. Next up, we check to see if the current waypoint distance is greater than the value of the `MIN_WAYPOINT_DISTANCE` field on line 26. If so, the code on lines 26–136 is executed. If not, the hover racer's turning angles are reset to zero on lines 138–140.

Take a look at lines 27–65; the angle from the hover racer's current position to the center of the current and the next two waypoints is calculated here. There is a debugging call on lines 45–47 and lines 62-64 to display the AI logic in the form of green lines connecting the car to the two waypoints we're working with here. On lines 66–130, if the car is moving fast enough and the turning angle is high enough, the `aiIsLargeTurn` flag is set to true. The final rotation, turning, value is calculated on lines 135–136. This method essentially steers the hover racer based on its relative distance to the next three waypoints and the angles involved.

Demonstration: PlayerState

I've set up a very detailed demonstration for the `PlayerState` class. Open the Unity editor and go to the "Project" panel. Find and open the "Scenes" folder. Next, locate and open the scene named "Main13Demonstration". Play the scene in the Unity editor, and you'll notice a ton of car state debugging information on the screen. The demo scene is set up to run itself if you click any of the track buttons on the start menu. I suggest letting the arcade demo mode, AI race, run while monitoring the debugging values shown on the screen. This is really useful to see how the car's AI is calculating what to do.

This demonstration scene is also set up to show the car's AI calculations with regard to turning, waypoints, and speed. If you let the race run in AI mode and click on the "Scene" panel, you'll notice that there are green lines emanating from the hover racers and a little purple line that indicates the forward direction vector. These lines indicate the AI calculations based on the current and upcoming waypoints. That brings us to the conclusion of this class review. Don't worry if you didn't absorb everything the first time around. There's a lot going on here. Take your time with it.

Chapter Conclusion

In this chapter, we reviewed part 1 of the Player and Game State Classes review. This chapter has been all about classes that track or capture the state of the game. Let's take a moment to summarize the material we've reviewed in this chapter.

1. PayerInfo: A subtle state class. This `MonoBehaviour` is used to provide the associated player's index, in the array of active players, which facilitates looking up `PlayerState` data from the main `GameState` object instance. This class is used to connect objects in the game to players in the game.

2. TrackScript: This class is a `MonoBehaviour` that resides on the `GameState` object, the Unity game object that holds references to important game and player data. It defines a few attributes about the current racetrack.

3. PlayerState: A very important state class, the `PlayerState` class is a `MonoBehaviour` that is used to track all kinds of information about the state of the player it's associated with.

Because this is only part 1 of the game and player state review, we didn't get to look at the GameState class. This class is another very important class; it's essentially the brain of the entire game. As such, it's fairly complex, and I thought it best to dedicate an entire chapter to its review. You've almost completed a detailed review of every class in the game! Once we're done with the GameState review, we'll go over some tips on how to make your next game "professional." Then we'll have some fun and build a new track to race on. Stay tuned!

CHAPTER 10

Player and Game State Classes Part 2

In this chapter, we'll continue our review of the game's state classes by looking into the game's brain, the GameState class. This class is complex and long, so take a deep breath and prepare yourself. We have our work cut out for us. Let's get to it.

Class Review: GameState

Well, we've somehow managed to review almost all the classes in the entire game, in detail, with some pretty decent demonstration scenes. We just got done reviewing one of the longest, most important classes in the game, and we have one more to review that's just as complex. The playerState class is updated by track interactions that lead to hover racer modifiers, it also receives some information from user input.

All of this data is organized, shared, stored, and presented by the GameState class and the game's HUD screen. The class is responsible for connecting the active hover racer to the game's HUD so that all of the modifiers, state fields, and notifications are displayed properly. This class is also responsible for managing the different menu screens and enforcing game states. We'll follow the review steps listed here:

1. Enumerations

2. Static/Constant/Read-Only Class Members

3. Class Fields

4. Pertinent Method Outline/Class Headers

5. Support Method Details

© Victor G Brusca 2022
V. G Brusca, *Advanced Unity Game Development*, https://doi.org/10.1007/978-1-4842-7851-2_10

6.   Main Method Details

7.   Demonstration

The first review section we'll take a look at is the enumerations section.

Enumerations: GameState

The GameState class has two enumerations for us to peruse. They are used in game state management and in preparing the track.

Listing 10-1. GameState Enumerations 1

```
public enum GameStateIndex {
    FIRST,
    NONE,
    MAIN_MENU_SCREEN,
    GAME_OVER_SCREEN,
    GAME_PAUSE_SCREEN,
    GAME_PLAY_SCREEN,
    GAME_EXIT_PROMPT
};

public enum GameDifficulty {
    LOW,
    MED,
    HIGH
};
```

The first enumeration listed, GameStateIndex, is used to help manage the game's current state. It also helps when changing states. In this case, a game state represents a unique screen in the game. For instance, the start menu is one state, while the help menu and the actual game are other game states. Notice that there are entries for a NONE state, a FIRST state, and a state for each menu screen. The next enumeration listed is the GameDifficulty enumeration that is used to help track the game's current difficulty. In the next section, we'll take a look at the class' static members.

Static/Constant/Read-Only Class Members: GameState

The GameState class has a few static and read-only class members we need to review.
Let's take a look.

Listing 10-2. PlayerState Static/Constants/Read-Only Class Members 1

```
private static bool FIRST_RUN = true;
public static bool ON_GUI_SHOW_CAR_DETAILS = false;
public static bool ON_GUI_SHOW_EXIT_BUTTON = false;
public static bool SHOW_WAYPOINT_OUTPUT = false;
public static readonly float START_GAME_SECONDS = 5.0f;

public static readonly float TRACK_HELP_SECONDS = 2.0f;

public static readonly int DEFAULT_TOTAL_LAPS = 10;
```

The FIRST_RUN field is a Boolean flag that indicates if this is the game's first run. The
following field is used in the "Main13Demonstration" scene. If the ON_GUI_SHOW_CAR_
DETAILS field is set to true, a lot of player and game state information will be displayed
on the screen. The next field, ON_GUI_SHOW_EXIT_BUTTON, is used to control the display
of a debug exit button. Next, the SHOW_WAYPOINT_OUTPUT field is used to control the
waypoint debugging output.

The START_GAME_SECONDS field controls the number of seconds shown before the
race starts. Similarly, the TRACK_HELP_SECONDS field holds the number of seconds the
help notifications are displayed. Lastly, the DEFAULT_TOTAL_LAPS field is used to hold the
default number of laps for each racetrack. That brings us to the end of the static/read-
only class member review. In the next review section, we'll cover the class' remaining
fields.

Class Fields: GameState

The GameState class is an important centralization and state management class, and as
such, it has a large number of class fields for us to review. We'll go through them in detail
here. We're going to omit the class' internal variables from the review as these fields are
used as local method variables. There's a lot of material we have to cover, so take your time
with it. Don't get frustrated if you don't absorb it all in one reading. It may take a little time
to really get comfortable with this class. Let's look at the first set of fields, shall we?

Listing 10-3. GameState Class Fields 1

```
//***** Class Fields *****
public ArrayList players = null;
public PlayerState p0;
public PlayerState p1;
public PlayerState p2;
public PlayerState p3;
public PlayerState p4;
public PlayerState p5;
public PlayerState currentPlayer = null;
```

The players field is an ArrayList instance used to hold an array of PlayerState object instances for the game's active players. This includes both human and AI-controlled players. Notice that the game is configured to support six players. The last entry is the currentPlayer field that references the PlayerState of the current player. The current player is the player whose state and cameras are plugged into the game's display. The next set of variables we'll peruse is a somewhat random assortment of class fields and associated responsibilities.

Listing 10-4. GameState Class Fields 2

```
//***** Internal Variables: Start *****
public int[] positions = null;
public bool sortingPositions = false;
public int currentIndex = 0;
public int player1Index = 0;
public LapTimeManager lapTimeManager = null;
public int totalLaps = DEFAULT_TOTAL_LAPS;
public int gameSettingsSet = 0;    //track type
public int gameSettingsSubSet = 0; //track difficulty
public bool debugOn = false;
public bool forceGameStart = false;
public bool scsMode = false;
private GUIStyle style1 = null;
private GUIStyle style2 = null;
```

```
public WaypointCompare wpc = new WaypointCompare();
public ArrayList waypointRoutes = null;

public ArrayList waypointData = null;
public AudioSource audioBgroundSound = null;
private AudioSource audioS = null;
private bool nightTime = false;
private bool player1AiOn = true;
private bool prepped = false;
private bool ready = false;
private bool startGame = false;
private float startGameTime = 0.0f;
public bool gameWon = false;
public bool gameRunning = false;
public bool gamePaused = false;
```

The first field listed in this set, positions, is an array of integers used to store the hover racers' position indexes, properly ordered. In this way, the lead car in the race can be found at index zero. The next field is a Boolean flag that's used to indicate the positions array is currently being sorted. The subsequent two fields seem redundant, but upon close inspection, we'll see they aren't. The currentIndex field represents the array index of the current, active, player in the array of available players. The next field, player1Index, is the index of player one which defaults to zero. So while these two fields seem like duplicates, keep in mind that the current player index can change but the index of player one will always be zero.

The next field in the set should be familiar. It's an instance of the LapTimeManager class and is used to manage the set of lap times stored in the game's preferences. The field is aptly named lapTimeManager. The totalLaps field represents the total number of laps for the current racetrack configuration. This value is set based on the track's associated TrackScript, the type of race, and the race's difficulty. The next two fields listed, gameSettingsSet and gameSettingSubSet, are class fields used to set the track's type and difficulty. The next field, debugOn, is used to turn on the GameState class' debugging text. This field works in conjunction with the ON_GUI_SHOW_CAR_DETAILS static class field we reviewed previously.

The forceGameState field is a Boolean flag that's used to bypass certain normal GameState class functionality and is used by most of the game's demo scenes. This value is usually set via the Unity editor's "Inspector" panel and saved as part of the scene's configuration. The scsMode field is used to help set the game up so that a screenshot can be taken of the game without triggering certain menu screens like the game pause menu screen. The style1 and style2 fields are instances of Unity's GUIStyle class and are used by the class' OnGUI method to display debugging information directly to the game's screen.

The wc class field is an instance of the WaypointCompare class and is used to sort the array of waypoints for the given track. The next field is an ArrayList instance that stores the different waypoint routes found on the current track. I should mention that the game, in its current state, doesn't use waypoint routes so this field won't be too well supported. The next field, waypointData, is used to hold all the waypoint entries found on the track. The next two entries are used by the class' audio responsibilities. The first, audioBgroundSound, is used to hold the track's background music. The second entry, audioS, is used to hold the menu sound effect. When a menu screen receives user input, it plays a sound effect to indicate the input event. In many cases, the menu screen will ask the game state class to play the menu sound effect.

Subsequently, the next five class fields are Boolean flags used to indicate something about the current state of the game. The nightTime field is a Boolean flag set by the track's TrackScript MonoBehaviour and its headLightsOn field. The next entry, player1AiOn, is a Boolean flag that indicates the player one car should be controlled by AI. This presents itself when the game first loads, and the "arcade" style AI race takes place. The prepped field is used to indicate that the game has been properly prepared by initializing all the PlayerState instances in the players array. Once this flag is set to true, calls to the class' Prep method will be escaped.

The ready Boolean field is a flag that indicates the game is ready to begin. The startGame field is used to indicate if the race is starting and the countdown timer should be started. The next field, startGameTime, is used to track the countdown that starts the race. The last three fields in this set are the gameWon, gameRunning, and gamePaused Boolean flags. The gameWon field indicates that the current player has finished the race. It doesn't necessarily mean that they came in first place. Subsequently, the gameRunning field indicates that the game is running, as you might have expected. And lastly, the gamePaused field indicates that the game is running but has been paused.

Listing 10-5. GameState Class Fields 3

```
//***** Track Help Variables *****
public bool trackHelpAccelOn = false;
public float trackHelpAccelTime = 0.0f;
public bool trackHelpSlowOn = false;
public float trackHelpSlowTime = 0.0f;
public bool trackHelpTurnOn = false;
public float trackHelpTurnTime = 0.0f;

//***** Track Settings *****
public int raceTrack = 0;
public bool easyOn = false;
public int raceType = 0;
public int waypointWidthOverride = 6;
public int waypointZeroOverride = 1;
public bool trackHelpOn = false;
private TrackScript trackScript = null;
public GameDifficulty difficulty = GameDifficulty.LOW;
public GameStateIndex gameStateIndex = GameStateIndex.FIRST;

//***** Camera Variables *****
private GameObject blimpCamera = null;
public string sceneName = "";
public Camera gameCamera = null;
public Camera rearCamera = null;
```

The next set of class fields for us to review is listed previously. The first group of fields in the set is the "Track Help Variables" group. The first field in this group, trackHelpAccelOn, and the following entry, trackHelpAccelTime, are used to turn on the help notification image and track its display duration. Similarly, the next four fields listed are used to control the help slow down and help turn notifications if they are triggered by the current player. The next group of fields for us to look at is the "Track Settings" group.

The "Track Settings" group starts with the raceTrack field. This field is a numeric representation of the track we're currently racing on. The easyOn field is a Boolean flag indicating if the current race has a difficulty setting of easy. The succeeding field, raceType, is used to indicate the mode of the current race. The next two fields are used to normalize some aspects of the track's waypoints. The waypointWidthOverride is used to set a standard width for waypoints on the current track.

In a similar fashion, the waypointZeroOverride field is used to override the Y position of waypoint markers that are positioned with a Y value of zero. The trackHelpOn field is a Boolean flag that's used to control if the track supports displaying help notifications. The next two entries, difficulty and gameStateIndex, are used to manage the track's difficulty settings and the game's states. The last group of fields to review in this set are the camera fields. The blimpCamera field is a GameObject instance that's used to reference the game's blimp camera feature. The next field in the list, sceneName, is a string that represents the name of the current scene. Lastly, the gameCamera and rearCamera class fields are used to support the game's standard and rear-view camera. We have one more set of class fields to review before we can close out this review section.

Listing 10-6. GameState Class Fields 4

```
//***** Menu System Variables *****
private GameObject gamePauseMenu = null;
private GameObject gameStartMenu = null;
private GameObject gameOverMenu = null;
private GameObject gameExitMenu = null;
private GameObject gameHelpMenu = null;
public GameHUDNewScript hudNewScript = null;
public GameOverMenu gameOverMenuScript = null;

//***** Touch screen Variables *****
public bool accelOn = false;
public bool newTouch = false;
public bool touchScreen = false;

//***** Input Variables *****
private bool handleKeyA = false;
private bool handleKeyD = false;
private bool handleKey1 = false;
private bool handleKey2 = false;
private bool handleKey3 = false;
private bool handleKey4 = false;
private bool handleKey5 = false;
private bool handleKey6 = false;
```

The first group of fields in this set are the "Menu System" fields. There are five entries representing the different menu screens supported by the game. The hudNewScript field is a reference to the script component that is associated with the game HUD. The next field gameOverMenuScript is a reference to the script component associated with the game over menu screen. Note that in the cases where we need more granular control, we get references to the MonoBehaviour instance. In other cases, it's enough to have a reference to the associated game object.

Following this group, we have the "Touch Screen" fields. The accelOn entry is a Boolean flag that indicates touch screen acceleration input is active. The newTouch field indicates that a new touch interaction is occurring. The last entry in this group, touchScreen, is a Boolean flag indicating that touch screen input is active. The last group of fields for us to review is the "Input" group. This set is self-explanatory. Each entry enables or disables the input from certain keyboard keys. This brings us to the conclusion of the class fields review section. In the next section, we'll take a look at the pertinent method outline and class headers review section.

Pertinent Method Outline/Class Headers: GameState

The GameState class' method outline has a laundry list of methods for us to review. No worries, we'll omit simple support methods from the detailed review to speed things up a bit. We'll still list them here. We just won't review them in any detail due to their simplicity. Let's jump to it.

Listing 10-7. GameState Pertinent Method Outline/Class Headers 1

```
//Main Methods
public void PauseGame();
public void UnPauseGame();
public void FindWaypoints();
public void SetCarDetails();
public void ResetGame();
public void SetCarDetailsByGameType(PlayerState player);

public void SetActiveCar(int j);
public void PrepGame();
public void OnApplicationPause(bool pauseStatus);
```

```
void Start();
void Update();

//Support Methods
private int GetOnGuiPosY(int idx, int rowHeight);
public void OnGUI();

//Support Methods Menu Is Showing
private bool AreMenusShowing();
public bool IsHelpMenuShowing();
public bool IsPauseMenuShowing();
public bool IsEndMenuShowing();
public bool IsStartMenuShowing();
public bool IsExitMenuShowing();
public bool IsTrackHelpOn();

//Support Methods Show/Hide Menu
public void HideHelpMenu();
public void ShowHelpMenu();
public void HidePauseMenu();
public void ShowPauseMenu();
public void HideExitMenu();
public void ShowExitMenu();
public void HideStartMenu();
public void ShowStartMenu();
public void HideEndMenu();
public void ShowEndMenu();

//Support Methods Misc. 1
public void PlayMenuSound();
public void PrintWaypoints();
public ArrayList GetWaypoints(int index);
public void ToggleDebugOn();
public void ToggleCurrentCarAi();
private bool PlayerStateIdxCheck(int idx);
public PlayerState GetPlayer1();
public PlayerState GetCurrentPlayer();
public PlayerState GetPlayer(int i);
```

```
//Support Methods Track Features On/Off
private void TurnOffArmorMarkers();
private void TurnOnArmorMarkers();
private void TurnOffGunMarkers();
private void TurnOnGunMarkers();
private void TurnOffHealthMarkers();
private void TurnOnHealthMarkers();
private void TurnOffInvincMarkers();
private void TurnOnInvincMarkers();
private void TurnOffHittableMarkers();
private void TurnOnHittableMarkers();
private void TurnOffOilDrumStackMarkers();
private void TurnOnOilDrumStackMarkers();
private void TurnOffFunBoxMarkers();
private void TurnOnFunBoxMarkers();

//Support Methods Misc. 2
private void AdjustTagActive(bool active, string tag);

public void LogLapTime(PlayerState p);
public void StartDemoScene();
public int GetPosition(int idx, int currentPosition);
public void SetPositions();
public int PlayerStateCompare(int i1, int i2);
```

Take a moment to look over the methods associated with this class. Let your imagination go and try to envision the class and its methods in use. We'll review these methods in just a bit. Before we move on, let's look at the class' import statements and declaration.

Listing 10-8. GameState Pertinent Method Outline/Class Headers 2

```
using System.Collections;
using UnityEngine;
using UnityEngine.SceneManagement;

public class GameState : MonoBehaviour {}
```

In the following review section, we'll cover the class' support methods.

Support Method Details: GameState

The first set of support methods we'll look at are simple and direct. I'll list the methods here for you to look at. I won't go into any detail reviewing them due to their simplicity. Please make sure you review and understand these methods before moving on.

Listing 10-9. GameState Support Method Details 1

```
01 private int GetOnGuiPosY(int idx, int rowHeight) {
02    return (idx * rowHeight);
03 }
```

```
01 private bool AreMenusShowing() {
02    if (IsStartMenuShowing() == true || IsEndMenuShowing() == true ||
      IsHelpMenuShowing() == true || IsExitMenuShowing() == true) {
03       return true;
04    } else {
05       return false;
06    }
07 }
```

```
01 public bool IsHelpMenuShowing() {
02    if (gameHelpMenu != null) {
03       return gameHelpMenu.activeSelf;
04    } else {
05       return false;
06    }
07 }
```

```
01 public bool IsPauseMenuShowing() {
02    if (gamePauseMenu != null) {
03       return gamePauseMenu.activeSelf;
04    } else {
05       return false;
06    }
07 }
```

```
01 public bool IsEndMenuShowing() {
02     if (gameOverMenu != null) {
03         return gameOverMenu.activeSelf;
04     } else {
05         return false;
06     }
07 }
```

```
01 public bool IsStartMenuShowing() {
02     if (gameStartMenu != null) {
03         return gameStartMenu.activeSelf;
04     } else {
05         return false;
06     }
07 }
```

```
01 public bool IsExitMenuShowing() {
02     if (gameExitMenu != null) {
03         return gameExitMenu.activeSelf;
04     } else {
05         return false;
06     }
07 }
```

```
01 public bool IsTrackHelpOn() {
02     return trackHelpOn;
03 }
```

```
01 public void HideHelpMenu() {
02     if (gameHelpMenu != null) {
03         gameHelpMenu.SetActive(false);
04         UnPauseGame();
05     }
06 }
```

```
01 public void ShowHelpMenu() {
02     if (gameHelpMenu != null) {
03         gameHelpMenu.SetActive(true);
```

```
04        PauseGame();
05    }
06 }
```

```
01 public void HidePauseMenu() {
02    if (gamePauseMenu != null) {
03        gamePauseMenu.SetActive(false);
04        UnPauseGame();
05    }
06 }
```

```
01 public void ShowPauseMenu() {
02    if (gamePauseMenu != null) {
03        gamePauseMenu.SetActive(true);
04        PauseGame();
05    }
06 }
```

```
01 public void HideExitMenu() {
02    if (gameExitMenu != null) {
03        gameExitMenu.SetActive(false);
04        UnPauseGame();
05    }
06 }
```

```
01 public void ShowExitMenu() {
02    if (gameExitMenu != null) {
03        gameExitMenu.SetActive(true);
04        PauseGame();
05    }
06 }
```

```
01 public void HideStartMenu() {
02    if (gameStartMenu != null) {
03        gameStartMenu.SetActive(false);
04    }
05 }
```

```
01 public void ShowStartMenu() {
02     if (gameStartMenu != null) {
03         gameStartMenu.SetActive(true);
04     }
05 }
```

```
01 public void HideEndMenu() {
02     if (gameOverMenu != null) {
03         gameOverMenu.SetActive(false);
04     }
05 }
```

```
01 public void ShowEndMenu() {
02     if (gameOverMenu != null) {
03         gameOverMenu.SetActive(true);
04     }
05 }
```

```
01 public void PlayMenuSound() {
02     if (audioS != null) {
03       audioS.Play();
04     }
05 }
```

```
01 public void ToggleDebugOn() {
02     if (debugOn == true) {
03         debugOn = false;
04     } else {
05         debugOn = true;
06     }
07 }
```

```
01 private bool PlayerStateIdxCheck(int idx) {
02     if (players != null && idx >= 0 && idx < players.Count) {
03         return true;
04     } else {
05         return false;
06     }
07 }
```

```
01 public PlayerState GetPlayer1() {
02     return (PlayerState)players[player1Index];
03 }
```

```
01 public PlayerState GetCurrentPlayer() {
02     return (PlayerState)players[currentIndex];
03 }
```

```
01 public PlayerState GetPlayer(int i) {
02     if (i >= 0 && i < players.Count) {
03         return (PlayerState)players[i];
04     } else {
05         return null;
06     }
07 }
```

```
01 private void TurnOffArmorMarkers() {
02     AdjustTagActive(false, "ArmorMarker");
03 }
```

```
01 private void TurnOnArmorMarkers() {
02     AdjustTagActive(true, "ArmorMarker");
03 }
```

```
01 private void TurnOffGunMarkers() {
02     AdjustTagActive(false, "GunMarker");
03 }
```

```
01 private void TurnOnGunMarkers() {
02     AdjustTagActive(true, "GunMarker");
03 }
```

```
01 private void TurnOffHealthMarkers() {
02     AdjustTagActive(false, "HealthMarker");
03 }
```

```
01 private void TurnOnHealthMarkers() {
02     AdjustTagActive(true, "HealthMarker");
03 }
```

```
01 private void TurnOffInvincMarkers() {
02    AdjustTagActive(false, "InvincibilityMarker");
03 }
```

```
01 private void TurnOnInvincMarkers() {
02    AdjustTagActive(true, "InvincibilityMarker");
03 }
```

```
01 private void TurnOffHittableMarkers() {
02    AdjustTagActive(false, "Hittable");
03 }
```

```
01 private void TurnOnHittableMarkers() {
02    AdjustTagActive(true, "Hittable");
03 }
```

```
01 private void TurnOffOilDrumStackMarkers() {
02    AdjustTagActive(false, "OilDrumStack");
03 }
```

```
01 private void TurnOnOilDrumStackMarkers() {
02    AdjustTagActive(true, "OilDrumStack");
03 }
```

```
01 private void TurnOffFunBoxMarkers() {
02    AdjustTagActive(false, "FullFunBox");
03 }
```

```
01 private void TurnOnFunBoxMarkers() {
02    AdjustTagActive(true, "FullFunBox");
03 }
```

```
01 public void StartDemoScene() {
02    PlayerPrefs.SetInt("GameStateIndex", 5);
03    PlayerPrefs.Save();
04    ResetGame();
05    SceneManager.LoadScene(SceneManager.GetActiveScene().name);
06 }
```

```
01 public int GetPosition(int idx, int currentPosition) {
02     int i = 0;
03     int l = 0;
04     l = positions.Length;
05
06     for (i = 0; i < l; i++) {
07         if (positions[i] == idx) {
08             return (i + 1);
09         }
10     }
11
12     return 6;
13 }
```

```
01 public void SetPositions() {
02     sortingPositions = true;
03     System.Array.Sort(positions, PlayerStateCompare);
04     sortingPositions = false;
05 }
```

The class support methods, listed previously, are straight forward, so I'll leave them for you to review on your own. In the succeeding listing of support methods, we'll review the methods to explain how they function. These support methods are a little bit more complex, so they deserve a little bit more attention. I should quickly mention that I haven't listed the OnGUI method in either the main or support method lists. This is because the method is fairly long, and it does little more than print debugging values to the screen. The review of this method is optional. I'll leave it to your discretion.

Listing 10-10. GameState Support Method Details 2

```
01 public void PrintWaypoints() {
02     if (waypointData != null && waypointData.Count > 0) {
03         ArrayList data = (ArrayList)waypointData[0];
04         int l = data.Count;
05         WaypointCheck wc = null;
06         for (int j = 0; j < l; j++) {
07             wc = (WaypointCheck)data[j];
```

```
08          if (SHOW_WAYPOINT_OUTPUT) {
09              Utilities.wr(j + " Found waypoint: " + wc.waypointIndex + ",
                Center: " + wc.transform.position);
10          }
11      }
12  }
13 }
```

```
01 public ArrayList GetWaypoints(int index) {
02    if (waypointData == null) {
03      return null;
04    } else {
05      if (index >= 0 && index < waypointData.Count) {
06          return (ArrayList)waypointData[index];
07      } else {
08          return null;
09      }
10    }
11 }
```

```
01 public void ToggleCurrentCarAi() {
02    PlayerState player;
03    player = GetCurrentPlayer();
04
05    if (player1AiOn == true) {
06      player1AiOn = false;
07    } else {
08      player1AiOn = true;
09    }
10
11    if (player1AiOn == true) {
12      player.aiOn = true;
13      player.cm.aiOn = true;
14      player.fpsInput.aiOn = true;
15      player.mouseInput.aiOn = true;
16      player.offTrackSeconds = 5.0f;
```

```
17    } else {
18        player.aiOn = false;
19        player.cm.aiOn = false;
20        player.fpsInput.aiOn = false;
21        player.mouseInput.aiOn = false;
22        player.offTrackSeconds = 10.0f;
23    }
24
25    if (forceGameStart) {
26        player.offTrackSeconds = 10000.0f;
27        player.wrongDirectionSeconds = 10000.0f;
28    }
29 }
```

The first set of more complex support methods up for review is listed previously. We have two waypoint methods and one AI-related method to review. The first method listed, PrintWaypoints, is used to list all the waypoints associated with the default route. If the waypointData field is defined and populated, line 2, then we load the default route's waypoints on line 3 of the method. For each waypoint in the data found, we print out a summary of its settings, lines 7–10. The next waypoint for us to review is the GetWaypoints method. If the waypointData field is defined, then we find the set of waypoints for the given route index. If the index of data is not defined, then the method returns a null value. The last method for us to review in this set of methods is the ToggleCurrentAi method.

This method is used to toggle the AI state of the current player's car. Note that AI flags are then set on all the input classes associated with the current player. The last bit of code is only run if the forceGameStart Boolean is set to true. We set some large timing values to prevent the off-track and wrong direction modifiers from triggering. There are a few more support methods for us to look at. I'll list them here.

Listing 10-11. GameState Support Method Details 3

```
01 private void AdjustTagActive(bool active, string tag) {
02    GameObject[] gos = GameObject.FindGameObjectsWithTag(tag);
03    int l = gos.Length;
```

```
04    for (int i = 0; i < l; i++) {
05        gos[i].SetActive(active);
06    }
07 }
```

```
01 public void LogLapTime(PlayerState p) {
02    string time = p.time;
03    int timeNum = p.timeNum;
04    int lap = p.currentLap;
05    int track = raceTrack;
06    int type = gameSettingsSet;
07    int diff = gameSettingsSubSet;
08
09    LapTime lt = new LapTime();
10    lt.time = time;
11    lt.timeNum = timeNum;
12    lt.lap = lap;
13    lt.type = type;
14    lt.diff = diff;
15    lt.track = track;
16
17    lapTimeManager.AddEntry(lt);
18    lapTimeManager.CleanTimes();
19    lapTimeManager.FindBestLapTimeByLastEntry();
20    PlayerPrefs.SetString("LapTimes", lapTimeManager.Serialize());
21 }
```

```
01 public int PlayerStateCompare(int i1, int i2) {
02    if (!PlayerStateIdxCheck(i1) || !PlayerStateIdxCheck(i2)) {
03        return 0;
04    }
05
06    PlayerState obj1 = (PlayerState)players[i1];
07    PlayerState obj2 = (PlayerState)players[i2];
08
```

```
09     if (obj1.currentLap > obj2.currentLap) {
10        return -1;
11     } else if (obj1.currentLap < obj2.currentLap) {
12        return 1;
13     } else {
14        if (obj1.aiWaypointIndex > obj2.aiWaypointIndex) {
15           return -1;
16        } else if (obj1.aiWaypointIndex < obj2.aiWaypointIndex) {
17           return 1;
18        } else {
19           if (obj1.aiWaypointTime < obj2.aiWaypointTime) {
20              return 1;
21           } else if (obj1.aiWaypointTime > obj2.aiWaypointTime) {
22              return -1;
23           } else {
24              return 0;
25           }
26        }
27     }
28 }
```

The last set of support methods, listed previously, is an assorted group. The first method listed is very useful. The AdjustTagActive method is used to locate all the GameObjects that have the specified tag. These objects have their active flag set to the provided argument value, line 5. The succeeding method listed is used to add a lap time to the player's log of lap times. On lines 2–7, the values needed to store the lap time are set based on the provided PlayerState values, p, and the track's current configuration. Next, on lines 9–15, a new LapTime object instance is created, and the object's fields are set based on the prepared method variables. The lap time is added to the game's lap time manager on line 17. The lap times are cleaned on line 18, and the best lap time is determined with a method call on line 19. Lastly, the player preferences are updated with the new, serialized, value from the lapTimeManager field on line 20.

The last method we'll review in this section is the PlayerStateCompare method. This method is used to compare two players to determine which player is in which position in the current race. First off, the provided player indexes, i1 and i2, are checked for validity on lines 2–4. On lines 9–27, the order of the two players in the race is determined by the current lap, then the current waypoint index, and lastly the fastest lap time. That brings us to the conclusion of this review section. Up next, we'll take a look at the class' main methods.

Main Method Details: GameState

The GameState class has a few main methods for us to review. Let's jump into some code!

Listing 10-12. GameState Main Method Details 1

```
01 public void PauseGame() {
02     gamePaused = true;
03     Time.timeScale = 0;
04
05     if (players != null) {
06         iPg = 0;
07         pPg = null;
08         lPg = players.Count;
09         for (iPg = 0; iPg < lPg; iPg++) {
10             pPg = (PlayerState)players[iPg];
11             if (pPg != null) {
12                 pPg.PauseSound();
13             }
14         }
15     }
16
17     if (audioBgroundSound != null) {
18         audioBgroundSound.Stop();
19     }
20 }

01 public void UnPauseGame() {
02     gamePaused = false;
03     Time.timeScale = 1;
04
```

```
05      if (players != null) {
06          iUpg = 0;
07          pUpg = null;
08          lUpg = players.Count;
09          for (iUpg = 0; iUpg < lUpg; iUpg++) {
10              pUpg = (PlayerState)players[iUpg];
11              if (pUpg != null) {
12                  pUpg.UnPauseSound();
13              }
14          }
15      }
16
17      if (audioBgroundSound != null) {
18          audioBgroundSound.Play();
19      }
20  }
```

```
01  public void FindWaypoints() {
02      GameObject[] list = GameObject.FindGameObjectsWithTag("Waypoint");
03      ArrayList routes = new ArrayList();
04      int l = list.Length;
05      WaypointCheck wc = null;
06      int i = 0;
07      int j = 0;
08
09      for (i = 0; i < l; i++) {
10          if (list[i].activeSelf == true) {
11              wc = (list[i].GetComponent<WaypointCheck>());
12              if (wc != null) {
13                  if (routes.Contains(wc.waypointRoute + "") == false) {
14                      routes.Add(wc.waypointRoute + "");
15                  }
16              }
17          }
18      }
19
```

```
20    ArrayList waypoints = new ArrayList();
21    ArrayList row = new ArrayList();
22    l = routes.Count;
23
24    for (i = 0; i < l; i++) {
25       row.Clear();
26       int l2 = list.Length;
27       for (j = 0; j < l2; j++) {
28          if (list[j].activeSelf == true) {
29             if (waypointWidthOverride != -1) {
30                if (list[j].transform.localScale.z < 10) {
31                   list[j].transform.localScale.Set(list[j].transform.
                      localScale.x, list[j].transform.localScale.y,
                      waypointWidthOverride);
32                }
33             }
34
35             if (waypointZeroOverride != -1) {
36                if (list[j].transform.localPosition.y == 0) {
37                   list[j].transform.localScale.Set(list[j].transform.
                      localScale.x, 1, waypointWidthOverride);
38                }
39             }
40
41             wc = (list[j].GetComponent<WaypointCheck>());
42             if (wc != null) {
43                if ((wc.waypointRoute + "") == (routes[i] + "")) {
44                   row.Add(wc);
45                }
46             }
47          }
48       }
49
```

```
50        object[] ar = row.ToArray();
51        System.Array.Sort(ar, wpc);
52        row = new ArrayList(ar);
53        l2 = row.Count;
54
55        for (j = 0; j < l2; j++) {
56            wc = (WaypointCheck)row[j];
57            wc.waypointIndex = j;
58        }
59
60        waypoints.Add(row);
61    }
62
63    waypointRoutes = routes;
64    waypointData = waypoints;
65 }
```

The first set of main methods for us to look at contains the game's pause and unpause methods as well as the waypoint loading method. Let's take a look! The PauseGame method is used to stop the game if the game's window loses focus. This can be tested in the Unity editor by running the main game and switching to another application while it's running. Notice that the gamePaused Boolean flag is set true, line 2, and the value of the Time.timeScale field is set to zero.

This has the effect of stopping the game engine, line 3. If the array of active players is defined, the loop control variables are set on lines 6–8. The loop iterates over the game's players and pauses the audio for each one, lines 9–14. Subsequently, on lines 17–19, the background music is paused. The second method listed in the set is the UnPauseGame method. This method reverses the game's pause method. Review this method carefully and note that the time scale is restored to one. The last method listed is responsible for finding and preparing all of the track's waypoints. All Unity GameObjects with the "waypoint" tag are located on line 2. A temporary route ArrayList and some loop control variables are set on lines 3–7. Next, on lines 9–18, we loop over all the waypoints and add any unique waypoint routes to the routes array. On lines 20–22, we prepare a few method variables. The row variable is used as a temporary holder for waypoint data, while the waypoints variable holds finalized waypoint data.

We loop over the known routes on line 24, the temp variable is reset on line 25, and a new length variable is set on line 26. Then on line 27, we loop over the list of known waypoints. If the waypoint is active, we then check if we have to apply the waypoint width override, lines 29–33, and the waypoint zero override, lines 35–39. The WaypointCheck script component is set on line 41. If the waypoint is a member of the waypoint group, we add it to the row variable, lines 42–46. On lines 50–52, we sort the waypoints we've found and reset the row variable. The l2 variable is set on line 53, and the route waypoint indices are reset on lines 55-58. On line 60, the route waypoints are added to the waypoints variable. Lastly, on lines 63–64, the waypoint data found is stored in class fields waypointRoutes and waypointData.

Listing 10-13. GameState Main Method Details 2

```
01 public void SetCarDetails() {
02     PlayerState player = null;
03     int i = 0;
04     int l = players.Count;
05
06     for (i = 0; i < l; i++) {
07         if (PlayerStateIdxCheck(i)) {
08             player = (PlayerState)players[i];
09             if (player != null) {
10                 if (i == player1Index) {
11                     gameCamera = player.camera;
12                     player.camera.enabled = true;
13
14                     rearCamera = player.rearCamera;
15                     player.rearCamera.enabled = true;
16                     player.audioListener.enabled = true;
17
18                     if (player1AiOn == true) {
19                         player.aiOn = true;
20                         player.cm.aiOn = true;
21                         player.fpsInput.aiOn = true;
22                         player.mouseInput.aiOn = true;
```

```
23                  } else {
24                      player.aiOn = false;
25                      player.cm.aiOn = false;
26                      player.fpsInput.aiOn = false;
27                      player.mouseInput.aiOn = false;
28                  }
29              } else {
30                  player.camera.enabled = false;
31                  player.rearCamera.enabled = false;
32                  player.audioListener.enabled = false;
33                  player.aiOn = true;
34                  player.cm.aiOn = true;
35                  player.fpsInput.aiOn = true;
36                  player.mouseInput.aiOn = true;
37              }
38              player.waypoints = GetWaypoints(0);
39          }
40      }
41   }
42 }
```

```
01 public void ResetGame() {
02     gamePaused = true;
03     Time.timeScale = 0;
04
05     prepped = false;
06     ready = false;
07     startGame = false;
08     startGameTime = 0.0f;
09     gameRunning = false;
10     gameWon = false;
11
12     Time.timeScale = 1;
13     gamePaused = false;
14 }
```

```
01 public void SetCarDetailsByGameType(PlayerState player) {
02     int idx = player.index;
03     player.player = GameObject.Find(Utilities.NAME_PLAYER_ROOT + idx);
04     player.player.transform.position = GameObject.Find(Utilities.NAME_
       START_ROOT + idx).transform.position;
05
06     player.maxSpeed = PlayerState.DEFAULT_MAX_SPEED;
07     player.gravity = PlayerState.DEFAULT_GRAVITY;
08
09     player.maxForwardSpeedSlow = 50;
10     player.maxSidewaysSpeedSlow = 12;
11     player.maxBackwardsSpeedSlow = 5;
12     player.maxGroundAccelerationSlow = 25;
13
14     player.maxForwardSpeedNorm = 200;
15     player.maxSidewaysSpeedNorm = 50;
16     player.maxBackwardsSpeedNorm = 20;
17     player.maxGroundAccelerationNorm = 100;
18
19     player.maxForwardSpeedBoost = 250;
20     player.maxSidewaysSpeedBoost = 60;
21     player.maxBackwardsSpeedBoost = 30;
22     player.maxGroundAccelerationBoost = 120;
23
24     if (idx != player1Index) {
25         if (difficulty == GameDifficulty.LOW) {
26             player.maxSpeed = PlayerState.DEFAULT_MAX_SPEED;
27             player.maxGroundAccelerationNorm += 5;
28         } else if (difficulty == GameDifficulty.MED) {
29             player.maxSpeed = PlayerState.DEFAULT_MAX_SPEED + 5;
30             player.maxForwardSpeedNorm += 10;
31             player.maxGroundAccelerationNorm += 10;
32         } else if (difficulty == GameDifficulty.HIGH) {
33             player.maxSpeed = PlayerState.DEFAULT_MAX_SPEED + 10;
34             player.maxForwardSpeedNorm += 15;
```

```
35              player.maxGroundAccelerationNorm += 40;
36              player.maxForwardSpeedBoost += 15;
37              player.maxGroundAccelerationBoost += 15;
38          }
39      } else if (idx == player1Index) {
40          player.maxSpeed += Random.Range(0, 12);
41          player.maxForwardSpeedNorm += Random.Range(0, 6);
42          player.maxGroundAccelerationNorm += Random.Range(0, 6);
43          player.maxForwardSpeedBoost += Random.Range(0, 6);
44          player.maxGroundAccelerationBoost += Random.Range(0, 6);
45      }
46 }
```

```
01 public void SetActiveCar(int j) {
02      if (debugOn == false) {
03          Utilities.wr("Method SetActiveCar says: debugOn is false,
            returning.");
04          return;
05      }
06
07      PlayerState player = null;
08      int l = players.Count;
09      for (int i = 0; i < l; i++) {
10          player = (PlayerState)players[i];
11          if (player != null && player.player != null) {
12              if (j == i) {
13                  currentIndex = i;
14                  currentPlayer = (PlayerState)players[currentIndex];
15                  player.camera.enabled = true;
16                  player.rearCamera.enabled = true;
17                  player.audioListener.enabled = true;
18              } else {
19                  player.camera.enabled = false;
20                  player.rearCamera.enabled = false;
```

```
21                  player.audioListener.enabled = false;
22              }
23          }
24      }
25 }
```

The first method listed in this set of main methods is the SetCarDetails method. This method is used to configure each car as an AI- or player-controlled car. On lines 2–4, the method prepares some local variables used to loop over the array of active players. The loop begins on line 6, and if the PlayerState instance, player, is not null, then we process that player on lines 9–39. With regard to this code block, the first branch of code on lines 10–28 is applied to the car that is supposed to be controlled by the human player. On lines 11–165, the hover racer is plugged into the game's HUD. If this car should be AI controlled, then it's configured as such on lines 19–22. Otherwise, the code on lines 24–27 turns AI off for this car. The remaining hover racers are all configured to be AI controlled on lines 30–36.

The next main method listed is the ResetGame method. Direct your attention to lines 2–3 of the method. Notice that the game is marked as paused and the game's time scale is set to zero. On lines 5–10, the method resets key class fields. At the end of the method on lines 12–13, the game paused marker is set to false, and the time scale is returned to a value of one. The third method listed in the set is the SetCarDetailsByGameType, which is used to prepare each hover racer with the correct settings taking into account the current game type. The first line of code gets the player's index from the passed in PlayerState instance, line 2. The player's GameObject and Transform are reinforced on lines 3 and 4. The hover racer's maximum speed, gravity, and speed settings for slow, norm, and boost speeds are set on lines 6–22. If the car's index is not the player one index, then we adjust the car's configuration based on the difficulty of the track, lines 25-38.

The last block of code on lines 40–44 configures the car for the human player. That brings us to the last method in this set, the SetActiveCar method. This method is used to set the currently active player in the race. This doesn't make the car AI or human controlled, but it does connect the car into the game's HUD. To check this feature out, run the "Main13Demonstration" scene in the Unity editor and try pressing the number keys on the keyboard, numbers 1 through 6. You'll notice that you can switch to different cars using this feature. Getting back to the code, notice that the method is escaped if debugOn Boolean field is set to false.

If not, loop control variables are prepared on lines 7–8. We loop over the current set of players, and if the current player is defined, we set it as the game's current player and the game will now display the car's camera, rear-view camera, and blimp camera, which are adjusted accordingly. On lines 19–21, the hover racer is set to the nonactive mode if it doesn't match the specified player index. There are a few main methods left to review in the GameState class. The next one that we'll cover is the all-important PrepGame method. This method is called by a number of classes to ensure that the game and its players are properly configured. Due to the length of the method, we're going to review it in blocks. Let's take a look at the first block of the method.

Listing 10-14. GameState Main Method Details 3

```
001 public void PrepGame() {
002     if (prepped == true) {
003         return;
004     }
005     prepped = true;
006
007     //Prep waypoints and track script settings
008     FindWaypoints();
009     trackScript = GetComponent<TrackScript>();
010     totalLaps = trackScript.laps;
011     nightTime = trackScript.headLightsOn;
012     sceneName = trackScript.sceneName;
013
014     //Prep menu screens
015     if (hudNewScript == null) {
016         if (GameObject.Find("GameHUD") != null) {
017             hudNewScript = GameObject.Find("GameHUD").GetComponent<GameHUD
                NewScript>();
018         }
019     }
020
021     if (hudNewScript != null) {
022         hudNewScript.HideAll();
023     }
```

```
024
025        if (gameOverMenuScript == null) {
026            if (GameObject.Find("GameOverMenu") != null) {
027                gameOverMenuScript = GameObject.Find("GameOverMenu").
                   GetComponent<GameOverMenu>();
028            }
029        }
030
031        if (gameOverMenuScript != null) {
032            gameOverMenuScript.HideWinImage();
033            gameOverMenuScript.ShowLoseImage();
034        }
035
036        if (audioBgroundSound == null) {
037            if (GameObject.Find("BgMusic") != null) {
038                audioBgroundSound = GameObject.Find("BgMusic").
                   GetComponent<AudioSource>();
039            }
040        }
041
042        if (gamePauseMenu == null) {
043            gamePauseMenu = GameObject.Find("GamePauseMenu");
044            if (gamePauseMenu != null) {
045                gamePauseMenu.SetActive(false);
046            }
047        }
048
049        if (gameStartMenu == null) {
050            gameStartMenu = GameObject.Find("GameStartMenu");
051            if (gameStartMenu != null) {
052                gameStartMenu.SetActive(false);
053            }
054        }
055
```

```
056     if (gameOverMenu == null) {
057         gameOverMenu = GameObject.Find("GameOverMenu");
058         if (gameOverMenu != null) {
059             gameOverMenu.SetActive(false);
060         }
061     }
062
063     if (gameExitMenu == null) {
064         gameExitMenu = GameObject.Find("GameExitMenu");
065         if (gameExitMenu != null) {
066             gameExitMenu.SetActive(false);
067         }
068     }
069
070     if (gameHelpMenu == null) {
071         gameHelpMenu = GameObject.Find("GameHelpMenu");
072         if (gameHelpMenu != null) {
073             gameHelpMenu.SetActive(false);
074         }
075     }
076
077     //Prep player prefs default values
078     if (FIRST_RUN && gameStateIndex == GameStateIndex.FIRST) {
079         PlayerPrefs.DeleteKey("GameStateIndex");
080         if (PlayerPrefs.HasKey("EasyOn") == false && PlayerPrefs.
        HasKey("BattleOn") == false && PlayerPrefs.HasKey("ClassicOn") ==
        false) {
081             PlayerPrefs.SetInt("EasyOn", 1);
082             PlayerPrefs.SetInt("BattleOn", 0);
083             PlayerPrefs.SetInt("ClassicOn", 0);
084         }
085
```

```
086     if (PlayerPrefs.HasKey("LowOn") == false && PlayerPrefs.
        HasKey("MedOn") == false && PlayerPrefs.HasKey("HighOn") ==
        false) {
087         PlayerPrefs.SetInt("LowOn", 1);
088         PlayerPrefs.SetInt("MedOn", 0);
089         PlayerPrefs.SetInt("HighOn", 0);
090     }
091     PlayerPrefs.Save();
092   }
093
094   //Prep lap time manager
095   string tmpStr = PlayerPrefs.GetString("LapTimes", "");
096   lapTimeManager = new LapTimeManager();
097   if (tmpStr != null && tmpStr != "") {
098       Utilities.wr("Found lap times: " + tmpStr);
099       lapTimeManager.Deserialize(tmpStr);
100   }
101
```

The main focus of this method, as the name indicates, is to prepare the game for a race. Let's go through the different responsibilities one at a time. First off, the PrepGame method is escaped if it has already been called, lines 2–4. The waypoints are loaded, and any TrackScript values are applied in the prep waypoints section on lines 8–12. References to all of the menu system game objects are configured on lines 15–75. The code is straightforward. Each menu screen game object is loaded by name and subsequently deactivated if defined. Notice that on lines 16–18, a script component reference is created for the hudNewScript field. On line 27, the same process is used to load a reference to the gameOverMenuScript. Using these objects, we can call class methods that adjust the setup of the HUD and game over menu screens.

The next section of code on lines 78–92 is responsible for preparing the player preferences by setting some default values for the race type and difficulty. Next, in the code block on lines 95–100, the lapTimeManager is initialized, and the currently stored lap times, if any, are deserialized and made active in the lapTimeManager instance on line 99. We'll continue reviewing this method with the next block of code listed as follows.

Listing 10-15. GameState Main Method Details 4

```
102     //Prep difficulty
103     if (PlayerPrefs.HasKey("LowOn") == true && PlayerPrefs.
        GetInt("LowOn") == 1) {
104        difficulty = GameDifficulty.LOW;
105     } else if (PlayerPrefs.HasKey("MedOn") == true && PlayerPrefs.
        GetInt("MedOn") == 1) {
106        difficulty = GameDifficulty.MED;
107     } else if (PlayerPrefs.HasKey("HighOn") == true && PlayerPrefs.
        GetInt("HighOn") == 1) {
108        difficulty = GameDifficulty.HIGH;
109     }
110
111     //Prep track configuration
112     if (PlayerPrefs.HasKey("EasyOn") && PlayerPrefs.GetInt("EasyOn") == 1) {
113        gameSettingsSet = 0;
114        totalLaps = 2;
115        TurnOffArmorMarkers();
116        TurnOffGunMarkers();
117        TurnOffInvincMarkers();
118        TurnOffHealthMarkers();
119        TurnOffHittableMarkers();
120        if (difficulty == GameDifficulty.LOW) {
121           gameSettingsSubSet = 0;
122           TurnOffOilDrumStackMarkers();
123           TurnOffFunBoxMarkers();
124        } else if (difficulty == GameDifficulty.MED) {
125           gameSettingsSubSet = 1;
126           TurnOffOilDrumStackMarkers();
127           TurnOnFunBoxMarkers();
128        } else if (difficulty == GameDifficulty.HIGH) {
129           gameSettingsSubSet = 2;
130           TurnOnOilDrumStackMarkers();
131           TurnOnFunBoxMarkers();
132        }
```

```
133     } else if (PlayerPrefs.HasKey("BattleOn") && PlayerPrefs.
        GetInt("BattleOn") == 1) {
134        gameSettingsSet = 1;
135        totalLaps = trackScript.laps;
136        TurnOnArmorMarkers();
137        TurnOnGunMarkers();
138        TurnOnInvincMarkers();
139        TurnOnHealthMarkers();
140        TurnOnHittableMarkers();
141        if (difficulty == GameDifficulty.LOW) {
142           gameSettingsSubSet = 0;
143           TurnOffOilDrumStackMarkers();
144           TurnOffFunBoxMarkers();
145        } else if (difficulty == GameDifficulty.MED) {
146           gameSettingsSubSet = 1;
147           TurnOffOilDrumStackMarkers();
148           TurnOnFunBoxMarkers();
149        } else if (difficulty == GameDifficulty.HIGH) {
150           gameSettingsSubSet = 2;
151           TurnOnOilDrumStackMarkers();
152           TurnOnFunBoxMarkers();
153        }
154     } else if (PlayerPrefs.HasKey("ClassicOn") && PlayerPrefs.
        GetInt("ClassicOn") == 1) {
155        gameSettingsSet = 2;
156        totalLaps = 4;
157        TurnOffArmorMarkers();
158        TurnOffGunMarkers();
159        TurnOffInvincMarkers();
160        TurnOffHealthMarkers();
161        TurnOnHittableMarkers();
162        if (difficulty == GameDifficulty.LOW) {
163           gameSettingsSubSet = 0;
164           TurnOffOilDrumStackMarkers();
165           TurnOffFunBoxMarkers();
```

```
166            } else if (difficulty == GameDifficulty.MED) {
167                gameSettingsSubSet = 1;
168                TurnOffOilDrumStackMarkers();
169                TurnOnFunBoxMarkers();
170            } else if (difficulty == GameDifficulty.HIGH) {
171                gameSettingsSubSet = 2;
172                TurnOnOilDrumStackMarkers();
173                TurnOnFunBoxMarkers();
174            }
175        }
176
177        //Prep game state
178        if (!FIRST_RUN && PlayerPrefs.HasKey("GameStateIndex") == true) {
179            gsiTmp = PlayerPrefs.GetInt("GameStateIndex");
180            if (gsiTmp == 0) {
181                gameStateIndex = GameStateIndex.FIRST;
182            } else if (gsiTmp == 1) {
183                gameStateIndex = GameStateIndex.NONE;
184            } else if (gsiTmp == 2) {
185                gameStateIndex = GameStateIndex.MAIN_MENU_SCREEN;
186            } else if (gsiTmp == 3) {
187                gameStateIndex = GameStateIndex.GAME_OVER_SCREEN;
188            } else if (gsiTmp == 4) {
189                gameStateIndex = GameStateIndex.GAME_PAUSE_SCREEN;
190            } else if (gsiTmp == 5) {
191                gameStateIndex = GameStateIndex.GAME_PLAY_SCREEN;
192            } else if (gsiTmp == 6) {
193                gameStateIndex = GameStateIndex.MAIN_MENU_SCREEN;
194            }
195        }
196
197        if (gameStateIndex == GameStateIndex.NONE || gameStateIndex ==
       GameStateIndex.FIRST) {
198            gameStateIndex = GameStateIndex.MAIN_MENU_SCREEN;
199        }
```

300

```
201     if (gameStateIndex == GameStateIndex.MAIN_MENU_SCREEN) {
202        player1AiOn = true;
203        ShowStartMenu();
204        HidePauseMenu();
205        HideEndMenu();
206     } else if (gameStateIndex == GameStateIndex.GAME_OVER_SCREEN) {
207        player1AiOn = true;
208        ShowStartMenu();
209        HidePauseMenu();
210        HideEndMenu();
211     } else if (gameStateIndex == GameStateIndex.GAME_PAUSE_SCREEN) {
212        ShowPauseMenu();
213     } else if (gameStateIndex == GameStateIndex.GAME_PLAY_SCREEN) {
214        HidePauseMenu();
215        HideEndMenu();
216        HideStartMenu();
217     }
218
```

The class field, `difficulty`, is set based on the value of the player preferences for the current track difficulty. This value is used extensively in the next section of code in the method lines 112–175. The Hover Racers game has the ability to adjust the features of a track to reflect the race type and difficulty. This code is very direct. Trace through it and you'll see what track features are turned on or off based on the different track settings. This brings us to an important section of code on lines 178–217. This section of code is responsible for preparing the game state by hiding or showing the game's menu screens. The next block of code in this method is listed as follows.

Listing 10-16. GameState Main Method Details 5

```
219     //Prep blimp camera
220     if (blimpCamera == null) {
221        blimpCamera = GameObject.Find("BlimpCamera");
222     }
223
```

```
224     //Prep track settings
225     raceTrack = PlayerPrefs.GetInt("RaceTrack");
226     int tmp = PlayerPrefs.GetInt("EasyOn");
227     if (tmp == 0) {
228        easyOn = false;
229     } else {
230        easyOn = true;
231     }
232
233     raceType = PlayerPrefs.GetInt("RaceType");
234     Utilities.wr("RaceTrack: " + raceTrack);
235     Utilities.wr("EasyOn: " + easyOn);
236     Utilities.wr("RaceType: " + raceType);
237
238     if (PlayerPrefs.GetInt("RaceTrackHelp" + raceTrack) != 1) {
239        trackHelpOn = true;
240     } else {
241        trackHelpOn = false;
242     }
243
244     //Prep player positions
245     positions = new int[6];
246     positions[0] = 0;
247     positions[1] = 1;
248     positions[2] = 2;
249     positions[3] = 3;
250     positions[4] = 4;
251     positions[5] = 5;
252     players = new ArrayList();
253     players.AddRange(GameObject.Find("GameState").
        GetComponents<PlayerState>());
254
255     //Prep player states
256     int l = players.Count;
257     PlayerState player;
```

```
258    Transform t;
259    for (int i = 0; i < l; i++) {
260       Utilities.wr("Setting up player " + i);
261       player = (PlayerState)players[i];
262       if (player != null) {
263          player.index = i;
264          player.carType = i;
265          player.position = i;
266          SetCarDetailsByGameType(player); //sets the model and speeds
267
268          if (player.player != null) {
269             player.active = true;
270             player.controller = player.player.GetComponent<CharacterCon
                 troller>();
271             player.cm = player.player.GetComponent<CharacterMotor>();
272             player.camera = player.player.transform.Find("Main
                 Camera").GetComponent<Camera>();
273             player.rearCamera = player.player.transform.Find("Rear
                 Camera").GetComponent<Camera>();
274             player.audioListener = player.player.transform.Find("Main
                 Camera").GetComponent<AudioListener>();
275             player.mouseInput = player.player.
                 GetComponent<MouseLookNew>();
276             player.fpsInput = player.player.GetComponent<
                 FPSInputController>();
277
278             t = player.player.transform.Find("Car");
279             if (t != null) {
280                player.gun = (GameObject)t.Find("Minigun_Head").
                    gameObject;
281                player.gunBase = (GameObject)t.Find("Minigun_Base").
                    gameObject;
282             }
283
```

```
284            player.lightHeadLight = (GameObject)player.player.
               transform.Find("HeadLight").gameObject;
285            if (player.lightHeadLight != null && nightTime == false) {
286                player.lightHeadLight.SetActive(false);
287            } else {
288                player.lightHeadLight.SetActive(true);
289            }
290
291            player.totalLaps = totalLaps;
292            player.currentLap = 0;
293            player.aiWaypointIndex = 0;
294            player.aiWaypointRoute = 0;
295            player.waypoints = GetWaypoints(player.aiWaypointRoute);
296            player.flame = (GameObject)player.player.transform.
               Find("Flame").gameObject;
297            player.gunExplosion = (GameObject)player.player.transform.
               Find("GunExplosion").gameObject;
298            //TODO //player.gunExplosionParticleSystem = player.
               gunExplosion.GetComponent<ParticleEmitter>();
299            player.gunHitSmoke = (GameObject)player.player.transform.
               Find("GunHitSmoke").gameObject;
300            //TODO //player.gunHitSmokeParticleSystem = player.
               gunHitSmoke.GetComponent<ParticleEmitter>();
301
302            if (player.gunOn == true) {
303                player.gun.SetActive(true);
304                player.gunBase.SetActive(true);
305            } else {
306                player.gun.SetActive(false);
307                player.gunBase.SetActive(false);
308            }
309
310            player.flame.SetActive(false);
311            player.gunExplosion.SetActive(false);
312            //TODO //player.gunExplosionParticleSystem.emit = false;
313            player.gunHitSmoke.SetActive(false);
```

```
314                //TODO //player.gunHitSmokeParticleSystem.emit = false;
315                player.LoadAudio();
316            } else {
317                Utilities.wr("Player model " + i + " is
                   NULL. Deactivating...");
318                player.active = false;
319                player.prepped = false;
320            }
321        } else {
322            Utilities.wr("Player " + i + " is NULL. Removing...");
323            players.RemoveAt(i);
324            1--;
325        }
326
327        player.prepped = true;
328    }
329    SetCarDetails();
330
331    //Start game //line 324
332    ready = true;
333    FIRST_RUN = false;
334 }
```

At the start of this block of code, listed previously, the blimp camera is configured on lines 220–222. A few more track settings are processed on lines 225–242, and we've just about handled all the game preparation responsibilities. Next up, the player positions array is initialized for the default set of six hover racers. A player state object instance is loaded into the initialized player's ArrayList on lines 252 and 253. Now we have to configure each PlayerState object. If everything is set up correctly, we'll have six PlayerState objects, one for each player.

The next section of code, under the "Prep Player States" heading, is arguably the most important. This code is responsible for preparing all aspects of the players and their cars. Local variables are set on lines 256 to 258, and the array of players is iterated over starting on lines 259–261. The player's index, car type, and position are set on lines 263–265 with their models and speed values configured by a call to the SetCarDetailsByGameType method.

If the car's model is successfully loaded, then the code from 268 to 315 executes. If not, the array entry is deactivated by setting the prepped field to false. Carefully review this code and note how the PlayerState class has all its fields prepped; models, camera, and controllers are set here. The final setup is performed by a call to the SetCarDetails method, line 329. This method is responsible for setting up the main and rear-view cameras, audio listener, and AI or user input controls. The method returns after setting the ready field to true and the FIRST_RUN field to false. The game is now ready to run!

We've covered a ton of code so far in this chapter, but we're not out of the woods yet. There are a few remaining methods I want to discuss. The next set of methods to review is listed as follows.

Listing 10-17. GameState Main Method Details 6

```
01 public void OnApplicationPause(bool pauseStatus) {
02     if (AreMenusShowing()) {
03         if (pauseStatus == true) {
04             PauseGame();
05         } else {
06             UnPauseGame();
07         }
08     } else {
09         if (pauseStatus == true) {
10             if (gameStateIndex == GameStateIndex.GAME_PLAY_SCREEN) {
11                 ShowPauseMenu();
12             } else {
13                 PauseGame();
14             }
15         } else {
16             if (gameStateIndex == GameStateIndex.GAME_PLAY_SCREEN) {
17                 HidePauseMenu();
18             } else {
19                 UnPauseGame();
20             }
21         }
22     }
23 }
```

```
01 void Start() {
02     if (style1 == null) {
03         style1 = new GUIStyle();
04         style1.normal.textColor = Color.red;
05         style1.fontStyle = FontStyle.Bold;
06         style1.fontSize = 16;
07     }
08
09     if (style2 == null) {
10         style2 = new GUIStyle();
11         style2.normal.textColor = Color.black;
12         style2.fontStyle = FontStyle.Bold;
13         style2.fontSize = 16;
14     }
15
16     if (forceGameStart == true) {
17         if (SceneManager.GetActiveScene().name == "DemoCollideTrackHelp") {
18             PlayerPrefs.DeleteAll();
19             PlayerPrefs.Save();
20         } else if (SceneManager.GetActiveScene().name ==
           "DemoCollideScript") {
21             PlayerPrefs.DeleteAll();
22             PlayerPrefs.SetInt("BattleOn", 1);
23             PlayerPrefs.SetInt("HighOn", 1);
24             PlayerPrefs.Save();
25         } else if (SceneManager.GetActiveScene().name ==
           "DemoCarSensorScriptAutoPass") {
26             CarSensorScript.TRIGGER_SPEED_PASSING = 0.00f;
27         } else if (SceneManager.GetActiveScene().name ==
           "DemoCarSensorScriptGunShot") {
28             PlayerPrefs.DeleteAll();
29             PlayerPrefs.SetInt("BattleOn", 1);
30             PlayerPrefs.SetInt("HighOn", 1);
31             PlayerPrefs.Save();
```

```
32          } else if (SceneManager.GetActiveScene().name ==
            "DemoCameraFollowXz") {
33              GameStartMenu.TRACK_NAME_1 = "DemoCameraFollowXz";
34              GameStartMenu.TRACK_NAME_2 = "DemoCameraFollowXz";
35          } else if (SceneManager.GetActiveScene().name ==
            "Main13Demonstration") {
36              GameState.ON_GUI_SHOW_CAR_DETAILS = true;
37              debugOn = true;
38              PlayerState.SHOW_AI_LOGIC = true;
39          }
40      }
41
42      audioS = GetComponent<AudioSource>();
43      if (audioS == null) {
44          Utilities.wrForce("GameState: audioS is null!");
45      }
46 }
```

The OnApplicationPause method is a Unity game engine callback method that fires when the game loses focus. If there are menus showing and the pauseStatus is true, then we want to pause the game via a call to the PauseGame method, line 4. If not, we want to unpause the game via a call to the UnPauseGame method, line 6. If, however, there are no menus showing, then the code on lines 9–21 executes. In this case, if the pauseStatus is true and the game is on the main game screen, then we simply show the pause menu screen, line 11. If not, then we pause the game. Similarly, on lines 16–20, if the pauseStatus argument is false and the game is active, we call the HidePauseMenu method. Otherwise, we unpause the game, line 19.

The next method in this set is the Start method. The main responsibility of this method is to prepare a few things for the class. First, the method loads up some styles used in the OnGUI method to display debugging text on the screen, lines 2–14. Next, on line 16, if the game is configured as a demo scene, then the forceGameStart flag will be true. The code on lines 17–39 is used to prepare different demonstration scenes that the code supports. Lastly, on lines 42–45, the track's background music is loaded.

There is one last method in this class that we haven't covered, the Update method. Despite being quite a long method, the code is very simple. This method updates the game's HUD; recall that the Update method runs each game frame, to reflect changes to the current player's car as they race on the track and experience different interactions and have different modifiers triggered. Read over this method and make sure you understand how it functions before moving on. That brings us to the conclusion of the GameState class review. This means that we've looked over, in detail, just about every class, field, and method in the game.

Demonstration: GameState

The best way to demonstrate the GameState class is to open the "Main13Demonstration" scene and play it. While the arcade demonstration mode is running, use the number keys, 1–6, to jump between cars and note how the HUD automatically updates to display the state of the currently selected hover racer. Another good demonstration might be to just play the game and let all your knowledge of how the game works flow through your mind as you actually experience it through game play.

Chapter Conclusion

In this chapter, we finished looking at the player and game state classes by completing the GameState code review. This was no small feat. There's a lot going on in this class because it's the central control point for the entire game. Take a moment to pat yourself on the back. This brings us to the conclusion of the game's code review. We've covered all the game specifications outlined in Chapter 2, and at this point in the text, you should have a good understanding of how game objects, physics, collisions, and script components all interact to create a game. Don't get frustrated if you didn't absorb it all the first time around. There's a lot going on, and you may need to give yourself more time to really grasp it all.

CHAPTER 11

Making It Professional

Welcome to Chapter 11. If you've made it this far, then you've reviewed a tremendous amount of code. I think you've earned your stripes. We won't be reviewing much code at all in the remaining chapters, at least not of any great length. Instead, we'll be taking a close look at the Unity editor and the aspects of game creation that set your game apart from the rest of the pack. This chapter is all about the features, steps, and mechanics that make your game professional. We're going to cover the following topics and how they are addressed in Unity:

1. Build Settings

2. Input Mapping

3. UI/Menu System

4. Data Persistence

5. Memory Management

6. Sounds and Music

7. Static Objects

8. Tags and Layers

9. AI Opponents

10. Cameras

11. Project Settings

It's a fairly varied list of topics. Some of them, if approached in detail, could fill up an entire book on their own. We're going to keep things light and focus on the important, general, aspects of the topic at hand. The first topic we'll tackle is the build settings. This is a concise, Unity-specific topic that's perfect for our first discussion. And with that, let's get started.

311

© Victor G Brusca 2022
V. G Brusca, *Advanced Unity Game Development*, https://doi.org/10.1007/978-1-4842-7851-2_11

Build Settings

Unity build settings are used to choose the target platform, configure your build, and start the build and test process. It's an important part of any serious Unity project because it's used to create the development and production builds of your game. Unity supports a number of build targets, but we'll focus on the most common targets and the settings I think are the most important with regard to iterative development builds and the quality of production builds. I'm going to focus on the build settings that affect efficiency of both the game development process and the performance of the game itself. We'll look at some choice build settings for the following platforms:

1. Generic Platform

2. PC, Mac, and Linux Desktop

3. Universal Windows Platform (UWP)

4. iOS

5. Android

6. WebGL

There are other build targets supported by Unity that we won't cover here, but this review should put you in a place of knowledge and confidence with regard to managing the build settings for any platform.

Generic Platform Settings

The generic platform settings are a group of build settings that apply to all platforms.

Development Build: This setting is used to enable script debugging and Profiler support in your project's build. You might be wondering why you would use this option when you can debug and profile your game in the Unity editor. The truth is that target devices can and will behave differently than your development environment. It's important to start testing your game on target devices early, and often, in your project's development.

Script Debugging: This option is only available if the "Development Build" setting is activated and is not available on the WebGL platform. Enable this option if you want your script component code to be debugged. I personally enable options like this when there is debugging to be done. I try to keep my development testing as pure as possible.

Scripts Only Build: This is a very useful feature for projects that have a large number of assets. If your project build time is hampering your testing iterations, then try using this build option. In order to use this setting, you'll have to do a full build of the project. Once that's done however, you'll be able to rebuild the project, scripts only, to address code issues much faster. This setting requires that the "Development Build" setting is enabled.

Compression Method: The compression method setting is an important one. Depending on your target platform, you'll have some compression options you can set. Test them all. Find the one that works best on your target devices. Don't overlook this setting. The choice you make can have noticeable effects on your game's load time.

PC, Mac, and Linux Desktop Settings

This category of build settings applies to desktop build targets, as you might have guessed.

Architecture: This option is not available on macOS. It is available for Windows and Linux. Optimize this setting to match the architecture of your target device. Again, test different settings to find the best fit for your game.

Copy PDB Files: The copy PDB files option is only available if you're targeting the Windows platform. This is a useful setting for adding debugging information to your game builds. This can give you an edge when tracking down stubborn bugs that crop up during development. Needless to say, this setting should be turned off for production builds.

Create Visual Studio Solution/Create XCode Project: This setting is available for Windows and Mac respectively. While you might not need this feature in all cases, if you need more control over your resulting project, this feature may help. Use it if you want a project created that, when compiled, will produce your final product.

Universal Windows Platform (UWP) Settings

This section covers the UWP build settings. There are a few more options available than we'll cover here, so I encourage you to take a look at the Unity documentation for more information.

Architecture: The UWP version of this build setting has a few different targets for you to choose from. You can specify x86, x64, ARM, and ARM64 but only when used with Unity's "Build and Run" option. This is most likely due to the universal aspect of this platform. It most likely includes binaries for all of the architectures listed previously in the resulting development or production build. What this option does is allow you to work with a specific architecture for testing, debugging, and evaluation.

Build Type: This setting is used to control how your project is built with regard to UWP and Visual Studio. You can choose XAML, Direct 3D, or executable only. If you want to use Windows XAML with your project, you'll take a performance hit, but you'll be able to XAML elements in your project. This is probably an uncommon choice for most games. The Direct 3D option offers the best performance and presents the game in a basic application window. The last option, executable only, is an interesting feature. This setting hosts the project in a prebuilt executable that doesn't generate a Visual Studio project. Use this option to lower your build times so you can iterate faster and get your testing and debugging done a lot quicker.

Build Configuration: This build setting only applies to Unity's "Build and Run" feature. The setting's options are the same as those in the Visual Studio project that Unity generates. The debug option includes debugging symbols and enables the Unity Profiler. The release option has no debugging code but also enables the Profiler. Lastly, the master option is fully optimized for a release build. Use this build setting to get your game optimized and ready for publication.

Deep Profiling: This option is used to profile all of your script code including recording function calls. Use this setting to pinpoint performance issues in your game, but be wary; it uses a lot of memory and might not work as expected with very complicated scripts.

Auto Connect Profiler: Automatically connects the Profiler to the game build. This setting requires that the "Development Build" option is enabled.

iOS Settings

The iOS platform has a lot of build settings that overlap with the platforms we've already covered, so we won't go over them again here. We will, however, review some iOS-specific options.

Run in XCode: This option is only available on macOS and is used to specify the version of XCode used to run the resulting project.

Run in XCode as: This option can be used to help you debug your iOS game by allowing you to specify if the project runs in debug or release mode. Use this feature if you need to debug your code and want to use XCode to do so. You can also use it to run release builds to check functionality in XCode before you start your device testing.

Symlink Unity Libraries: This option lets you reference Unity libraries instead of copying them into the project. Using this feature reduces the resulting XCode project size and helps you iterate faster due to quicker project build times.

Android Settings

Similar to the iOS settings, the Android build settings overlap partially with the options we've already reviewed, so we won't cover them again here. We'll focus on the settings that help you optimize and test your game.

Texture Compression: The Android platform supports the following texture compression formats at the time of this writing: DXT, PVRTC, ETC, ETC2, and ASTC. The default setting is ETC, but you should be aware of the capabilities of your target devices and choose a setting that offers you the best balance of support and efficiency.

ETC2 Fallback: I won't go into detail on this setting. If you are using the ETC2 texture compression format, be aware of this option. It can help make your game run more efficiently on devices that don't support ETC2 and OpenGL ES 3.

Run Device: This build setting lets you specify the target attached Android device which you can then use to test and debug your builds.

WebGL Settings

The WebGL platform has a number of build settings that overlap with the options we've already covered. You can apply that knowledge when configuring the build settings for this platform.

Input Mapping

Input mapping, in my opinion, is an essential aspect of a professional game. By using input mappings, you create an abstraction layer between the input and your game. This allows you to map similar inputs to one input label. Why do I need this for my game? Well, if you're going through the trouble of building a game, why limit its input to one or two directly mapped inputs. Take the time to refine and use input mappings to seamlessly support multiple inputs. The following screenshot demonstrates such an input mapping configuration used in the Hover Racers game.

Figure 11-1. *Input Mapping Example*

The image depicts multiple raw inputs mapped to an input label

As you can see in the previously listed image, we've mapped keyboard input and joystick input to the same label, "Horizontal." Now, let's take a look at some input code and see how the label is used.

Listing 11-1. Input Mapping in Use

```
01 if (Input.GetAxis("Turn") < 0.0f) {
02     if (Input.GetAxis("Horizontal") < 0.0f) {
03         transform.Rotate(0, -1.75f, 0);
04     } else {
05         transform.Rotate(0, -1.25f, 0);
06     }
07 }
08
```

```
09 if (Input.GetAxis("Turn") > 0.0f) {
10     if (Input.GetAxis("Horizontal") > 0.0f) {
11         transform.Rotate(0, 1.75f, 0);
12     } else {
13         transform.Rotate(0, 1.25f, 0);
14     }
15 }
```

Notice in the previously listed code that the "Horizontal" input mapping is used regardless of the input source. The player can be using a keyboard, controller, or mouse to make the hover racer turn; we don't care which. Take the time to work on your game's input! A great game can be ruined by bad controls. Conversely, a game that might not look like much can be really fun and addictive to play if the controls are implemented correctly.

UI/Menu System

The menu system is another one of those features that can really detract from your game if it's not implemented well. Users are accustomed to fairly competent UI in their games. This is something you should keep in mind when building your game. The menu system should be simple and intuitive. Limit the number of options and information on any given menu screen to make things easy for your players to understand what's going on.

Aside from providing the menu system in the actual game as a solid example to work from, I want to talk about two aspects of the Unity UI system that will help you get up and running faster. The first is setting up a new Canvas, and the second is setting up a Panel with some buttons. We'll also go over connecting those buttons to an associated script component. Open up the main project and create a new scene named "MyMenuSystemSample." Open the scene and you'll be greeted by a default, somewhat blank "Hierarchy" panel.

Right-click in the "Hierarchy" panel and select the "UI" section of the context menu and then select the Canvas entry. You'll see two editions to the hierarchy: a Canvas and an EventSystem object. We'll focus on the Canvas object for now. Select it and direct your attention to the "Inspector" panel. Expand the "Canvas" entry and set the "Render Mode" to "Screen Space – Overlay." This will display the menu on top of whatever is on the screen and is a good starting point for your menu system. Check the "Pixel Perfect" option if you want to make sure the menu graphics are scaled as cleanly as possible. Make sure the "Target Display" is set to "Display 1."

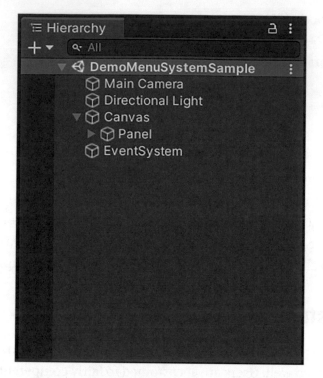

Figure 11-2. *Canvas Hierarchy Example*

An image snippet depicting the hierarchy after adding a Canvas and Panel object

Next, expand the "Canvas Scaler" entry and set the "UI Scale Mode" to the "Scale with Screen Size" value. We're going to set things up so that the menu screen is centered and scales up and down with the game's screen size. The "Reference Resolution" entry should match the dimensions that were used to create your menu screen assets, specifically the background image being used. In this case, we'll set the "X" value to 640 and the "Y" value to 960. The "Screen Match Mode" should be set to "Match Width or Height," and the "Match" option should have a value of 0.5. This is an even balance between width and height. Lastly, the "Pixels Per Unit" entry should match the pixel density of the original menu background image. In this case, set it to 326.

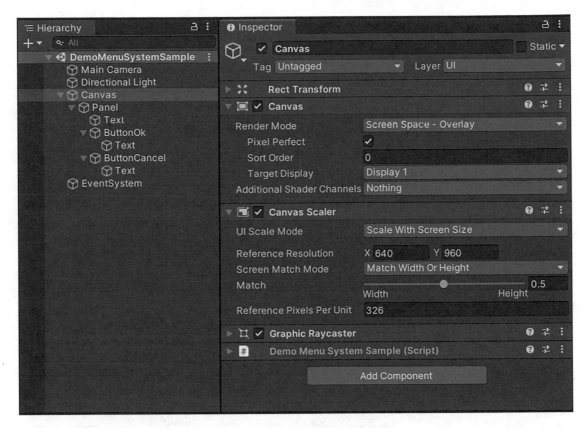

Figure 11-3. *Canvas Hierarchy and Settings Example*

A screenshot depicting the completed demo scene hierarchy and focusing on the Canvas' settings

Now we're going to add a Panel object to our Canvas. Select the Canvas object in the hierarchy and right-click on it. Select the "UI" option and then select the "Panel" entry. Your Canvas object will now have a Panel child object. Select the new child object and direct your attention to the "Inspector" panel. Expand the "Rect Transform" entry and set the "Width" and "Height" values to 460 and 240, respectively. These are the natural dimensions of the background image we'll use.

We want our menu scenes to stay centered, so we'll work on the "Anchors" and "Pivot" options next. The "Min" and "Max" anchor values for "X" and "Y" should be set to 0.5. These values represent a percentage, 0.0 to 1.0 or 0% to 100% if you want to think about it that way. Now set the "Pivot" values for "X" and "Y" to 0.5 as well. This will set the pivot and anchor points to the center of the menu. The "Rotation", "PosY", "PosX", and "PosZ" fields should all be set to zero.

Let's take a look at the `Panel` object's "Image" entry in the "Inspector" panel next. Expand it and select the "Source Image" option, click the selection button, and in the resulting popup window, type in "menu" and find the entry named "MenuPanel_512x512." You may need to reset the "Rect Transform" entry's "Width" and "Height" values after this step, so be sure to double-check them. Set the "Image Type" option to "Sliced" and check the "Fill Center" checkbox.

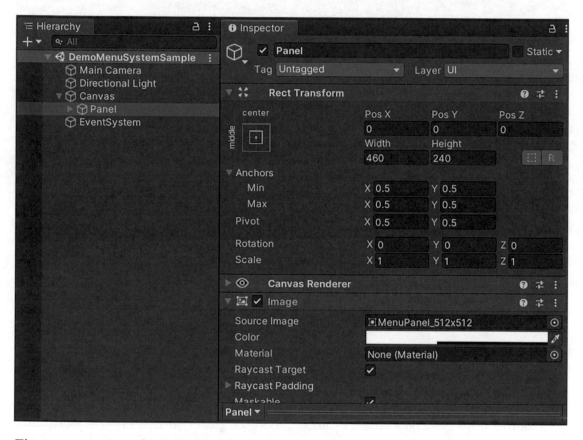

Figure 11-4. *Panel Hierarchy and Settings Example*

A screenshot showing the Panel object's "Rect Transform" and "Image" settings

The last thing we'll do in this section is add menu screen features, some text, and two buttons. Then we'll connect the buttons to a script, run a few tests, and call it a day.

Step 1: Add a Text Object

- Select the Panel object from the hierarchy and right-click it.

- Select the "UI" option and then select the Text entry. A new Text object will be added as a child of the Panel object.

- Select it and direct your attention to the "Rect Transform" section in the "Inspector" panel.

Step 2: Configure the new Text Object

- Set the value of the "PosY" field to 60.

- Now scroll down to the "Text" section and expand it. Change the value of the "Text" field to "Hello World." Change the "Font Style" to "Bold" and the "Font Size" to 20.

- Under the "Paragraph" subsection, set the "Alignment" option to centered text.

Step 3: Add two Button Objects

- Follow the same process you used to add the Text object to the Panel except add two Button objects this time. All three UI elements should be child objects of the Panel.

Step 4: Configure Button Objects

- Rename the first Button object as "ButtonOk" and name the second button as "ButtonCancel."

- Select the ButtonOk object and expand the "Rect Transform" section in the "Inspector" panel. Set the value of the "PosX" field to –90. Do the same thing for the ButtonCancel object except use a value of 90.

The simple menu screen is shaping up nicely. Notice that the two buttons are inherently parent objects. Expand the first button and select the Text child object. Set its "Text" value to "Ok." Repeat this step for the second button except set its "Text" value to "Cancel."

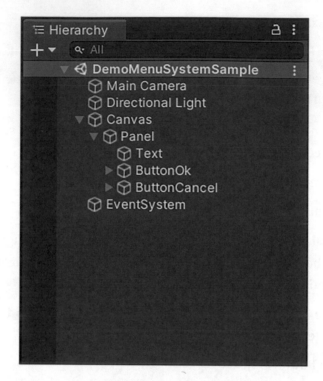

Figure 11-5. *Panel Hierarchy with UI Elements Example*

An image snippet depicting the scene's hierarchy with Panel object and UI elements added

We're going to add a script component to the Canvas object. Select the Canvas object in the hierarchy. Now, go to the "Project" panel and search for the following string, "DemoMenuSystemSample". Locate the script component with that name and add it to the Canvas object. Next, right-click on the Canvas object and select the "Properties..." entry. Move the resulting popup off to the side a bit. Select the ButtonOk object and expand the "Button" section in the "Inspector" panel.

Scroll down to the "On Click" section and click the "+" button. Set the type of the resulting row entry to "Editor and Runtime." Drag the "Demo Menu System Simple" script component from the properties popup to the "Object" field of the "On Click" row entry. Change the value of "No function" to "DemoMenuSystemSample" selecting the "BtnOkClick" function. Do the same thing for the cancel button except this time select the "BtnCancelClick" function. We have everything all wired up. Take it for a spin and check the logs for indications of which button was clicked. A demonstration of this simple screen can be found by opening the "DemoMenuSystemSample" scene.

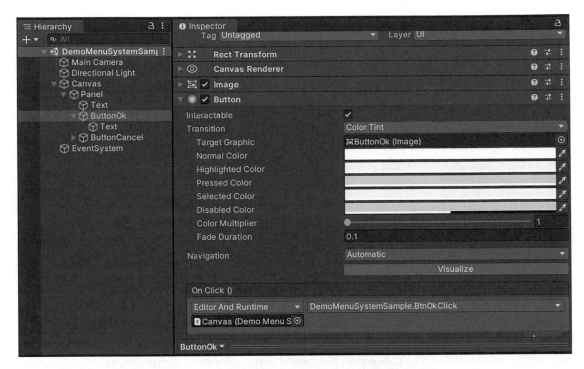

Figure 11-6. *Panel Hierarchy and Settings Example*

A screenshot depicting the configuration of the ButtonOk object

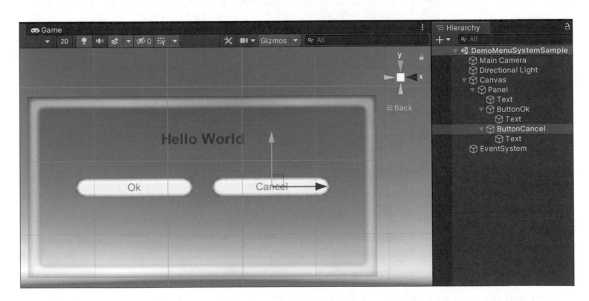

Figure 11-7. *Finished UI Hierarchy Example*

A screenshot depicting the hierarchy and scene of the completed UI demonstration

Data Persistence

We covered data persistence during our review of the Hover Racers code base. This is a simplified form of data persistence that uses the Unity APIs `PlayerPrefs` class. While it's great for storing simple data, it might not be the best solution for complex information. Serialization techniques, like the kind that we used to store track time data, might be an option, but you shouldn't use it for large amounts of data or for very complex data. In those cases, you should explore writing and reading data files.

Memory Management

Since you're writing your Unity game in C#, a memory-managed language, then you don't have to worry about memory management, right? Wrong. Garbage collection uses resources, and the more work the garbage collector has to do, the greater chance it has to disrupt the smooth frame rate of your game. Make sure to keep track of the methods that run every frame and keep the creation of hanging objects, objects that aren't referenced anywhere else and are lost at the completion of the method, to a minimum.

In the Hover Racers game, we used private class fields as a replacement for local method variables to circumvent the garbage collector. This approach can quickly become cumbersome however and is not recommended for more complex methods, classes. Keep memory management on your mind when coding and you're halfway there. Clean up any remaining issues by profiling your game and scrutinizing methods and classes that are involved with the Unity engine's `Update` method, or other frequently firing methods like collision callback methods.

Sounds and Music

This may seem obvious, but I'll go over it anyway. Sound effects and music are very important to any game, including yours. Don't worry if you aren't able to create audio resources. There are a ton of places, Unity store included, where you can get access to great music and sounds. Generally speaking, every interaction from the player, sometimes through their character, should elicit some kind of sound effect. You should also find a decent background track and ambient sounds if applicable. I know this is a lot to add onto a game build, but if you keep it in mind and use placeholders during development, you'll be in a great place when the time comes to polish and refine your project.

Static Objects

If you select any GameObject in the Unity editor and check that object's configuration in the "Inspector" panel, you'll notice a little check box next to the label named "Static" in the top right-hand corner of the panel. If an object in your game doesn't move or interact with characters or AI opponents and doesn't interact with other objects, you should mark it as static. Doing so will increase the efficiency of your game as static objects are escaped from certain runtime calculations.

Tags and Layers

Tags and layers are great features for organizing interactions in your game. You can find the management screen for them under the "Edit" ➤ "Project Settings..." main menu option. Select the "Tags and Layers" entry on the left-hand side of the resulting settings window. Tags are reference names you can assign to one or more GameObjects. For example, all of the hover racers in the game have the tag "Players." Tags help you identify specific GameObjects and can aid in programmatically connecting game objects to script fields.

Layers in Unity are used to define which GameObjects can interact with each other. As noted in the Unity documentation, they are most commonly used by Camera objects to render only part of the scene and by lights to illuminate only parts of the scene's contents. We do not really use layers in the Hover Racers code base. However, if you look at the blimp camera, top right-hand side of the game screen, you can imagine a scenario where the camera doesn't display a full rendering of the track, as it does now. For instance, it could be configured, using layers, to only show certain objects and nothing more. Keep these features in mind during your game's development.

AI Opponents

Now this is a bit of a tough subject. First off, AI, in this case, is a bit of a misnomer. Currently, and perhaps for a little while still, game AI is not true artificial intelligence or machine learning. In the same way that certain physics calculations can be approximated and thereby simplified, game AI is meant to mimic a human player as closely as possible and in doing so appear intelligent. In the not-too-distant future, every decent computer will have dedicated AI/ML hardware similar to the way GPUs work today, and in some cases, they already exist. Look into Google's TPU and Apple's M1 chip.

But for now, we'll have to live with approximated and simplified game AI. This is a huge topic and is heavily reliant on the type of game you're making. One of the main aspects of a game AI implementation is mimicking user input and managing that input to create a realistic AI player. With this in mind, you might want to abstract the input handling from the actual input so the same functionality can be achieved programmatically.

When implementing the Hover Racers' AI, we have the benefit of simplicity. The hover racers have a set, designated, place where they can move, the racetrack. Without it, you'll have to use pathfinding techniques like A* or Unity's navigation mesh system. Furthermore, the racers can only speed up, slow down, or turn. The track's waypoint system tells them what direction to move in, where the track's center point is, how much to turn, and when to slow down. That's everything we need for decent AI opponents in this game. I recommend thinking and planning for AI very early on in your project.

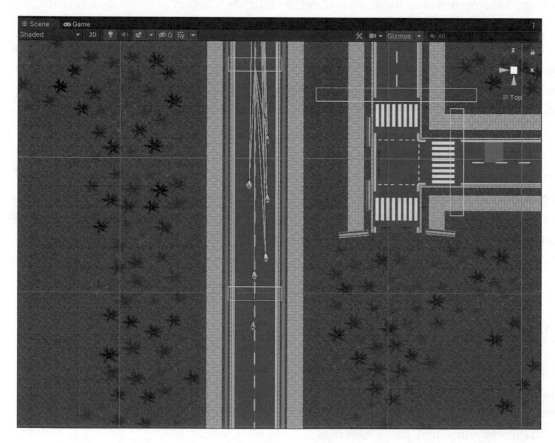

Figure 11-8. *Hove Racer AI Logic Example*

A screenshot depicting the AI opponent's calculation that determines where to move and how much to turn

Cameras

Cameras can be an awesome addition to your game. A lot of games implement two or more cameras to provide different views of the current level. That navigation HUD on your favorite FPS is most likely a camera set to only see a specific layer of objects that are used to depict a simplified version of a player's environment or location on a given level. Adding cameras to your game in new and unique ways can really make your game stand out. For an example of how to position and size your cameras, check out the "Main13" or "Main14" scene, the main game scenes for this project.

Project Performance

Last but not least, there are the Project Settings. There are a lot of settings involved with your Unity project, a few we've touched upon already. There are more than I can hope to address in this text. I would, however, like to spend a little bit of time discussing the "Quality" settings. You can find the Project Settings as an option under the "Edit" entry in the main menu. The "Quality" section can be selected from the left-hand side of the resulting popup window.

Take the time to test these settings to get the correct balance of quality and performance for your game. You can check how your game performs under the hood by using a few Unity performance monitoring tools. The first such tool we'll look at is the "Game" panel's "Stats" feature. Open up the main game scene, "Main13" or "Main14," and run the game in the Unity editor. Notice that there is a "Stats" button on the top-right hand side of the panel. Click it and you should see something similar to the following screenshot.

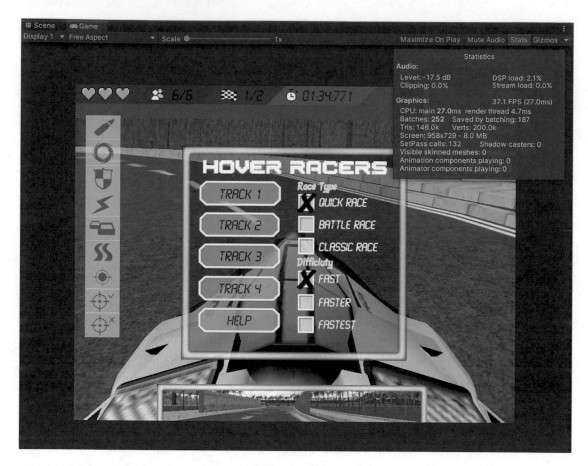

Figure 11-9. *Hove Racers Stats Example*

A screenshot depicting the scene statistics dialog

This little popup has a lot of useful high-level information about your game and can be used to identify issues with your project. "Why is my game only running at 30 FPS?" you ask. Good question. To get a truer picture of your game's performance, stop the game and click the "Maximize on Play" button, located next to the "Stats" button. Now start the game back up and open the "Stats" popup once again. An example of this feature is as follows.

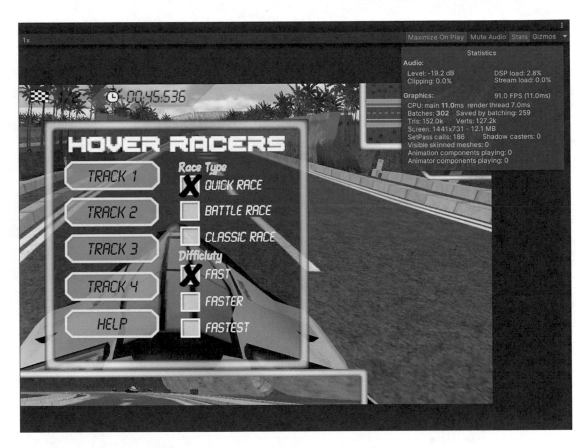

Figure 11-10. *Hove Racers Maximized Stats Example*

A screenshot depicting the main game running in the Unity editor, maximized,
with the statistics popup showing

Take a look at the frame rate in the previously listed image. Note that it's running
at 91 frames per second at 1441 × 731 pixels. That's not too shabby. Plan to check your
game's performance at regular intervals, especially after adding new features and
game mechanics. But what happens if I detect performance issues during testing in the
Unity editor? The statistics popup isn't giving me enough information to approach the
problem. Fear not! The Unity Profiler can help. The Profiler can be found at the following
main menu location: "Window" ➤ "Analysis" ➤ "Profiler." Let's run the game again and
watch the data flow into the Profiler's graphs and summary sections. Take a look at the
following example screenshot.

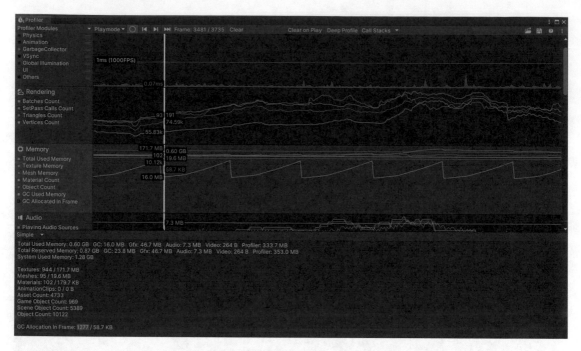

Figure 11-11. *Hove Racers Profiler Example*

A screenshot depicting the Unity profiler with data from a run of the Hover Racer's game

Take time to play with the Profiler. Toggle the different metrics on the left-hand side to pinpoint what's causing your game to misbehave. Clicking on the graphs will bring up details in the window's bottom panel. You can access information about how much time the garbage collector is taking up, how much time certain method calls are taking to complete, etc. The Profiler is a powerful tool. Developers who know how to use it can address inefficiencies in their game competently and quickly. Be one of those developers.

Chapter Conclusion

That brings us to the conclusion of the chapter. In this chapter, we took a look at a number of topics that I feel will help you make your next Unity game just that much better. We talked about a variety of topics that address things like game efficiency and refining aspects of your implementation. Let's review those topics here.

Build Settings: In this section, we covered some key build settings and pointed out some useful options that can affect your game's performance. We also discussed many options available to help you test and debug your game on a bunch of different platforms, listed subsequently.

1. Generic Platform Settings

2. PC, Mac, Linux Desktop Settings

3. UWP Settings

4. IOS Settings

5. Android Settings

6. WebGL Settings

Input Mapping: The input mapping section discusses setting up your inputs so they are abstracted by the input mapping feature. We talked about, and looked at, how multiple inputs that function the same when applied to a game can all share the same label. This effectively creates an abstraction layer allowing you to code against the input label and not directly against the input sources.

UI/Menu System: In this section, we talked about how a solid UI can enhance your game and provide a good experience for your players. We also stepped through the process of building a simple two-button menu screen with attached script for handling button click events and provided a complete demonstration version of said scene for you to peruse.

Data Persistence: We took a moment to touch on the subject of data persistence and mentioned the `PlayerPrefs` class that's used by the Hover Racers game. We also talked briefly about using Serialization/Deserialization techniques to store slightly more complex data. And lastly, we recommended using data files for highly complex and/or larger amounts of data.

Memory Management: With regard to memory management, we laid out some ideas on how to control garbage collection as is implemented in the provided game project. We also stressed the importance of being aware of and proactively addressing how your code affects the garbage collector.

Sounds and Music: In this section, we talked about well... sounds and music. We recommend having sound effects for all player interaction, background music, and ambient sounds whenever possible. We also mentioned using place holders during development, allowing you to focus on the game's code while giving you the flexibility to polish and refine your game's sounds at a later time.

Static Objects: The static objects section is a reminder to take the time to make objects in your game static whenever possible. You can view this feature in use as the Hover Racers game project uses static objects in both the "Main13" and "Main14" scenes. Take a look and see.

Tags and Layers: In this section, we briefly touched on tags and layers and talked about how you can use them in your game. The Hover Racers code base uses tags frequently to help identify certain game objects programmatically.

AI Opponents: The AI opponents section laid out some general ideas about game AI and talked about the specific implementation as it applies to the Hover Racers game.

Cameras: In this section, we discussed cameras and how they can be used to enhance your game. We also mentioned checking how the multiple camera setup of the game was implemented.

Project Settings: There are a ton of project settings, and it would take quite a bit of time and many pages of text to cover them all. What we did was focus on the "Quality" section of the project settings and used that as a segue into the Unity editor's Stats popup and Profiler tool.

I hope this chapter has provided you with some food for thought. At the very least, you'll have a few things to keep in mind as you build your next great game or refine your current one. In the next chapter of this text, we'll take a look at how to add a new racetrack to the Hover Racers game!

CHAPTER 12

Adding a New Racetrack

We've reviewed the code top to bottom. You've seen every game mechanic and interaction, and now we're going to build a new track in the Unity editor and plug it into the game. This will reinforce the concepts you've learned through the code review process and show you where the GameObjects meet the code so to speak. We'll proceed step by step, adding prefab game objects to the scene, building out a new racetrack, and then finally adding the track to the game by connecting it to the game's start menu screen. Well, we have our plan laid out for us, so let's get to it!

Track Environment and Cleanup Script

The first thing we're going to do is create a new scene named "MyTrack15" and open it. Once that's done, we'll need a place for our new racetrack to exist. Let's direct our attention to the "Hierarchy" panel. Right-click inside the panel and select "Create Empty." Rename the new GameObject to "Features." Perform this operation two more times and create the following two objects: "Menus" and "SceneOther." Move the default Main Camera and Direction Light game objects into the SceneOther object you just created. Your hierarchy panel should have the following entries at the root of the hierarchy.

Figure 12-1. *New Racetrack Hierarchy Example 1*

Image snippet depicting the scene's hierarchy at this point in the new racetrack development process

© Victor G Brusca 2022

V. G Brusca, *Advanced Unity Game Development*, https://doi.org/10.1007/978-1-4842-7851-2_12

We'll use these empty GameObjects almost like folders in a filesystem. This is perfectly fine from a performance perspective and is actually a great way to keep your project's game objects organized. To set up a simple environment for the racetrack, we'll create an instance of an existing prefab object in our scene. In the "Project" panel, find the "PreFabs" folder and locate the entry named "Board." Drag it up to the "Hierarchy" panel and drop it into the "Features" game object. Repeat this process for the prefab named "Destroyer." Your hierarchy should look similar to the following.

Figure 12-2. *New Racetrack Hierarchy Example 2*

Image snippet depicting the scene's hierarchy after adding the Board and Destroyer objects

We need the "Board" game object to be slightly wider. Select it in the hierarchy and change the "Scale X" value in the inspector from 1 to 1.5. That'll make the board a little wider for our track to fit inside of it. Your setup should look like the following screenshot. The Destroyer game object should be much larger than the board and positioned below it.

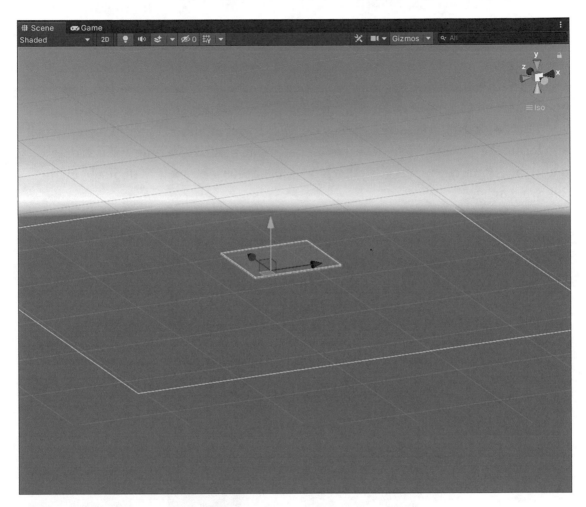

Figure 12-3. *New Racetrack Scene Example 1*

Screenshot depicting the Board and Destroyer game objects and their relative positioning

Obviously, it doesn't have to match exactly, but your setup should be similar to that shown in the previously listed screenshot. In the next section, we'll set up the racers and the game state object and associated scripts.

Hover Racers and the GameState Object

In this section, we'll add the racers, the game state object, and associated scripts to the scene. There will still be a few more steps we need to work through before we have a fully functional and integrated racetrack, but this will bring us one step closer to that goal. We'll start with the hover racers starting set. Direct your attention to the "Project" panel and locate the "PreFabs" folder. Search for the prefab named "StartingSet" and drag it into the "Hierarchy" panel such that it is a root GameObject entry as depicted in the following image.

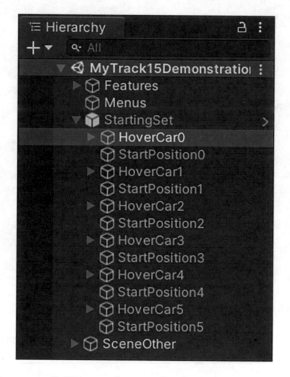

Figure 12-4. *New Racetrack Hierarchy Example 3*

An image snippet that depicts the scene hierarchy after adding the StartingSet object

Perform the same steps except this time find the prefab named "GameState" and drag it into the hierarchy such that it is a child of the SceneOther object. The following image depicts the current scene hierarchy. You should have a matching setup in your hierarchy panel.

Figure 12-5. *New Racetrack Hierarchy Example 4*

Image snippet depicting the hierarchy after adding the GameState object

We'll have to adjust the position of the StartingSet object. Select it and adjust the "Position Y" value to –66. You could have slightly different positioning, so if the value –66 doesn't bring the racers close to the board's surface, use the "Scene" panel and reposition them, so they are close to the board's surface but not touching it. Next, expand the SceneOther parent object and select the Main Camera child object. In the "Inspector" panel, click the checkbox to the left of the name field to deactivate the camera.

While we're at it, let's toggle the static flag for a few scene objects we know won't be moving. Expand the Features game object and set the Board and Destroyer game objects to be static if they aren't configured that way already. Apply the static flag to all child objects if prompted to do so. Let's test the scene. Click the play button; you should see the board through the player's camera. Wait for a few seconds and you'll be able to control the racer. This is similar to the demonstration scenes you've worked with previously. When we're done setting things up, there will be a countdown displayed that indicates the passing of this time. For now, we'll just have to make do with waiting a few seconds.

After running the scene, if the hover racer floats down at the start of the scene, then it's a little too high. Adjust the StartingSet down a bit and test it out again. Similarly, if the racer bounces up into the air at the start of the scene or falls below the board's surface, then the racer is a little too low. Adjust the StartingSet up a bit and test it out again. Remember, scene changes made while the scene is running, scene demonstration, are lost when the scene demonstration is stopped. Make the adjustments once you've stopped the scene so they will be stored properly and persist. Make the adjustments when the scene is running to test them out at runtime. Next up, we'll tackle the track and waypoints.

Track and Waypoint Objects

The new track is starting to take shape. We have a lot of GameObjects and script components all set up. We can run the scene and drive around, but things are quite barren. Just a big empty gray board and not much else. Let's add a track and waypoints to our board. I've created a simple track for us to use. Normally, you would drag the track models or prefabs over to the hierarchy to set up a racetrack. In this case, I've done the work for you.

Direct your attention to the "PreFabs" folder in the "Project" panel and locate the "SimpleTrack" prefab. Drag and drop the prefab into the hierarchy such that it becomes a child of the Features game object. Set the location of the SimpleTrack object to "X" = 35, "Y" = 0, and "Z" = -9. You can have a slightly different positioning to your board, and if so, don't worry, just move the track so that it's in the center of the board. Make sure the road is visible and the track isn't hovering above the board's surface. A screenshot of the setup is as follows.

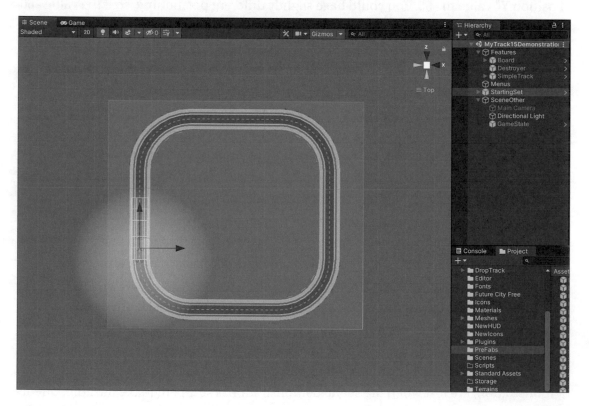

Figure 12-6. *New Racetrack Scene Example 2*

A screenshot depicting the scene with track centered inside the board

Now that we have a track, let's reposition the hover racers to a good starting point for this particular track. Set the StartingSet object's position to "X" = -430, "Y" = -66, "Z" = -254. This should position the racers as indicated in the previously listed screenshot. If your objects were positioned differently to begin with, then don't use the values listed here. Instead, reposition the cars by using the Unity editor such that it is similar to the setup shown.

Let's add the track's waypoints next. Locate the "SimpleWaypoints" prefab and drag it into the hierarchy so that it's a direct child of the Features game object. Adjust the position of the waypoints, if need be, such that they align with the track's turns and straightaways. Adjust the position of the StartingSet so that the hover racers are in between the waypoints on that side of the track. There's one last thing I wanted to do before we move on to the next section.

Expand the SceneOther parent game object and select the GameState child object. Expand the "TrackScript" script component entry in the "Inspector" panel. Set the "Laps" field to a larger number; because this track isn't that large, we'll use more laps than usual. Use something like eight laps. The following image depicts the current setup of the scene. You should have something very similar in your scene.

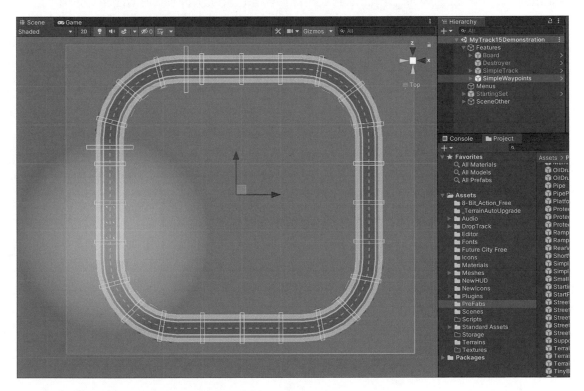

Figure 12-7. *New Racetrack Scene Example 3*

A screenshot depicting the scene with board, track, and waypoints configured and a starting set of hover racers

I should mention that the race type will override the laps you just configured in some cases. If you look into the list of waypoints on the track, you'll notice that some of them are there to trigger help notifications. One such help notification waypoint, TrackHelpTurn, actually turns off the track help notification system and should be the last such waypoint on the track. Otherwise, it will prematurely turn off help notifications. I also want to point out that the StartingSet, containing all the hover racer, is positioned after the last waypoint but before the first waypoint. Make sure you have a similar setup in your scene.

Jumps, Boosts, Menu Screens, and More

In this section, we'll add some interesting features to the track. We'll also add the menu screens to the track and connect our track to the starting menu. Notice how we've been able to add new features and functionality to the track and it just plugs into the game seamlessly. The scene was playable as soon as we added hover racers to the board. If you recall from the code review chapters, the code is designed to react to missing script components and game objects by shutting down a class that couldn't be properly configured. This allows us to build out the new racetrack in phases with a functional scene at the end of each phase. Keep in mind you can always comment out these checks on release builds of the project to ensure the highest performance.

To add a set of new track features including boosts, jumps, fun boxes, and battle mode markers, go into the "PreFabs" folder in the "Project" panel and locate the "SimpleFeatures" prefab. Drag the entry to the hierarchy so that it is a child of the Features parent game object. Make sure that the new track objects are properly aligned with the track as shown in the following image.

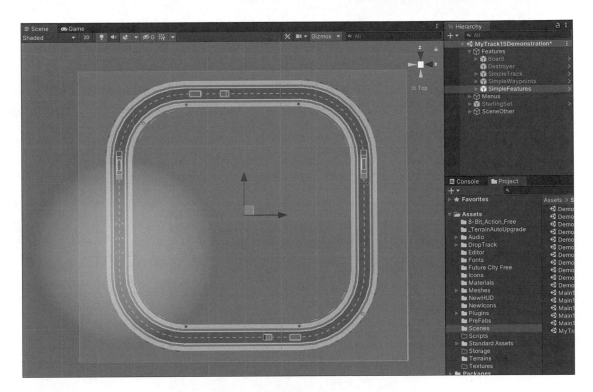

Figure 12-8. *New Racetrack Scene Example 4*

A screenshot depicting the track with boosts, jumps, fun boxes, and battle mode markers configured

We're going to do the same thing for the following prefabs, BgMusic and BlimpCamera, except we're going to drag and drop them into the SceneOther parent object such that they are direct children of the SceneOther parent game object. Adding these objects to the scene will enable background music and blimp camera functionality to the scene. Next up, we'll add in the menu system and configure the code to run your track from the start menu. In order to get the menu system setup, we need to drag and drop the following prefab objects into the Menus parent game object in the scene hierarchy:

- GameExitMenu

- GameHelpMenu

- GameHUD

- GameOverMenu

- GamePauseMenu

- GameStartMenu

We're going to need an EventSystem object to get the UI/Menu System up and running properly. Right-click on the Menus parent game object and select the "UI" option and then select the EventSystem entry. You should have an EventSystem game object as a child of the Menus parent along with all the supported menu screens. You should have a setup similar to the following screenshot.

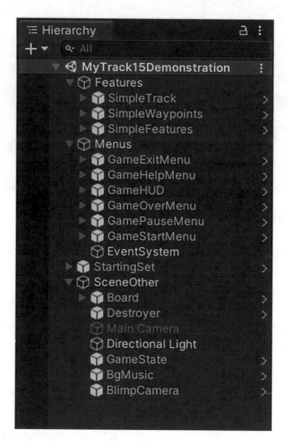

Figure 12-9. *New Racetrack Hierarchy Example 5*

An image snippet depicting the hierarchy of the scene after configuring the menu system

Take a moment to think about what we've done so far to get the racetrack up and running. We're mainly working with prefabs, but this is just to save time and cut down on the number of steps needed to get things up and running. The phases of development are the same; they are just condensed to speed things up a bit for us. The last thing we need to do is plug our new track into the menu system code so that we can use it as part of the game and then take it for a test spin.

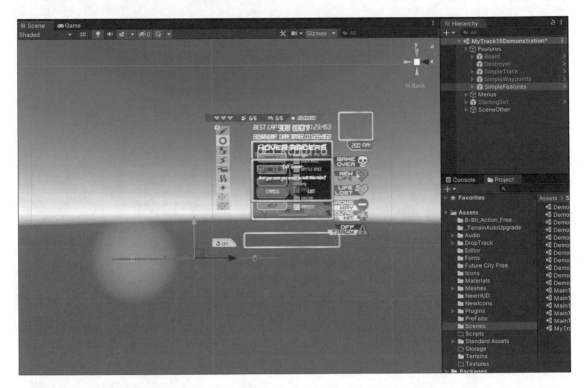

Figure 12-10. *New Racetrack Scene Example 5*

A screenshot depicting the current state of the scene with menu system configured

To connect our new racetrack to the game, open up the GameStartMenu and GameOverMenu classes for editing. Alter the TRACK_NAME_4 class fields in each class and replace the scene name listed with that of the scene you're working on. If you've adhered to the text closely, then the name would be "MyTrack15." We'll also need to add the scene to the project build configuration. To do so, open the build settings from the following menu location: "File" ➤ "Build Settings." At the top of the resulting window is a list of scenes included in the build process for the project. Make sure you have the "MyTrack15" scene open and click the "Add Open Scenes" button. You can drag the scene entry up or down in the list to reposition it if need be.

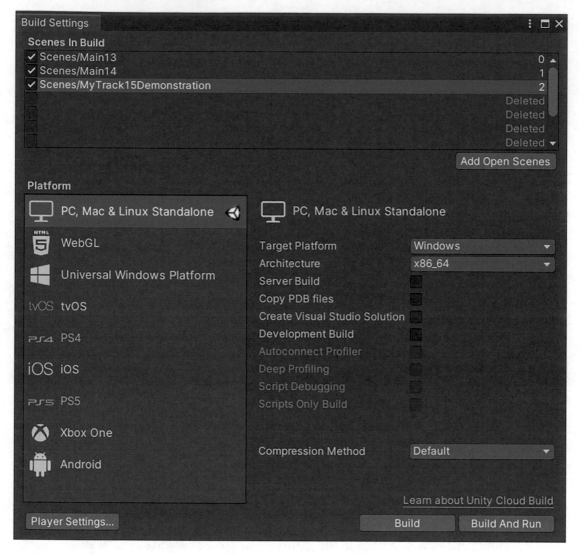

Figure 12-11. *New Racetrack Build Settings Example*

A screenshot depicting the list of scenes included in the project's build settings

A demonstration version of this racetrack, for comparison and debugging purposes, can be accessed by using the "Track 3" button on the start menu. Congratulations! You've successfully added a new racetrack to the game!

Chapter Conclusion

That brings us to the conclusion of this chapter. We saw how to use prefab objects to speed up racetrack creation in the Unity editor. Prefabs allow us to use preconfigured objects as building blocks, greatly cutting down on development time. Notice that all the different scripts we've reviewed in detail are associated with the correct game objects and can plug into our core game code as we drag and drop them into the scene's hierarchy.

This is done by design. All of the method escape code we've reviewed, and we've mentioned that phrase quite a bit, is used to shut down unused or improperly configured classes in the code base to keep the game as functional as possible throughout the track development process. Let's review the steps we used in creating the new racetrack.

Track Environment and Cleanup Script: In this phase of the track's development, we created a simple place for our track to exist. We also add a destroyer script to handle deleting objects that have accidentally fallen off the board. Try it yourself. If you hit a jump after triggering a boost modifier, you can manage to fly off the board. See what happens when you do.

Hover Racers and the GameState Object: This section of the track's development process added the starting set of hover racers to the board and created an instance of the game's brain, the GameState object with associated GameState script component. At this point in the track's development, you'll be able to demonstrate the board and drive around the scene.

Track and Waypoint Objects: Adding the track pieces and the waypoint objects turns on a number of features on the track under development. The AI opponents now begin to race around the track, and features like off-track, wrong way, and stuck racer support are now enabled.

Jumps, Boosts, Menu Screens, and More: What good is a hover car racetrack if it doesn't have some jumps and other cool aspects to it? In this phase of the track's development, we finalize things by adding background music, the blimp camera, the game's menu screens, and a number of boosts, jumps, fun boxes, and battle mode markers to the racetrack. Lastly, we connected the track to the game by registering it with the menu system.

Take a moment to think about the track creation process we've just completed. Look through the different game objects and see what scripts are in use. Think back to our review of those scripts and try to connect the functionality you see, when racing the track, to the code that drives it.

CHAPTER 13

Conclusion

Welcome to the conclusion of this text! If you're reading this, then I'll assume you completed an in-depth review of a full, fairly complex, Unity racing game. That's nothing to shrug off. It's a serious challenge to review that much material and build your own addition to the game, a little demonstration racetrack. You overcame that challenge and I commend you. Let's take a moment to review some of the things we've managed to accomplish together over the course of this text.

Accomplishments

We've managed to cover a lot of ground together in this text. We started with the basics and got our Unity development environment up and running. We took the book's included game project for a test spin and then got serious and reviewed, in detail, a ton of code. Here are some of our notable accomplishments from this journey.

Game Specifications: We took a professional approach to the game development process and outlined all the different interactions that power the game mechanics encountered while racing on a track. The concepts are described as diagrams with supporting text to clearly describe the relevant game situation.

Simple Interaction Scripts: You got to look at the simpler interaction scripts that powered the on-track and bounce barrier game mechanics in detail. These classes showed us how the code interacts with game objects via collision handlers and gave us simple examples, demonstration scenes, we could visualize through game play.

Complex Interaction Scripts: The complex interaction scripts power the game's battle mode and a number of collision-related game mechanics like boosts, jumps, and battle mode markers. Things got a bit more complicated, but we reviewed the code in detail and got a chance to look at the code in action by trying out different demonstration scenes.

© Victor G Brusca 2022
V. G Brusca, *Advanced Unity Game Development*, https://doi.org/10.1007/978-1-4842-7851-2_13

Helper Classes: We took an in-depth look at helper classes as used by the game's code base. This gave us a great example of how regular C# classes can mix with script components to handle esoteric tasks like sorting and serializing/deserializing data.

Code Structure: While we didn't address this directly, it has been there behind the scenes all along. We reviewed the base class that is used by almost every script component in the code base. We also saw, as part of the menu system classes, specialized base classes that centralize the similar functionality of a few menu screens. Lastly, we gained familiarity with the overall structure of the game's code base and classes.

Project Structure: A good example of an organized project structure, including organizing resources and game objects in the "Project" and "Hierarchy" panels, is expressed through the Hover Racers project itself. It's definitely worth taking the time to review the project as a whole with an eye toward the organizational aspects of the project, hierarchy, and code.

Input Classes: Together we reviewed all the various input classes, including input mappings, that power the Hover Racers game. This provides you with a great, working example of handling input from keyboard, mouse, controller, and touch screen sources. The game project provides a great example of handling abstracted input from different sources. Be sure to review this aspect of the text as it's sure to come in handy in the future.

AI Opponents: You got to see AI opponent implementation firsthand. Initially with the implementation of waypoints to guide AI-controlled racers and subsequently with abstracted input handlers and AI-specific input methods that mimic user input. Game AI is always a challenge, and the rule I go by is to cheat as much as possible by providing as much data as possible to your AI-controlled characters. My second rule of thumb, mentioned previously, is to abstract input handlers from the actual functional code so it can be used by AI logic and human players alike.

Menu System Classes: We reviewed menu system classes demonstrating how you can connect script components associated with menu screens to the rest of your game via game state and player state classes. We also built a simple menu screen demonstrating basic positioning, resizing, and script-based event handling.

Game and Player State Management: You got to see firsthand a project wide implementation of game state control via the use of the `BaseScript` class' initialization methods. We saw how every main script component extended this class and was to "turn off" every instance of the class if a configuration error was detected. This feature, when properly applied, adds stability to the code and allows the game to function when script components or game objects are missing from the scene. We experienced this in Chapter 12 when building a new racetrack for the game. You also got to experience the centralization benefits of this approach as every main script component in the code base established a reference to the GameState object and associated script.

Unity Tips: We went over a number of Unity tips you can use to make your next game that much better. We covered tips to increase efficiency and speed up build times so you can iterate faster and get more testing and debugging done. We also talked about passive tips, things you should keep in mind when building your game.

Adding a New Track: You gained some direct experience working with prefab objects to build out a new track for the Hover Racers game. What you may not have realized is that each track is in fact a complete game. The main menu screen provides buttons that allow you to jump, for lack of a better word, to the different main scenes in your game. This exercise showed us how Unity GameObjects, with associated script components, work together with the code base to make a complete game.

Acknowledgments

- Katia Pouleva: A fantastic artist who created a lot of the Hover Racers game art and also cleaned up all of the screenshots in this text.
Link: https://katiapouleva.com

- Jacek Jankowski: Creator of the "Simple Modular Street Kit" used in the "Main13" scene and other demonstration scenes.
Link: N/A

- Unity Technologies: Creator of the "Shanty Town: Concrete Wall Rough" and "Shanty Town: Concrete Pipe" models used in the game's main scenes.
Link: N/A

- Reikan Studio: Creator of the "Hover9k" original model used for the hover racers in the game.
Link: N/A

- BOXY KU: Creator of some awesome music used as the background songs in the Hover Racers game.
Link: https://assetstore.unity.com/packages/audio/music/electronic/electronic-future-city-free-21756

- Duane's Mind: Creator of the "Concrete Barrier, Wooden Pallet & Oil Drum Props" model used on both main tracks and in some demonstration scenes.
Link: https://assetstore.unity.com/packages/3d/props/industrial/concrete-barrier-wooden-pallet-oil-drum-props-2698

- Publisher 971: Creator of the "Concrete Barrier" used in the game's two main scenes, "Main13" and "Main14."
Link: N/A

- Guy Cockcroft: Creator of the "8 Bit Retro Rampage: Free Edition" used in some of the sound effects in the game.
Link: https://assetstore.unity.com/packages/audio/sound-fx/8-bit-retro-rampage-free-edition-7946

- MoppySound: Creator of the "8-Bit Action Free" used as a source of some of the sound effects in the game.
Link: https://assetstore.unity.com/packages/audio/music/electronic/8-bit-action-free-19827

Where You Go from Here

There are a lot of directions you can go in from here. Please allow me to make a few suggestions.

Modify the Existing Game: You can add new game mechanics driven by new game objects and interactions between them and the existing set of objects. You can create new tracks to race on or perhaps add multiplayer support to the Hover Racers game. The sky's the limit.

Add Particle Effects to the Game: The original particle effects that were used to add a dust cloud to the racers, a fire streak that triggers on boost modifiers, and a cloud that explodes when the racer's cannon fires, were deprecated so I commented them out but left the comments in place. A great exercise would be to add new updated particle effects to the game.

Create an Entirely New Racing Game: Use the Hover Racers project as the starting point for a new racing game or throw the whole thing out and start from scratch; you can always use it as a reference when needed.

Add New Models, Music, and Sound Effects: Hit the Unity asset store and look for new models, music, or sound effects and add them into the game.

Create a Totally New Game: Take the knowledge you've gained and start working on the game you always wanted to make.

Saying Goodbye

Well, it's time for me to get going. I hope this book helps you on your game development journey and has provided you with some amount of knowledge, entertainment, or wisdom. I wish you the best of luck and success in all your future endeavors! Ciao, ciao.

Index

© Victor G Brusca 2022
V. G Brusca, *Advanced Unity Game Development*, https://doi.org/10.1007/978-1-4842-7851-2

Printed in the United States
by Baker & Taylor Publisher Services